China's Dream

To Flemming Christiansen, with gratitude for his
support over the years.

China's Dream

The Culture of Chinese Communism and the Secret Sources of Its Power

Kerry Brown

polity

First published in 2018 by Polity Press
Reprinted 2019

Polity Press
65 Bridge Street
Cambridge CB2 1UR, UK

Polity Press
101 Station Landing
Suite 300
Medford, MA 02155, USA

ISBN-13: 978-1-5095-2456-3
ISBN-13: 978-1-5095-2457-0 (pb)

A catalogue record for this book is available from the British Library.

Library of Congress Cataloging-in-Publication Data

Names: Brown, Kerry, 1967- author.
Title: China's dream : the culture of Chinese communism and the secret sources of its power / Kerry Brown.
Description: Cambridge, UK ; Medford, MA : Polity, 2018. | Includes bibliographical references and index.
Identifiers: LCCN 2018007932 (print) | LCCN 2018029569 (ebook) | ISBN 9781509524600 (Epub) | ISBN 9781509524563 (hardback) | ISBN 9781509524570 (paperback)
Subjects: LCSH: Zhongguo gong chan dang. | Communism–Social aspects–China. | China–Social policy. | Social change–China. | China–Social conditions–2000- | BISAC: POLITICAL SCIENCE / Globalization.
Classification: LCC JQ1519.A5 (ebook) | LCC JQ1519.A5 B75 2018 (print) | DDC 306.20951–dc23
LC record available at https://lccn.loc.gov/2018007932

Typeset in 10.5 on 12 pt Sabon by Toppan Best-set Premedia Limited
Printed and bound in the UK by CPI Group (UK) Ltd, Croydon

For further information on Polity, visit our website: politybooks.com

Contents

Chronology

1911–12	Fall of the Qing Dynasty through the Xinnai Revolution. Establishment of the Republican government.
1919	May Fourth Student Movement, a rebellion by young intellectuals promoting modernization in China.
1921	First Congress of the Communist Party of China, held in Shanghai and Jiangsu.
1927	Savage purge of Communists by the ruling Nationalists; retreat of the main Communist movement from Shanghai to the rural areas in Jiangxi.
1932	Marco Polo Bridge incident, marking Japanese interference in Chinese affairs.
1935–6	Long March, led by newly dominant Communist Party leader Mao Zedong, taking the Party to a northern refuge to counter Nationalists' attacks.
1937–45	Sino-Japanese War.
1946–9	Civil War between the Nationalists and the Communists.
1949	Establishment of the People's Republic of China under Communist rule after their victory in the Civil War. Nationalists flee to Taiwan and establish a government there.
1950–3	Korean War.
1953	Launch of First Five-Year Plan, introducing planned economy into China.
1956	Hundred Flowers Campaign, which results in the first major clampdown against intellectuals and 'rightists'.

1957	Launch of the Great Leap Forward, to accelerate China's industrial development, setting ambitious new growth targets. First signs of Sino-Soviet rift as a result of de-Stalinization in the USSR.
1959–61	The great famines, which led to the deaths of as many as 50 million people.
1964	China successfully tests hydrogen bomb.
1966–76	The Great Cultural Revolution.
1967	Felling of Liu Shaoqi, until then President of China.
1971	Death of Lin Biao, Mao's chosen successor, while trying to flee to the USSR on a plane.
1976	Death of Mao Zedong, and fall of the 'Gang of Four' radical group around him.
1978	Announcement of reforms to open up the Chinese economy, tolerate the market, and promote entrepreneurialism, at the Third Plenary of the Eleventh Party Congress. Deng Xiaoping emerges as paramount leader.
1981	Announcement of the Resolution on Party History, which criticizes the Cultural Revolution as a 'mistake'. Introduction of Special Economic Zones which allow manufacturing for export and foreign investment.
1989	Tiananmen Square uprising, which is put down by the Deng Xiaoping leadership. Appointment of Jiang Zemin as Party Secretary.
1991	Collapse of the Soviet Union.
1992	Deng Xiaoping Southern Tour, reaffirming commitment to reforms and openness despite the setback of Tiananmen in 1989.
2001	China's entry into the World Trade Organization.
2002	Appointment of Hu Jintao as Party Secretary.
2008	China hosts Olympics in Beijing. Tibet uprising.
2009	Widespread unrest in Xinjiang region, in the north-west of the country.
2010	China becomes world's second largest economy, overtaking Japan.
2012	Appointment of Xi Jinping as Party Secretary.
2017	Start of Xi Jinping's second term as Party Secretary.

Abbreviations

CCDI	Central Commission for Discipline Inspection
CCTV	China Central Television
CPC	Communist Party of China
CPPCC	Chinese People's Political Consultative Conference
PLA	People's Liberation Army
PRC	People's Republic of China
SOEs	state-owned enterprises
WTO	World Trade Organization

Preface

China is just a geography. A place with borders and territorial limitations. Why does it merit special attention?

While the argument in this book is about China, and things that happen in that geographical place, underlying its contents there is an overarching generic question. This is about how it is that twice in the twentieth century China managed to take what were regarded as universal rules, and transformed and adapted them in ways which were exceptional.

The first was the importation of Marxism-Leninism with its stress on urban revolution, and the upending of this so that in China it ended up being an agrarian-based phenomenon.

The second was the use of capitalist economic methods after post-Mao reforms in 1978, and the development of a society which has become increasingly wealthy, where all expectations that it would also introduce political, democratic reforms have, so far, not been met.

These two great moments of innovation have created a China in the twenty-first century which is convinced it is exceptional, and that it uses models which are relevant only to it. It stands as the great inconvenience to Western universalist ideas. That gives what it has done not just a local but a global significance, because it undercuts ideas which are a necessary part of the Western Enlightenment mentality.

For this reason, the phenomenon described in this book is of significance way beyond being a description of a behaviour of a particular geography and the frameworks it might fit into. It is about the attempt to create a different form of modernity, a bespoke one – one which is hybrid, guided by moral and intellectual sources of thinking utterly different in their history and development from the West. Those are the questions that have prompted, and guided, the writing of this book.

Acknowledgements

I would like to express my thanks to Louise Knight and Nekane Tanaka Galdos at Polity Press for commissioning and then steering this book through to publication. It has been stimulating and highly congenial to work with them. I would also like to thank Justin Dyer for his copy-editing. I am also grateful for comments received on the first draft of this book from Simone van Neuwenhuizen, Siv Oftedal, Cindy Yu, Jolita Pons, Julia Lovell, James Miles, Jasper Becket, and from two anonymous reviewers. They have helped enormously in shaping the book.

About the Author

Kerry Brown is the Director of the Lau China Institute at King's College London and Associate for Chinese Affairs at Chatham House. With 30 years experience of life in China, he has worked in education, business and government, including a term as First Secretary at the British Embassy in Beijing. He writes regularly for the *Times Literary Supplement, The Observer, The Diplomat* and *Foreign Affairs*, as well as for many international and Chinese media outlets. He is the author of ten books on China, including the Amazon-bestselling *CEO China: The Rise of Xi Jinping*, and *The New Emperors*.

Introduction

On a summer's afternoon in 2014, while still based at the University of Sydney, I came back to Europe to go to a seminar in Copenhagen. Attending seminars is part of the rhythm of everyday life for academics. It is a thing we are habitually expected to do. But there was something unusual about this particular event. For a start, there was the heavy security before going into the building where the meeting was due to take place. Then there was the slight matter of the secrecy around the reasons for the gathering and the sense of expectation that had preceded it. Finally, there was the composition of the meeting: a seminar being attended by a hybrid audience of researchers, scholars, and officials rather than simply from one of these groups alone.

Arriving in Denmark from the UK the evening before the event, I remember glancing through the preparatory notes that had been sent to me while back in London. The theme we were due to discuss was a grand one: 'The Chinese Communist Party and the World'. The attendees on the hosting side were simply named as 'Scholars of the Communist Party'. This designation carried with it an unsettling ambiguity: were those included either all united by focussing on the Communist Party of China (CPC) as their object of research, or actually working for and in it? As for the composition of the visitors, the attendees were briskly listed as: 'Members of the Central Committee and International Liaison Department of the Communist Party of China'. The agenda was tightly structured and the strictures about how it was to be conducted clear: to make sure that no one went beyond their allotted ten minutes. No ambiguity there.

Around lunchtime the next day, on the second floor of an inconspicuous building on one of the campuses, we were told to line up in an orderly queue. Liu Yunshan, one of the most senior leaders of the CPC, a man who sat on its seven-strong Politburo, the summit of power in the country, suddenly appeared from the sole lift servicing the school. A retinue of bodyguards and various severe-looking officials followed in his wake. He proceeded to move down the line of twenty or so people waiting to greet him, hastily shaking their hands before moving on. The most I could say in those few seconds of one-to-one interaction when my time came before he was whisked was that I had spent two years over a quarter of a century ago in the region of China he had grown up in – Inner Mongolia. For the next two hours after that all we did, as a group, was to talk about the party he was a member of: what our understanding of this organization was, its history, its current status, and its vision for the country it was still enjoying a monopoly of political power in.

It's worth pointing out that in the power geography of contemporary China, figures like Liu were far more remote than their equivalents in Western contexts. Even at a relatively low level of administration, leaders of the prefecture or province (China has five levels of government from the centre down to townships) often seem to live in a different universe to what in common parlance is called 'the old hundred names' (*laobaixing*), the general public. They get driven around in special cars, live in designated and highly protected compounds, and move around the world with a corridor cleared before them for safe passage by security personnel. Those few who try to penetrate this wall uninvited from the outside world are dealt with harshly. It is a zone of control. At Liu's level, he would never take a plane on which members of the general public rode, travel along streets which had not been carefully traffic-managed, or have anything remotely like spontaneous (and therefore difficult to predict) interaction with the people he was meant to be serving. Access to him would be carefully controlled by a formidable phalanx of bureaucrats, screening everything he looked at and everyone he spoke to. Our access that day was exceptional, and highly unorthodox, a testimony to the ways in which, for all the distrust and suspicion shown towards them, foreigners, for Chinese politicians at least, were still accorded a different, and sometimes privileged, space.

Liu had been of interest to me for a number of years. His key role was management of propaganda and ideology, standard functions for any Communist party. I had actually met him once before this encounter, at a similar conference in Beijing in 2010. At that time, he had merely been a member of the full Politburo of twenty-four people, not yet sitting on the Standing Committee. Through his responsibility for propaganda – messaging, or, in the gentler language the Party had started to use in recent years, publicity – he had been in charge of Xinhua, the most important news agency, and other formal information agencies. It was he who had been responsible for the vast soft-power harvest that was meant to have come from the 2008 Olympics held in Beijing. But in the years after this, he had had a tough time. Blamed for poor management of news during the disastrous 2010 train crash that had killed so many in Wenzhou, a district of Zhejiang province on the coast, he had also been accused by more hawkish members of the Party's grassroots of being a latent leftist, someone who had authorized, covertly or overtly, the construction of a spate of Mao Zedong statues springing up across the land.

In a political elite remarkable for its homogeneity in terms of ethnicity, gender, and age, Liu was also, at least in one respect, the odd man out. He had uniquely been a journalist, serving as a correspondent for the official state news agency mentioned above, Xinhua, in the early 1980s during the flowering of the reform era after the death of Mao in 1976. He was assigned to the Inner Mongolian Autonomous Region, which was a tough area to get by in, bitterly cold in winter, horribly scarred by environmental problems, with the heavy use of fossil fuels to power the factories blighting the air with thick smog. Added to this was a complex history. When Liu had been an adolescent and young man, it had witnessed a local manifestation of the Cultural Revolution, the tumultuous radical campaign instigated by Mao from 1966 to 1976 which will figure a great deal in this book. This had seen a large number of cadres of Mongolian ethnicity singled out for particularly brutal treatment. (Despite the region's name, Mongolians only constituted 10 per cent of the local population, the rest being Han.) Official figures released in the 1980s said up to 22,000 had perished. Many tens of thousands more were injured. I got to know a small number of these nearly three decades after the event when living in the provincial capital, Hohhot. For some, their lives had been a project of survival ever since that time.

The 2010 meeting that I had attended was held in the Great Hall of the People, a vast ceremonial building in the centre of the capital. If Liu was under intense political pressure then, he did not betray any nervousness. The small group I was with that met him were participating in discussions at the International Liaison Department nearby, the part of the Party that specialized in liaison with foreign political parties and academics. The focus of this meeting was Party building and communication. The era of Hu Jintao, President and Party leader since 2002, was coming to a close. For eight years under his direction,

China had grown stronger, more prominent, and yet, despite these achievements, more silent. As one commentator said to me at a conference held in London at about the same time, over this period it seemed to have acquired the body of an elephant and the voice of a mouse. In the middle part of the decade, Liu himself had berated officials at the Central Party School in Beijing, the closest thing the country had to a think-tank, about how the language used by officials was stiff, unappealing, and left most people emotionally cold. While China itself as a country and a society was vibrant, dynamic, and full of excitement and action, the Party seemed to have been left adrift, its central leaders spouting a language that sounded like it was being spoken in the faded voices of people recorded from another age.

In any political system, communication matters. But it has to operate on two levels: emotional and rational. Soon after joining the British Foreign Office a decade earlier, I remember we were given a speech-writing course. The tutor that day remorselessly came back to the issue of how an effective speech needed not only to be accurate and have a good argument but also to reach the emotions of the people being addressed. Few British politicians, she sighed, were really able to do this. Ironically, the one example she did think succeeded was the then Chancellor of the Exchequer, Gordon Brown. As Britain was to find out some years later, his rhetorical skill was not one he was able to maintain while leading people as Prime Minister. In that role he seemed too stiff and controlling.

British politicians, and their equivalents in other multi-party systems, at least have some latitude in the register they can use when speaking in public, and some agency over their choice of vocabularies and tone. Chinese leaders have a much narrower space to operate in. As became clear during the seminar before meeting Liu in 2010, the Party was in a mini-crisis regarding its relations with the wider public. Even though it had 88 million members, that still constituted less than 7 per cent of China. And the real movers and shakers in this group were vastly smaller. How did this minority relate to the wider world around it? How did it justify its right to rule, and not just rule, but to have an uninterrupted monopoly on power? Its language clearly needed an overhaul. It sounded outdated even to insiders. The afore-mentioned Hu Jintao was the high priest of this, someone who never referred to any personal biography in his public utterances, and who was infamous for robotically spewing forth statistics and slogans. His favourites were 'scientific development' and 'harmonious society'. Neither meant much to anyone without a solid background in contemporary Chinese understanding of Marxism-Leninism, a tiny demographic.

Liu himself in the Great Hall of the People in 2010 was frank about these communication problems. Every day in China since reform and opening up from 1978, he said to the assembled scholars, there had been changes. He mentioned a place he had recently revisited after a year-long gap. It was unrecognizable because so much building and new infrastructure had been constructed. I could sympathize with the sense of bewilderment. In Hohhot, the capital of the region he and I had once worked in, I had found myself a few years earlier so wholly disorientated by the rebuilding that I had been unable to find a single familiar sight from which to get my bearings. The old, run-down, but at least human and idiosyncratic city I had been so familiar with in the mid-1990s had been wiped out by a pageant of newness. Indeed, in the 2000s, during the boom years after China's entry to the World Trade Organization (WTO) in 2001, this had been the story everywhere. Even a Politburo member had been confounded by this pace of change.

But Liu proceeded to make a clarification. There were the physical changes, the changes to the world we can see, which he had just illustrated. But there were other changes which we could not see, the changes, he said, in people's hearts. And there things were even less easy to make sense of. The challenge of somehow understanding these two realms in China and the links between them was a theme that had haunted our conversations in the days before meeting Liu. Since WTO entry, the CPC had created the space for Chinese people to embark on a wealth generation spree the world had never seen the likes of before. Over this period, the Party became the ultimate Midas, with everything it touched turning to gold. Inner Mongolia, poor and backward when I lived there, was now booming, enjoying thirty-plus percentage point growth rates from 2006 onwards because of a commodities bonanza (the region was rich in coal and minerals). The smoggy, often ice-covered streets Liu had been familiar with as a young journalist, and I had known in their final years, had indeed been resolutely swept away and replaced by gleaming marble, smooth tarmac, and well-lit roads. Everything had changed on every level it seemed, apart from one thing: the unique, powerful position of the Party in society. And the Communists had done this despite unleashing a revolution since the turn of the millennium that had resulted in a China that, to all intents and purposes, looked ever more capitalist.

Dealing with a world pervaded by change and transformation was one of the contributing reasons for why Chinese elite political leaders in their speeches sounded like they were using language, and referring to a world, that had been left behind. Everything had moved on, except them. Even before they could start to say something, they had to make formulaic respectful mentions of previous leaders and their thought systems, things that many in their audience no longer felt interested in or attached to: 'Mao Zedong Thought, Deng Xiaoping Theory, the Three Represents, scientific development...'. The list seemed to go on and on. And then they had to intersperse their statistics-laden speeches with formulas acknowledging their commitment to creating the primary stage of socialism, observing the mass line, delivering socialism with Chinese characteristics so that they could achieve a moderately prosperous society in an all-round way by 2021 – a date which marked the much-anticipated centenary of the foundation of the Party. What was this strange sub-dialect they were speaking?

One of the greatest issues was how often this language sounded alien, stodgy, and remote. There were already politicians who were willing to dissent and use a more natural register. One of them, the princeling[1] Bo Xilai, had managed to be appointed Party boss of the massive south-western city of Chongqing since 2007. There, he had promoted traditional 'red song' campaigns, harking back to the glory years of the Party propaganda effort under Mao Zedong, and his era of leadership from the 1930s up to 1976. Bo had backed these theatricalities up with housing policy ideas that seemed more equitable and a savage crackdown on mafia, which had gone down well with a law-abiding, hard-working local middle class. But perhaps the most impressive thing about him was not what he did, but how he spoke. Unlike any of the leaders around him, he talked and looked like a human being, not a political machine. As a politician from Europe shrewdly pointed out to me in 2011, after he had been granted a meeting with the great man himself, 'He is the only leader in contemporary China who a foreign politician can relate to, because he speaks to the emotions and feelings of the Chinese people.'

Making this appeal to people's hearts was clearly becoming a higher priority for the Party's leaders as the twenty-first century ran on. In many ways, now that it is over, the Hu era can be seen as one where the Party lacked emotional engagement with the public. It was happy to just let them grow rich. This was a missed opportunity, something clearly recognized from 2012 with the elevation of a far more political leadership replacing the previous generation of administrators and technocrats. Under the man guiding this, Xi Jinping, appealing to public emotions of pride at what China had achieved, national sentiment, and aspirations for a better life offered massive new opportunities for refreshing the Party's legitimacy and broadening its appeal. Almost from his first day in power, Xi took the lead in this, deploying a much more direct mode of expression, utilizing slogans like the China Dream that appealed to feelings and nothing else.

The visit by Liu Yunshan to Denmark in 2014 was already two years into this new era. The key tasks for the leadership were then clear. Alone of the reduced membership of the Politburo Standing Committee (it had gone down to seven members from nine in the era to 2012), Liu, with his solid background over the last two decades in propaganda and thought management, was the ultimate defender of the faith – the man tasked with squaring the circle of ensuring the Party remained faithful to its historic allegiance to Marxism-Leninism, while somehow communicating in a more natural and direct way with a population where perhaps 99.9 per cent did not know, care about, or believe a word of what lay in the voluminous works of Marx. For this vast group the principal drivers appeared, at least on the surface, to be personal material enrichment, creation of strong, supportive networks, and acquiring the sort of physical goodies that lay at the heart of lives well lived in Western developed economies, lives they could see directly through touring abroad. As this book will attempt to show, things were in fact far more complex than this. But that was at least the way they seemed.

A central issue in addressing this problem of what language the Party should use which best expressed its evolving identity and reconnected it with the greater society around it was to decide and then spell out what the CPC itself was. This question rarely got asked, either because the organization had been around so long people inside and out of it had forgotten why they should raise it, or because, were a question like this to be posed in the wrong way, it would be construed as dissenting, radical, and therefore problematic. For people around Xi, however, some clarity about the Party's function, its core beliefs, and its values which wasn't just stagnant verbiage was crucial. Failing to be clear about the answers to these risked sleepwalking into the sort of deadly complacency that had caused decline and then demise for others. In particular, Xi's people (the generation of leaders around him who became influential after he came to power) were mindful of the collapse of Communist parties exercising power in a similar way in the old Soviet Union and elsewhere from the late 1980s onwards. Their fate was taken as a great warning. Grow stagnant, fail to keep up with society, and this was what could happen.

So far, China has managed to buck the trend. Only five such systems have survived to 2018 – those of North Korea, Vietnam, Cuba, and Laos being the other ones. But in terms of size and importance, China clearly overshadows them all. A large part of its success had been due to its adaptability and hybrid nature. Its system lived happily with notions of the market having a role in the economy and more liberal attitudes to social development, much of which would have been pure heresy in the Maoist era, while still maintaining a socialist political structure. But this had been achieved at a high cost to the Party, forcing it to contort and change its posture so it seemed almost to be pointing in two directions at the same time, with a rhetoric which said one thing, and working in a reality which indicated another. It couldn't continue to square the circle for ever. It needed to preserve some valid function and an overall narrative of its right to rule which, even if at a very high level, explained and justified these inconsistencies. Failing to do that ran the risk that the Party would be rendered irrelevant or, worst of all, swept away just as others had by the very forces of growth and change it had encouraged in the first place. Dealing with these massive challenges meant it needed to understand much better what it was, what it did, and why it had to have a role in the future of the society it was in charge of politically.

In the 2014 meeting, one thing became strikingly clear. Whatever Liu and his colleagues might have thought the CPC was, it didn't resonate with the scholars sitting across the table from them. As the discussion progressed, there were clearer and clearer signs that on seemingly the same issue both had massively divergent vocabularies and understandings. One of the attendees put forward the idea that the CPC operated in a 'fragmented authoritarian' context. Another called it 'resilient and adaptive'. The more labels accumulated, the more the Chinese side looked perplexed. It was like they were wondering to themselves whether they had come to the wrong room, and it was not a group of experts on the CPC they were in a meeting with, but a random, ill-informed selection of the public who had just wandered in off the street.

This was not to cast any aspersion on the expertise of the attendees. They had all read deeply in the available literature. They had looked at the work of scholars like Andrew Nathan, David Shambaugh, Yongnian Zheng, and Kenneth Lieberthal, all of whom in an earlier era had wrestled with this question of how best to describe the CPC, the same question referred to above. They too had wondered what kind of a thing it was, with its hybrid approach of creating a capitalist-looking economy, but controlled by a one-party system. Leninist capitalism seemed an oxymoron. But with the CPC's stress on tight organization for the Party, and its function as the elite vanguard of the ongoing revolution, there seemed no other appropriate phrase. And yet the terms created after long, patient, and hard work by these scholars were clearly unrecognizable to the very people in the organization they were meant to be applied to.

That in itself raised a number of profound issues. The day I sat in the seminar with Liu Yunshan and saw the increasing mismatch between both sides, my first thought was why there were no common vocabularies they shared. In any discipline area, the first move is usually to tightly define key terms used. But here were scholars on one side and key actors in the subject of their research on the other clearly fundamentally disagreeing on what language could best be used about them. This was not just a matter of the inevitable differences between English and Chinese languages. Although a lot could be blamed on that, it struck me that focussing too much on that aspect alone was a red herring. The issue was not the words used, or any doubt about the concepts being referred to. It was that the Chinese side understood these ideas being applied to them, and also absolutely disagreed they were correct. The CPC, as one official said, was neither fragmented, nor authoritarian. So how could this term be of any use? It was simply wrong. They had not been seen right. They had been misunderstood.

Beyond this was an issue of intellectual and cultural context and the clash between two viewpoints. Scholars from outside of China (be they ethnically Chinese or non-Chinese), inhabiting what is broadly called the Western academy, the great tradition of self-critical, analytic research and investigative discourse that this embodies, could simply assert that the members of the CPC were free to think what they liked, and be as unhappy as they wanted about the terms being used about them. That didn't matter. The main thing was that these were ideas arrived at by rigorous analysis of empirical evidence, and they had some claim to be objective. Factoring in the beliefs and ideas of the subjects was irrelevant. In the end, the claims to objectivity trumped everything else. QED!

Ironically, Chinese officials like Liu had, in recent years, protested more and more vehemently against what they called Western universalism, and the habit of the West (and here this means the largely US-led world of multi-party, developed, democracies) to impose categories from its own intellectual history harking back to the Ancient Greeks on a China that had its own traditions of thinking going back even further and which stood as a viable alternative to these of the West. These protests had largely been interpreted outside of China (and sometimes within) as another example of the way the CPC politicized everything – issuing edicts like Document Number Nine in early 2013 which forbade university lecturers from opining on liberal values and universalist discourse in classrooms. This approach also meant that the CPC was able to defend its understanding of human rights and values as being valid within its own traditions, and not available to being attacked by outsiders. It was, in essence, a profoundly defensive position, based on a strong assertion of exceptionalism. The divergences internally and externally of the sort discussed above about the best mode of description of the Party itself were symptomatic of this profound, and seemingly deepening, divide.

Despite this, surely the beliefs, attitudes, and convictions of the subjects of a discourse, the people who were actually Party members, those who were in the Party's contemporary elite and were the custodians of its mission, did matter. There had to be some way of factoring their viewpoints into a more comprehensive, dynamic view of the Party. Discounting their voices and airily imposing external criteria of understanding and evaluation seemed arrogant at best, and at worst simply wrong. E.P. Thompson had famously said in his monumental history of the English working class that his aim was to restore a voice to those who had never been given one.[2] In a very different context, the CPC was often studied with the voices of its key agents either silenced, excluded, or, more problematically, mediated in a way which was unrecognizable to the original actors – at least in external discourse.[3] The overriding assumption was that as people involved in a project that was unsustainable (the creation of perpetual one-party rule), its actors were probably wrong about how they understood their role, and being deluded, using the weird language and terms they did, in a capitalist society at odds with the socialist rhetoric they were saddled with, their own views could be ignored.

Liu Yunshan that day presented some kind of attempt to rectify this. He gave a simple overview of what he called the 'five dimensions in understanding the Communist Party of China'.[4] In essence this put forward the internal view of what the Party was and how its members understood it, at least in their own terms. This was also clearly how they wanted the outside world to understand their self-conception. There was little ambiguity or self-doubt in Liu's position. He stated categorically that 'to study [contemporary] China, one must study the CPC'. And 'to study socialism with Chinese characteristics one must also study the CPC'. That made it clear. The CPC is comprehensive. It is an entity guided by ideology and by a belief system, and this ideology and belief system are not dead rhetoric but a part of its core nature and identity – it's 'raison d'être'. On Liu's reckoning, the CPC rested on five core pillars:

- *History*: The past century, through humiliation and foreign aggression, saw China try many different forms of governance, from constitutional monarchy, to imperial rule, to republican systems.

But none of these worked. Only, Liu stated, has Communism with Chinese characteristics really succeeded. The implication of this is very obvious: 'The leadership and governing position of the CPC is not self-appointed, but rather chosen by history.' The CPC is therefore the servant of destiny. We will come back to this issue of teleology later.

- *People*: The CPC is supported by 'the overwhelming majority of the people'. It does not represent vested interests, or narrow networks, but the greater good for the greatest number of people. 'If the people are happy with things, we will get down to [doing them].' Liu quoted the Pew research centre surveys that showed 85 per cent of Chinese were content with the direction of their country in 2012. This was a register of satisfaction, and was used by Liu as a basis for showing that, despite having no open elections, the Party still had a popular mandate.

- *Culture*: As stated above, the recent leaders of China have been zealous in locating sources of legitimacy in China's past and its cultural assets. 'One can find reference to the values and governing philosophy of the CPC in traditional Chinese culture,' Liu stated, referring to ancient philosophical concepts of benevolence, justice, and integrity and saying these were consistent with the core values of socialism. Moreover, the CPC 'promotes the integration of Marxist thought with traditional Chinese culture'. In a reappearance of the strong exceptionalist strand of Chinese elite discourse about the Party, he stated that the CPC was able to combine 'socialist values with the unique values of China'.

- *Practice*: The Party was pragmatic; it judged its ideas according to their concrete impact on the real world, not because of their abstract neatness. For this, the Party had to be organizationally coherent; it had to have strong principles of Party building, an idea of the mass line and close adherence to it in order to serve the people, and a strong sense of its own cultural and moral values.

- *The world*: Despite the stress on exceptionalism, Liu made clear that the CPC 'always puts a high premium on adopting a global perspective and world-wide vision'. The CPC was intrinsically international, maintaining relations with over 600 other political parties outside of China, and 'learning from the outside'. Deng Xiaoping, paramount leader from the period after Mao's death till the 1990s and regarded as the father of the Party's reform and opening up since 1978, once stated that as a Communist he was optimistic. This is something that became apparent in Liu's final comment. He stated that the CPC was 'future-orientated'.

From Liu's words, it was easy to conclude at least some things about the views of members from within about how they saw the organization they belonged to. The Party for them is pragmatic, unifying, diverse, and hybrid. It is exceptional to China, but highly interlinked to the outside world and they are aware that their country's problems all have an international dimension. The pragmatism of the Party means it constantly makes tactical space available to it to change its direction, move into different areas: one minute claiming uniqueness, the next unity with the outside world, when it needs to. Liu stated that 'political structures are so plural that there is no unified standard to justify all political parties'. This heads off demands by those ideologically trying to promote the creation of multi-party democratic systems in China.

There are some other characteristics of the CPC's position. It promotes the ideas of scientific solutions to problems, and the creation of a highly definite sense of modernity, involving the deployment of science in fulfilling people's material needs, giving them 'clothes to wear and food to eat and delivering the kind of standard of living that they now see prevailing in the US, EU and other developed countries'. But it also tries to link with the concept of an ancient cultural and philosophical tradition which it is fulfilling and embracing. Party leaders like Liu know that arguing about the inevitability of historical materialism and Marxist dialectics has nothing like the emotional appeal of nationalism, and the project of constructing a great, powerful state. This is why some have argued that the CPC's current stance is nothing more than nationalism with the odd sprinkling of Marxism in order to placate memories from the past. This book will show that things are more complicated than that. But the Party under Xi is certainly very keen to avail itself of the resources China's national past as a country offers, despite a position in its early years in power which was often antagonistic to many ideas and attitudes present in the country's long, complex imperial histories which preceded the Communist era in 1949.

In view of Liu's statements, it is easy to see why terms like 'fragmented authoritarian', 'consultative Leninism', or 'resilient and adaptive authoritarianism' were unappealing to the internal discourse of the Party about itself.[5] Liu's statement shows that within the upper levels of the contemporary Party, there is no self-conceptualization of being 'authoritarian', or 'fragmented', and no space for the idea of being Leninist, even though there is recognition of being consultative. Internally, Chinese Party elites deploy a wholly different set of concepts and vocabularies. And these concepts stand in stark variance to those of the outside world. In view of this stark difference in respective vocabularies describing the same thing – one deployed from within, one from outside – it seems the divide can never be breached. The Party is two things: one to its members, and another to those looking in on it. This is the root cause of the confusion between the understanding of the non-Chinese experts and those in Liu Yunshan's party the day the seminar was held in 2014.

The aim of this book is to do something about this great divide, the dichotomy between the Party's inner language and the language of the world outside about it. This is a particularly sharp challenge because it would be easy to accept the terms of a wholly defensive Party discourse about itself, presenting it uncritically, or on the other hand to accede to an external perspective which fails, as mentioned above, to take the views of the internal players more fully and properly into account. In order to avoid falling into either of these traps, I have adopted two main strategies in what follows. Firstly, I have taken some clues from the comments quoted from Liu above. As the man in charge of the ideological messaging of the CPC up to his retirement from the Standing Committee in 2017, his words and the words of people in a similar position to him (not that there are that many!) do carry weight. At least, we know when we listen to him that this is how the Party wants the outside world to understand it, even if we can't assume entirely safely that it is truly what it thinks about itself. We have therefore to pay very careful attention to these words, and use a specific method to understand and interpret them.

One of the most striking aspect of Liu's discourse, and one that will be critical to the argument of this book, is the way they indicate that the CPC regards itself as more than just a political entity. This marks a crucial area of dissonance from much analysis in English and other non-Chinese languages. There the assumption is that the Party is a political organization, and that all it does fits into the realm of politics. It is about power, about organization, about control over the military, budgets, and other sources of influence. In the end, it is a machine for one particular output: organizational prowess.

Of course, this is not to deny that a lot of what the CPC does is, by its nature, political. It learned the lessons of Leninist organization well. But it has pretensions that stray far beyond this. This helps partly to offer an explanation to the vexed question of why, so long after most other one-party Marxist-Leninist structures have fallen, the Party in China still remains in place. For it is clear from what Liu said in 2014 that the CPC in China has frontiers and an identity that reach into the realm of culture, ethics, philosophy, and towards almost spiritual, quasi-religious objectives, and ways of aligning itself with the contours of the earlier and still existing cultural dispositions of

China, which have proved more enduring and successful – so far – than, for instance, their equivalent in the Soviet Union.

One indication of this ambitiousness in terrains beyond the purely political and organizational was the way in which the Party in its early era from 1927 acquired a military arm and more defined structure, and its leadership was sometimes described as a state within a state – an idea that will be repeated several times throughout this book. The reason why this description is still so useful is that it alludes to the Party's pretensions to comprehensiveness. This was not just a narrowly political force, but something that carried a world-view, a new understanding of how to behave, how to shape society, how to construct a modern nation. These aspirations have been maintained to the present, despite the vast differences in the context the Party operates in and the powers available to it.

One obvious manifestation of this comprehensiveness is the way in which since coming to power in 1949 the Party has monopolized political ideas. In Europe, North America, and most other areas dominated by multi-party systems, lines are drawn across the spectrum from what is now called the left to the right wing. Most parties, in order to gain power through competitive elections, attempt to claim the centre ground. None at the moment say they are able to occupy all the various positions along the whole line. But in effect, the CPC does precisely that. It has annexed all the meaningful political territory. It eschews the need for alternatives. Those who chose to explore space beyond the boundaries of the Party in terms of political ideas wander into the dangerous domain of dissidence and illegality. They violate the Party's self-ordained norms. The Party says to everyone that it is a vast house, a home that all can come to reside in – a mansion with many rooms, and no need of any neighbouring separate domiciles. However diverse the occupants, they are all essentially in one structure and under one roof. For those who do not wish to reside in this mansion, the alternative is not to move to some lower or lesser nearby abode. It is simply to become homeless and dispossessed. Having such a dominant location, the CPC therefore had to supply a wide menu of services and fulfil a large number of needs which sprung from this. It had to answer not just organizational but spiritual and cultural questions. It had to assert that its power and existence accorded with some fundamental notion of reality and truth, and that it embodied a unifying view of humanity, actions, and beliefs which justified this monopoly. Democracies can accommodate scepticism and doubt through the competition of choices they offer. In the one-party system China used from 1949, the Party set itself up as embodying truth. Its world-view had been proved by history to be right in the act of granting it power. Such heady and grand justifications are not easily available in multi-party systems, if they are available at all.

As the various chapters of this book will show, the nature of the Party's ambitiousness and aspirations to be a comprehensive force that reached far beyond the boundaries of the purely political were recognized in much of the scholarship from earlier eras by those observing China from outside. Works by A. Doak Barnett, Franz Schurmann, Lucian Pye, and John Lewis, amongst others from the 1950s into the 1960s, are important secondary sources, and will be referenced later. In the Cultural Revolution from 1966, an absolutely crucial event by which to understand this desire for comprehensiveness and fulfilling aims far beyond the purely administrative, the desire was to fundamentally redraw what it was to be human in modern China, and to politicize the most intimate spaces of life and of the self. This involved a violent reappraisal of the nature of society, of its culture, belief systems, and underpinning ethical values, and of how modern Chinese related to their long, complex past. Perhaps this is not surprising. The clue, after all, was in the title of the vast movement – a *cultural* revolution, not merely a national one. The objective was to remake and remould this Chinese culture, to overturn its oppressive burden and seek new liberty from its stifling influence. This particular attempt resulted in widespread chaos, tragedy, and calamity. But it still offers a powerful example of the Party aspirations being more than just about functional issues, serving people's material lives and operating in the physical domain.

Even in the 1980s, when reform and opening up really got into their stride after the death of Mao, during the era of breakneck economic growth and a brief period of hopeful liberalism when the whole ethos of the Cultural Revolution seemed to be repudiated, spiritual pollution campaigns clamped down on those who tried to besmirch the Party's cultural grander mission and to dilute its thinking and values with those imported from outside. Somewhere along the way, the CPC annexed not just political space but the very notion of Chinese modernity, a modernity that had been attempted so many times in the last century and a half but always remained out of reach and remote. Its victory at the end of the Civil War against the Nationalists, the ruling party from 1911, was a victory for its vision of modernization over theirs. And while the Nationalists emigrated to the island of Taiwan and pursued a different path, the Communists, through control of so much more territory, could claim that they had a particular authenticity. They were the vanguard of Chinese modernity. They could speak with unique power and legitimacy about what it was to be Chinese but also modern. It is the culmination of this viewpoint, I will argue at certain points in this book, that we see today under Xi Jinping.

These links between a very distinctive link with Chinese culture and the sort of modernizing politics the Party felt it embodied were present right from the time of the organization's birth. They manifested themselves in movements like the New Culture campaign of the 1930s, and in the successful efforts to create indigenous Chinese-style Communist art and ideology with a style of propaganda flowing from it at Yan'an, the revolutionary base area from the late 1930s onwards. The CPC was inducting people into a new life-style. It was the means by which new ways of thinking, new attitudes, and a new sense of Chinese identity were promoted, and through which a different sort of Chinese culture was proposed which liberated people from the enslavement of adherence to past models and modes of thinking. The completeness of this mission is tangible in the ways in which from the time the CPC came to power in 1949, it undertook campaigns not just to reorganize the surface features of society, but also to reshape the character of Chinese people – to create the Maoist new men and women, in the image of the CPC's ideology and mission. Jiang Qing, Mao's fearsome demagogue wife, eventually called this a movement to 'touch the soul'. But it was also one that aimed to rebuild and restructure the soul. All of this occurred in a context in which the terminology of scientific Marxism-Leninism only mattered on the surface. Underneath, there were other manipulations, other strategies being pursued, which related to China and only China, and to the remoulding of its culture through the operations of the CPC.

I use the word 'culture' in this context with a high awareness of how broad its meaning is. The importance of this term, at least for this book, is the ways in which it involves understanding symbols and practices and the impact these have on people's thinking, and the conduct of their private and public lives. Culture is also about embracing stories and the language through which they are rendered. It also crucially involves consideration of one of the most important, but most under-analysed and under-theorized aspects of the Party's mode of operation: its ability to relate to, mobilize, and create emotions for those involved within it, or engaged with it. As Daniel Bell said in his 1976 classic *The Cultural Contradictions of Capitalism* (a book to which I will return later), culture is predominantly about a set of shared symbols, and the ways in which these are manipulated or used to create meaning. The Party from its inception has been masterly at working on at least one key area here: the devising of a national narrative involving modernity and progress. It has been adept at creating a raft of new meanings, new explanatory frameworks and stories by which Chinese people understand their lives and themselves within this framework. This will be a crucial theme throughout this book.

This is a vast subject, and so to make things digestible, this book will move through a number of discrete areas, using them to illustrate the way in which the CPC can be viewed as an entity for not just political but also cultural, ethical, and personal transformation in the country it controls and rules over. Viewing the Party in this context at least addresses the conundrum referred to above of how to deal with the divide between external and internal attitudes and under-standings about the CPC. For the outside view, from the Western academy, maintenance of objective 'universalist' standards is key, as is preservation of the discourses of political science. But this book grants greater space to the concept of the CPC and what it represents. It is freed from the tight bounds of just being recognized as a 'politi-cal party' and granted more space and a richer identity by acknowl-edging the aspirations and the very wide scope of its practices and identity noted above. And for internal views, there can be no complaint that it has not received a more exhaustive and ambitious framework within which to attempt to locate it. The Xi leadership refer to 'win win' outcomes. Here is 'win win' in practice!

The structure of this book will be thematic. The first two chapters will concern narratives and describe the way that the CPC asserts and understands the teleology of its own history. These will look at how the principal publicly acknowledged and memorialized moments of evaluation of that history over the last nine decades, before and after coming to power, have been crucial in shaping the Party's identity and mission, and how they gave it a purposeful narrative stressing its redemptive role. The conclusion here is that the CPC has a moral narrative in which its fundamental mission is to restore justice and dignity to Chinese people.

In the third and fourth chapters, there will be discussion of the Party and the ethical systems it has been associated with through its historic narrative. These will show how its early attempts to outline what a good cadre might be and the selflessness and sense of sacrifice for the organization and against the individual this demanded came into conflict in the post-Mao era. Such conceptions found themselves at odds with the rise of a marketized, individuated self in a Chinese society returning to the tight atomized networks which prevailed in the pre-Communist period, a place described as Deep China. (This concept will be described in more detail in Chapter 4.) In the last two decades, as the Party's own morality and that of society have diverged, there has been an attempt to unite these seemingly irreconcilable domains by stressing the imperative to support the CPC in its fulfilment of its moral narrative, as outlined in the first two chapters.

In the fifth and sixth chapters, there will be discussion of belief itself – ideology, and what it might mean in modern China, what sort of things Party members have to believe, and the ways they believe these things, the functional utility, as it were, of ideology. Once more, the increasing displacement of this against the wider society around China will be attended to. This will involve a discussion of language, and of the Party's attempts to create an appropriate language that carries its political and cultural goals, but one freighted with the internal commitments to selfless Party morality and a Marxist-Leninist belief system against a society largely now indifferent to these. The tactic here has been to utilize heavy nationalist symbols and ideas and to somehow link the Party to these broader missions.

In the final chapter, there will be a discussion of the Party and aesthetics, the ways in which it has since the earliest period become its own drama, one with a particular view of the utility of art to promote political messages around collectivism and selflessness, something that market China challenged when Chinese art became so commercially successful and more individuated and diverse in its messaging post-1978. As will become clear, the unifying theme across all these areas is that of obedience to a specific set of narratives – an historic one, a moral one, an ideological one, and finally an aesthetic one. All of these will finally be presented as parts of an integrated whole. These narratives, and they above all else, represent the comprehensiveness, and carry the ambition of the Party as it exists in Xi's China. Understanding them gets to the heart of understanding how CPC leaders and followers think about themselves.

This book attempts to create a richer and more flexible joint language and framework within which to view the CPC. It does not attempt to make judgements on whether the mission of the CPC from its foundation onwards was a correct one, and whether or not it is likely to succeed (though I do make comments about the sustainability of some of the postures of the Party under Xi, and offer criticisms of these). The main purpose here is to describe as objectively as possible the factors that matter to the CPC as an organization, and the ways these range far beyond a simply political framework into a broadly cultural, moral one. As this book will try to show, the CPC is most remarkable for its powers of concealment. It acts on the surface as one thing, but operates underneath as another. Unravelling this disguise will be the core theme of this book. This will primarily be achieved by lifting it from the purely political, and placing it in the context of a social cultural movement, and one with diverse elements. This is predominantly a descriptive account – the story of the stories of the Communist Party across a set of important domains. This will involve a multi-disciplinary approach. Again, that is justified by the fact that the Party's mission and identity operate in many areas, from the ideological to the moral to the economic and aesthetic. That demands a multi-pronged approach.

A final issue concerns sources. One hypothetical framework for understanding the CPC that I have used is that of a quasi-religious organization, answering a series of ethical and metaphysical questions which other political entities often steer clear of. Not only this, but the Party's answers to these are often monopolizing and complete in ways which differ from the more hesitant, contingent posture of others. To reinforce the appropriateness of this parallel, the Party does indeed have a series of canonical texts – texts which have played a seminal part in its development and are, in many cases, part of its identity now. Amongst these, the works of paramount elite leaders from Mao to Deng, and on to Xi, have played a key role. I have drawn heavily on these, and particularly on those of Mao and of Xi, largely because of the immense importance of the founder, and the topicality of the current incumbent. I have supplemented these with deployment of texts which had importance in key areas. Liu Shaoqi's treatise on cadre behaviour, for instance, will be attended to in the chapters on ethics, largely because this was such a formative and popular work, and one which to this day maintains its status in official training, as the epitome of the expression of standards of elite conduct.

In addition to these, the Party has also produced throughout its various phases a seemingly infinite amount of reports, statements, commands, and declarations. Any one period, whether the 1960s, the 1990s, or the 2000s, would fill a whole library. No one would, or could, read through these. Not least, they would have to endure extraordinary levels of repetition and dense, largely meaningless rhetoric. Even so, there are some texts, such as those around judgements of Party history issued in 1945 and 1981, which had great impact, and which again have become part of the identity of the CPC. There is, too, a hierarchy of prestige involved in this documentation. Those carrying the imprimatur of the Central Committee sit at the top. Those emanating from lower levels of government and leadership have less of a cachet. On the whole this book only looks at centrally issued material. There are archives for the Party in Beijing. But they remain closely guarded, and largely inaccessible even to Chinese scholars. So this book only uses publicly available material.

There is a question of counter-discourses, as I have presented critiques of the Party's moral status and its ethical posture after 1978.

Within official material, of course, the onus is on uniformity. There are no issues of heteroglossia there. The voice is largely controlled, and the content, interpretation, and analysis, where they are offered, are mostly herded into one framework, and supportive of conveying a sense of consensus and harmony. One of the most powerful, and forensic, counter-discourses I have set against this is that of the late dissident Liu Xiaobo. One of the main reasons for its inclusion is the cogency of his work. But there is the more practical reason that at least this 'subaltern' language is openly available, despite its censorship within China. There are, of course, many other dissident voices. But Liu's, for a whole number of reasons, from its prominence to its coherence and focus, seemed the most appropriate and representative. There are a diversity of other secondary sources which I have also used. Some have already been referred to. Others are explained in the text.

1

Redemption from the Dark Past

History matters to the CPC. Interest in historic narratives has been one of the constants about its behaviour since the very earliest era. It is almost as though both the Party's elite leadership and its members were telling themselves a story as events unfolded, then ordering and reordering events in hindsight, seeking to make a tale that was compelling, and that could then help them control the present and the future. But it was, as I will argue in this chapter, always a tale with a very specific ordering meta-narrative – and that was one of justice and retribution, and the workings out of a new political order based on this.

Of course, the Party is not alone in this addiction to searching in the past for information that can shape its current identity and give clues to its future development. Nations, communities, companies, and individuals are all in the business of seeking a coherent narrative that arises from how they came into being, grew, and developed. These can be the basis for helping them move into some kind of clearer future which is at least approximately shaped by contours created in the past. Such narrativizations of the past have been staples of human society since the start of recorded history, and reach back before, into the vast era of human existence in which anthropologists tell us it was oral, rather than written, stories that were told to link, integrate, and create meaning. In the structures and patterns about pasts we find materials for interpretation, from which arise meaning and significance – identifiers, keywords, subliminal or sometimes open and explicit messages. From the time of Herodotus and Homer onwards, stories have been the source of history, and history has been the source of identity and of ordering world-views.

For the CPC in the twenty-first century, there are two issues that give this question of the narratives, of the story it draws from history, a real sharpness. The first is the ways in which it has a dual, contrasting story about itself, with one strand running up to 1978, when the post-Mao economic reforms started, and one subsequent to this. These widely divergent stories, as we shall see, have involved a large amount of work for the Party in reinventing itself, in imposing wholly new objectives, but also, more flagrantly, sometimes, in the words of British journalist Louise Lim, employing amnesia about difficult parts like the Cultural Revolution, the great famines of the early 1960s, or (the particular focus of Lim's work) the 1989 revolt.[1] Forgetfulness was, as we will see, a reliable part of the Party's armoury as it created dynamic new narratives throughout the last nine decades since its foundation in 1921, rearranging and renegotiating its relationship to this past. The second issue is the ways in which the Party, in coming to power, and moving from a revolutionary to a governing force, had to present itself as the forger of a new history not just for itself but for the nation it now had custodianship over. For this reason, from 1949 there is little daylight between the CPC story and the national one. The two became intimately linked. Till recent times, again as I will argue later, the Party argued it had achieved the salvation of the country. It was the entity that helped China throw off the heavy burden of its imperial pasts. Over the last decade or so since the mid-2000s, however, the question has become more how the country is now saving the Party – and how the CPC has become parasitical on nationalist messages and missions that make it clear its justification is in delivering these rather than Marxist objectives.

These complex issues of self-definition and self-understanding are not helped by the fact that the Communist Party came to existence in China with a confused mission right from the first day it had members in the country, during the very earliest era of the Republican period from 1911 onwards. In essence, its early leaders knew what they didn't want, and what they disliked about the China they were living in and experiencing in their day-to-day lives. But there was widespread disagreement about what they were actually aiming for, and what sort of new China they were trying to promote. What was attractive about the creed of Communism as an international movement, particularly after its victory in the 1917 Russian Revolution, was the way it offered a body of ideas like dialectics and Marxist-Hegelian views of history, which asserted that there was such a thing as perpetual progress. History had a purpose. It was heading in a positive direction. The future was eventually going to be better than the past. In the abstract, at least, that offered hope to Chinese potential adherents of the new doctrine.

A whole series of terms were invented by which to make sense of how this positive history would develop and what sort of teleology it might have. The introduction of this set of ideas into China through translated works and word of mouth (the first Chinese students started to go to study in Russia around about the time of the revolutionary ferment there from 1911) had a momentous impact. It appealed to a very specific frustration that Chinese people experienced with their own history. The 1917 October Revolution in Russia vividly offered the example of a country breaking the heavy burden of the interminable, stifling past and bringing about modernization. The weight of conservatism and tradition was something that many young Chinese passionately felt was also suffocating their own culture and politics. The USSR therefore offered a viable blueprint for what they could do.

British sinologist William Jenner wrote in the early 1990s of the particularly tragic, constrictive burden of these layers of Chinese histories.[2] Communists, through their early existence in China, could provide concepts and frameworks that at least promised to start to shatter this and offer one route to liberation, showing that by dialectical progress this history would one day end. In the Communists' world-view, China's feudal, Confucian, imperial, highly conservative pasts, stretching right back into mythical and semi-mythical times like the Xia and the Shang over a thousand years before the Christian era, were not an object of pride and a source of confidence, but a prison. With the implementation of dialectical materialism, class theory, and the whole menu of other Marxist-Leninist ideas, the Party was able to claim the role of a potential saviour, one which held a key to breaking the pattern of the narratives which had dominated till then, leading Chinese into a more flexible, future-orientated, liberating story.

In the years in which the Party fought for power and tried to gain adherents, this was a powerful source of mobilization and incentive. It offered hope, the most potent and illusive quality of all. The new structure of history and its meaning derived from this interpretive framework was something that gifted the Party through its foundational years with a dynamic, inspirational vision of China, an ancient country freeing itself of the huge weight of this long past. The tragedy is that this was a noble ambition which became the source of a whole raft of new challenges once the Party came to power and could actually bring this dream about. Its implementation created divisions in society and often bloody conflict, uprooting people from the familiar with violent social movements instigated by leaders who knew what they didn't want, but offered only the haziest idea of what they were trying to replace the old world with. Getting rid of the burden of history proved to be like trying to rid people of their shadows while they stood under the sun. It undermined something fundamental about Chinese people in general – that their history was a constitutive element making them what they were, encoded in the language they used, and the family structures and societies they lived in. Its contestation was to prove profoundly painful and disorientating. In the end, it proved impossible without burying the very notion of what it was to be Chinese. The restoration of language about pride in the country's long past and its traditions under Xi Jinping from 2012, which will be attended to later, testifies to this failure.

Reappraisals of History: The Two Iterations

The importance of the CPC's attitude towards China's history and its role within that is proved by the privileged place grand statements about these issues occupy in both the current state constitution of the People's Republic of China (PRC), and that of the Party. They figure as brave attempts to settle an issue which, it is clear, is still unresolved and possibly will always remain so. The state constitution, agreed at the National People's Congress in 1982, and subsequently (but not comprehensively) revised several times since, places one specific narrative right at the start, in the preamble:

> After waging protracted and arduous struggles, armed and otherwise, along a zigzag course, the Chinese people of all nationalities led by the Communist Party of China with Chairman Mao Zedong as its leader ultimately, in 1949, overthrew the rule of imperialism, feudalism and bureaucrat-capitalism, won a great victory in the New-Democratic Revolution and founded the People's Republic of China. Since then the Chinese people have taken control of state power and become masters of the country.[3]

This distils many of the issues that will be addressed later: the notion of the Party as an entity that was engaged in struggle and what this meant; the forces it struggled against; and the specific role it had and continues to have as an actor in a history which is purposefully moving forward to a positive denouement. Curiously, the Party constitution also has a parallel narrative, what we might call a shadow one, which echoes, albeit incompletely, that of the state:

> Under the guidance of Mao Zedong Thought, the Communist Party of China led the people of all ethnic groups in the country in their prolonged revolutionary struggle against imperialism, feudalism and bureaucrat-capitalism, winning victory in the new-democratic revolution and founding the People's Republic of China, a people's democratic dictatorship. After the founding of the People's Republic, it led them in carrying out socialist transformation successfully, completing the transition from New Democracy to socialism, establishing the basic system of socialism and developing socialism economically, politically and culturally.[4]

These two statements, in documents that have a highly privileged political and administrative status in modern China, stand as the end results of a long period of consensus seeking, arising from internal and external debate by the CPC and the government. Their production involved a high degree of management of contention. But for all their surface simplicity and clarity there is an immense amount of complexity, as though there were vast spaces underneath the words, which, if they were to be torn apart by dissent, would overwhelm the language they contain and devour it. The past is, as the British novelist L.P. Hartley famously said, another country, but for the CPC, it is a particularly treacherous and dangerous one, full of doors that have been carefully closed and locked, and territories that are vigorously blocked off and policed. Much of this past is unfinished business. A great deal about how to interpret and understand it and give its lessons meaning in the present remains undecided. Despite the neatness of the constitutional utterances, therefore, these questions of the scrappiness and messiness of history within China, for the Party and for Chinese people, will remain live ones for many years ahead.

One means of getting some handle on the ways in which the consensus position of the modern CPC and the state as articulated in the two constitutions quoted above has come about is to look at two core documents produced in the last seven decades. The first of these, dating from 1945, is the 'Resolution on Certain Questions in the History of Our Party' adopted by the Seventh Central Committee. The second is the 'Resolution on Certain Questions in the History of Our Party since the Founding of the People's Republic of China', passed by the Eleventh Central Committee in 1981. (A third document, which we will examine in Chapter 2, is the official Party history produced by the Central Archives of the CPC School in 2011, a multi-volume work as yet untranslated into English.) Separated by several decades, and after different, but very marked, eras of change and transformation, they offer something like canonical texts which can explain the ways in which the Party has decided on a specific narrative, the different ways it has articulated this over time, and the sorts of language and ideological, cultural, and other practices and impacts that have flowed from these narratives once they were put in place.

Before looking at them in detail, it is good to devote some time to an initial discussion of the links between these documents, what they say about the Party's expression of its own history, and, most importantly, how they relate the settlement of historic issues to questions of legitimacy. From its following an ideology (Marxism-Leninism) which had a highly elaborated theory of history, the Party was always in the business of proving through practice and its own development that this theory was correct. But history had to have a moral direction too, something relating to its experience of modernity which was utterly crucial. The Party narratives therefore had a strong underlying link to notions about salvation, the delivery of justice, and the idea of a righteous ending. These served to address the very strong sense of victimhood that the country had suffered from its first brutal and unequal encounters with modernity from the 1839 Opium War onwards. China as a victim afflicted with a mindset that always placed it in a weaker position than others internationally was one explanation used by intellectuals like the writer Lu Xun for the ways in which, up to the end of the Qing Dynasty (1644–1911), the once great country (in their nostalgic view) had become the object of bullying, subject to unequal treaties enforced on it by others, fierce reparation demands, and colonial dismemberment (the ceding of Hong Kong island in 1841 being the most egregious of these). This marked a difference from, for instance, the USSR or other socialist countries. They had histories, for sure, but in China's case the length, complexity, and cultural strength of its history through a unified language and other shared attributes made it a much bigger factor. The USSR did not, for instance, have a vast dynastic past to look back on. And without this, for all its pre-revolutionary suffering, it did not experience the deep and prolonged shock that China did when it underwent its calamitous encounter with aggressive Western modernity. China's sense of history and the pride deriving from this was deeper, and the suffering it underwent when this was so badly challenged was therefore greater in magnitude. These played a much bigger role in the case of China than anywhere else where Communism took hold.

Modernity to Chinese from the late Qing onwards was seen as an alien movement, originating in the West, something which had just sneaked up on them with no proper warning. They were most envious of the fact that even though modernization was an intellectual and social process, it resulted in the very practical outcomes that came from the industrial revolution. This gave Great Britain and others military and commercial resources that led to power and influence far beyond their country borders. That phenomenon of the projection of power in new and unexpected ways meant that China was forced out from its period of untroubled prelapsarian stagnation under the Qing to one in which it was vulnerable to nations which had become rapidly much more powerful and had the capacity now to impede on its domestic space. Apart from Britain, Japan was the most significant of these. But the encounter of China, an undeveloped, largely agrarian state, with a militarized, modernized Japan was to prove much more brutal than that with Britain. The Sino-Japanese War from 1937 to 1945 was Armageddon for a country stuck in pre-modernity, fragmented, weak, and vulnerable, and showing through the decimation it was suffering the clear superiority a state that had engaged with industrialization much more effectively gained. The conflict led to the deaths of some 20 million Chinese, and the displacement of about 50 million. It destroyed what little industrial infrastructure the country had, leaving it in many places a bombed wasteland. It was a kind of national crucifixion.[5]

A great attraction of the message of the Communists was that they were able to offer, firstly, an explanation for why this calamitous history had happened (feudal oppression, colonial capitalist exploitation, the dominance of one class holding back others), and, secondly, a vision of how this history, despite its unbelievable darkness, could form the basis of a new future, one where finally things would turn out well. It was that particular interpretive framework and the feelings of hope that flowed from it, rather than any real subscription to Marxism-Leninism as a political philosophy per se, that was the greatest force propelling the early Communist movement forward. Elements of this idealism about the good news that history would end well filled the speeches of Chinese leaders from the era of Mao Zedong and continue right up to the present day, all derived from the primal source of this master narrative structure. An added attraction was that this theory of history had such practical utility. It transformed the pain from the past into a useful force for the world now, inspiring people to fight for change. And best of all, there was a self-fulfilling logic to the Party's position on history. The Party, even in the act of coming to power, was showing that its interpretation was right. It alone in China had understood the teleology of this history. Power had been delivered to it because it had this understanding. Any attacks on the Party were attacks not on a limited institution but on this historic narrative and its optimistic message. Dissenters were surrendering to the old pattern of defeat and pessimism, and were enemies of hope. This posture continues to this day. Attacking the Communist Party is seen as being about far more than just dissenting from its politics. It is about turning one's back on a vision of optimism and the rights of the Chinese people to have this, which the CPC says it embodies.

The 1945 Resolution, and that of 1981, are the highest-status documents that embody this vision of history and its moral meaning and direction. Their status derives from their being formally passed at Party Central Committee meetings, the most important forum for Party governance, to be accepted as collective declarations of views on what the organization's history was. But the context of their issuance marks a substantial difference. The 1945 Resolution was written and issued by a revolutionary party fighting to gain power. This gives it a hypothetical flavour. It was talking not just of things that had been, but of things to come. Its tone was prophetic. That of 1981 is the declaration of a party in power, the early aspirations partially delivered, and its stance vindicated. In 1981, however, there was the need for more urgent justification of its experience of rule and the ways this had diverged from the purity of its initial pre-power vision. In particular, there was the slight matter of the retrogressive calamity of the Cultural Revolution and the late Mao era, events which seemed to directly contradict the idea of progress and things daily getting better. Accommodating these in the grand interpretive narrative of ever-onward progress and showing that it was not incorrect were what mattered most in 1981.

The two resolutions differ in terms of the way in which they were drafted and produced. The 1945 one is regarded as being the work of Mao Zedong, and indeed occurs in his selected works, albeit as an appendix. It is therefore something intimately related to his leadership, directly emanating from him. The 1981 Resolution, however, to suit the style of the Deng leadership, was a much more collective document, drafted and worked on by others, as will be seen below, even though there was guidance and verbal input from the paramount leader. Despite this difference, both are linked by the historic contexts in which they occurred. They were each produced at critical moments of opportunity and potential change. The 1945 Resolution was issued as the Sino-Japanese War had drawn to a close; the 1981 Resolution occurred after a time of upheaval involving the Cultural Revolution and the crisis that this brought. They were documents seizing the chance offered by a new beginning after eras of tumultuous change, provoked by the need to make sense of the recent harrowing history, and what lessons could be drawn from it. They were also offering forms of justification, saying the positive direction of history was still valid despite the recent calamities that had happened. They were finally highly practical in intent, organized in order to legitimate and create space for a new way forward, sanctioning new ways of operating, some of which had already started (the rural reforms, for instance, were already underway in 1981).

1945

In 1945, sense needed to be made of the series of crises that had happened to the country leading up to the 1937 war in ways which validated and recognized the latent, but increasing, power of the CPC, which had formally existed since 1921, giving it a dominant position in a narrative where most others merely granted it marginal status. The Resolution starts this endeavour of shifting the Party to centre stage by offering a chronological view of this period organized into three phases: the First Great Revolution, the Agrarian Revolution, and the War of Resistance Against Japan.[6] The Party may have been weak and in its infancy, but by viewing this history so that it shows 'the integration of the universal truth of Marxism-Leninism with the concrete practice of the Chinese revolution', the CPC is granted unique powers of agency and understanding. The first broad phase (the 'First Great Revolution) was marked by the introduction of Communism and the international outlook it brought to the specific attendant conditions presiding in Republican China (since 1911). This gave a language and outlook to better understand the evil impacts of imperialism and feudalism and the injustices that flowed from these. The 1927 defeat of the Communists by the Nationalists and their retreat to the countryside marked a decade in which the Party as an increasingly agrarian rather than urban force (thus 'the Agrarian Revolution) created the infrastructure and specific ideology, along with a unified leadership, to be a Chinese-style anti-imperialist, anti-feudal force. From 1937, as part of a united front, the Communists engaged alongside the Nationalists in the struggle against the Japanese ('the War of Resistance'). This ended in victory in 1945. That year therefore historically marks the point in which the enemy for the Communists once more shifted back to being the Nationalists, and the struggle became a purely domestic one.

While this historic narrative with its three broad phases can be seen as an externally facing one, implanting the CPC within the broad movement of history, there was also the working out of contradictions within the Party itself which needed to be accounted for. This was a parallel process of historic rationalization and justification because from 1921 the CPC was all too frequently not a unified force. It was beset by what the document describes as three phases of leftism. The first was associated with one of the fathers of the Communist movement and the introduction of Marxist ideology into China, Chen Duxiu. The error of this group of leaders was to adhere too purely to the notion of China following the Soviet template of development and assuming that it was already a country like the USSR having an effective bourgeoisie and proletariat. They took the erroneous view, the document states, 'that Chinese society was already one in which capitalism was dominant and would develop peacefully'.[7] Such a view downplayed the importance of rural areas, and the ways in which people there, rather than in the cities, would be the real source of revolutionary change in China. The second leftist error, from 1929, associated with the figure of Li Lisan, was to fail to 'recognize the uneven development of the Chinese revolution' and to hold 'that the revolutionary crisis was growing uniformly in all parts of the country, that preparations should be made everywhere for immediate insurrections', and that the cities were the core places where this would occur.[8] A third left line, around 1935 and linked to the Zunyi meeting convened then, continued the problems of the previous ones in privileging urban struggle and trying (it was claimed) to rigidly impose the template of international Communist theory on the complex and distinctive situation of China. Behind all of this was a fierce struggle for domination between people like Wang Ming and what were called the 'Twenty-Eight Bolsheviks' with close links to Moscow, and those around Mao Zedong, who were for a more indigenous, specific model of revolution.

The conclusion of these various struggles over strategy, and the core political objectives that needed to be followed, was a crucial one. It is something that is declared in several places by the 1945 Resolution. This was that the situation in China was very specific, that it was exceptional, and that while Marxist theory was universal, there needed to be a careful and sensitive application of it to these distinctive conditions. The 1945 Resolution therefore figures partly as an argument in support of this assertion of exceptionalism. China's new democratic revolution, it states, 'renders it necessary for the revolution to go through a protracted, tortuous struggle before nationwide victory can be achieved'.[9] The complexity of the Chinese situation and the need for a bespoke approach is stressed throughout the document. It makes it clear from very early on, therefore, that Marxism is to be introduced and embraced within China on terms that accord with the country's unique circumstances. This refrain has continued to this day.

There was another important element beyond the question of how to interpret history and affirm the role of the CPC that comes clearly through the narrative set out in the 1945 Resolution. This was support for a philosophy of leadership, for the centrality and symbolic importance of a unified direction manifested in one person. Mao Zedong's name occurs throughout the text. His is 'the correct leadership', the line he had supported is marked as 'the correct' one – reflecting the ideology of 'the advanced elements of the Chinese proletariat'.[10] 'Comrade Mao Zedong has devoted himself to applying the universal truth of Marxism-Leninism to the investigation and study of the actual conditions of Chinese society.'[11] The role of Mao as an intellectual enlightener, the provider of the paradox of an indigenous version of universal truths, is one from which he was never to be removed after 1945. But in the years before, the competition for supremacy within the Party was often fierce, and Mao's final victory far more precarious than the 1945 Resolution ever remotely admits to. In fact, with its categorical and frequent expression of Mao's core role, the Resolution implicitly testifies to the fact that this process had not been an easy one, and that further affirmations of his personal victory were necessary.

Unified Party leadership was a strategic means to deal with another immensely problematic issue: the profound fragmentation of Chinese society, and its complex and often deeply differentiated key components. This impacted itself in the Party through factionalism – 'mountain stronghold mentality', as one frequently used expression puts it. Party discipline had been challenged by 'bureaucracy, patriarchalism ... individualistic heroism ... favouritism towards fellow-townsmen and schoolmates, factional squabbles ... all of which undermine the Party's ties with the masses and its internal unity'.[12] Subsequent history was to show that this remained a perpetual challenge for the Party – the forging of a collective identity and the search for the means by which to do that in a society riven by lower-level, more local allegiances. The most acute and eloquent analyst of the root cause of this was the great sociologist Fei Xiaotong, whose almost contemporaneous work *China from the Soil* of 1947 had argued that the country was an overwhelmingly agrarian one, one in which person-to-person relations were 'elastic', based on personal knowledge in tight-knit, small communities where everyone enjoyed close propinquity with others. Outsiders in this kind of China were people not from another country, or another province, but from the next village. Levels of trust were high within these small communities, and almost non-existent outside. The average Chinese person in the imperial era had few, if any dealings, with representatives from higher levels of the state. Power distances were vast. Family linkages were the most important, the most reliable, and the ones in which people were most deeply embedded. But they also, for the modernizing Communists, lay at the heart of the feudal social structures that held the country back. This is supplemented by work collected by Hong Kong-based psychologist Michael Bond in the 1980s, where the privileged status given to family relations above all else created 'nepotism and obligation networks; non-objective performance assessment; and paternalism'.[13] Such networks created a tendency to secrecy, enclosure, and tightness. Many of these qualities were inimical to the process of modernity, though of course some were useful in creating a powerful sense of ownership and obligation once they had been tamed and the CPC was presented as a kind of new family or kinship. A fresh set of allegiances needed to be created, therefore, blending the old with the new, with the Party under Mao as a family beyond the natural family itself.

That Communist ideology proposed a new set of relationships in this way was truly radical. These cut across traditional patterns in Chinese society. They were often antagonistic to them. They set far wider parameters for the sort of world that people lived in. This was possibly the most profound innovation that the new political movement brought: not the modernization of the economy, but an attempt to erode and then dismantle the tightly inter-networked, individual-focussed worlds people lived in without any sense of a larger, wider society around them. This issue of a profoundly complex web of linkages and allegiances based purely on the person was testified to by Mao himself, echoing the founding father of Chinese Nationalism in the 1920s, Sun Yatsen, who complained that Chinese people were like 'grains of sand' resisting any attempts to enlarge their social worlds and create spaces for impersonal action and responsibility by melding them together. 'China's backward and decentralized social environment', the 1945 Resolution states, 'with its clans and guilds', meant there was a tendency of the petty bourgeoisie to display traits reminiscent of individualism and sectarianism.[14] Searching for sources of unity became a paramount mission. Demanding allegiance to a unified leadership was one tactic, at least strategically, of achieving that, even though it shifted from being a means in the early Mao era to becoming an end during the personality cult of the Cultural Revolution.

The other strategic commitment that emanates from the 1945 document is less palatable and less openly stated. That was an adherence to forms of violence as a way of achieving change and the justification of that through what political results it brought. Mao had said famously that power grows from the barrel of a gun.[15] In the 1945 Resolution, the 'complex' and unique situation in China, the range of problems, the lack of unity, and the urgency all provided justifications for the Party to deploy force. The revolution, it was declared, should seek to make 'extensive use of the enemy's contradictions and to set up and maintain armed revolutionary base areas'.[16] 'In the Chinese revolution', the document continues, 'armed struggle is the main form of struggle' through an army composed of peasants.[17] The Red Army occupied a distinctive position in this political constellation, 'a peasant movement led by the proletariat'.[18] Peasant guerrilla warfare, the organization of revolutionary base areas with armed capacity, and the utilization of organized forms of violence were all legitimized in this narrative. They were means of empowering the Party physically to address the great injustices, rebalance the unequal forces in society, and rectify the power iniquities it had identified in its interpretation. This justification of the deployment of violence during its revolutionary phase was to create a culture which was highly problematic as the CPC transformed itself into a governing entity, one which needed to find less destructive, more sustainable ways of addressing social problems and facing down opposition. Throughout the Maoist period, however, no solution to this was forthcoming. Use of state-supported violence in order for the Party to achieve its ends, along with the continuation of the Red Army as its army rather than that of the state, all fortified this, because it meant there were never effective institutionalized entities that existed to restrain its darker tendencies.

The importance of seeing the most crucial forces in the new history as distinctively agrarian rather than urban in focus was a revolutionary reformulation in its own right. But this was the chief means of the Party asserting itself, because its identity after 1927 was so strongly rural. As a strategic move, it was a stroke of genius. After all, the environment in which the vast majority of Chinese had lived since the dawn of Chinese imperial development had largely either been ignored, excluded, or regarded as profoundly backward and problematic in the annals of official histories and most narratives prior to the twentieth century. Rural China was the ultimate problem: a place of potential unrest, threat, uprisings, and immense dislocations; the residence of 'the enemy within', being quelled or encircled by havens of urban sophistication. There were ways in which the Communist ideology imported from the Soviet Union simply sought to continue this marginalization of the rural areas, privileging urban proletariat forms of unrest, and placing them at the vanguard of the revolutionary movement. But the Maoist innovations defied this. The rural areas were revolutionary too, they showed; they could also serve as the source of vanguard forces. For that reason, from the 1930s, overtly or covertly, Mao and the party he was becoming increasingly influential in were accused of heresy, most of all by the USSR. Much of the leadership tension had been a result of Soviet-educated, and -inspired, potential leading cadres returning to China and trying to enforce a much more standard interpretation of Marxism onto the Chinese situation. For them, focus on cities and the emerging proletariat there was the priority. In this context, the 1945 document testifies to a further significant event: the victorious emergence of Mao as champion of the countryside in China, and of an ideology that was supportive of this.

Asserting the primacy of agrarian areas had important ideological implications, and ones which created internal tensions which were never properly resolved. For Marxism-Leninism to remain a coherent, universalist, scientific body of truths, it had to accommodate this new Chinese-originated development, one that seemed on the surface to contradict it. (In a similar way, Western modernization theories in a later era had the same kind of challenges posed to them by China's economic development and lack of any meaningful political democratizing reform.) The Maoist approach, as the 1945 Resolution made clear, was hybrid. It was interested less in the content of classical Marxism historiography, and more in the practical use to which it could be put. It liked the idea that events, revolutions, changes, and trends happened according to a predictive framework that ideology supplied, even if that ideology was not strictly one to be found in Marx. The main thing was that the underlying logic was broadly right. This gifted the CPC with an immense resource: the means to instil order on what superficially seemed a disorderly history, and thereby to manufacture narrative meaning. It provided rationality in a situation that often seemed chaotic and insane. Most importantly, this history had a moral teleology. Things were happening the way they were because they were leading towards a better point. Finally, the 1945 Resolution showed that the Party under Mao understood well one key factor: that whoever controls the narrative controls almost everything else, and that that ownership of the story of the present and the future begins with the right to tell a tale about the past. This was a lesson it was never to forget.

1981

As stated above, the Resolution of 1981 occurred at a specific juncture in the Party's history as a governing, rather than a revolutionary, entity. It remains to this day one of the most important announcements made as part of the post-1978 new settlement, a period marked as 'reform and opening up' inside China, and as 'the great transition' by some outside. The history of this era has largely been presented as a relatively unproblematic shift from one phase of the Party's era in power to another. But as the work of historians Frederick Teiwes and Warren Sun has shown, there was never some neat template of what to do after Mao's demise in 1976.[19] The solutions to China's problems at the time did not fall from heaven. There was an immense amount of contention and indecision, even over issues like rural reform and the break-up of entities as unpopular as production brigades and communes. Perhaps the only commonality amongst the various leaders was that things needed to change. Which direction to travel in remained open to debate. It was, in the words of a phrase often used at the time, a period for 'liberating of thought'.

One of the most difficult issues grappled with in 1981 was how to deal with precisely the situation which a document like the 1945 Resolution had been so instrumental in establishing: the effects of unified, charismatic leadership. Originally posited as a source of strength, under Mao it had progressively deteriorated to that of tyranny and oppression. In addition to this there was the continuing impact of adhering to an ideology which privileged rural areas despite the fact that now cities and urban economies were becoming more important for the country. Finally, there was the divisive impact of promoting a taxonomy of enemies in society which had reached its apogee in the Cultural Revolution, with an attendant tolerance, verging on enthusiasm, for violence as a tool for political change. These were very formidable issues over which to forge a new consensus, especially amongst a confused and often diverse new set of leaders, many of whom were gathered around the figure of Deng Xiaoping, but plenty of others who had a residual allegiance to different figures, from Hua Guofeng, the man initially chosen by Mao to be his successor, to Chairman Mao himself. Even the memory of Mao itself was a highly sensitive issue to deal with.

The Third Plenum of the Eleventh Party Congress in late 1978, held at the Jinjiang military hotel in Beijing (to this day off-limits to most foreigners), marked what is widely agreed to be the formal relaunch of the Party's programme, though at the time this was not widely recognized. There was enough space to recognize some limited forms of marketization, some entrepreneurialism, and some use of foreign capital. These had all been anathema prior to 1976 and Mao's death. But in terms of practicalities, that all lay in the future, with initiatives like the Foreign Joint Enterprise Law of 1979, the creation

of the first raft of Special Economic Zones from 1981, and a whole
series of other edicts and regulations. The struggle over this period
was how to connect the increasingly distant pre-1976 period with
what was happening in a China through the late 1970s and into the
early 1980s, which was wandering further and further away from the
way the country had been since 1949. Something that was particularly
difficult to manage was the issue of the Party and its ideology, its role
in society, and, above all else, the very practical problem of how it
dealt with its past.

As was shown in the previous section, in 1945 the Party that
had existed then had been a victimized, marginalized, underground
force, one that had been fighting within itself, and then with many
in the hostile environment around it, simply to survive, let alone
prosper. From 1949, with victory after the Civil War against the
Nationalists, it transformed into the government, in charge of a vast
country and population, and needing to construct rather than fight
and destroy. While in many senses a vindication, this also presented
it with formidable new challenges. Over the period from 1949 till
the death of Mao in 1976, the dominant ideological commitment
was the purging of society through class struggle, with the aim of
creating a utopian socialist land after the full Marxist-Leninist Maoist
programme had been introduced (tailored, as stated above, to Chinese
characteristics). The main means of achieving this were a series of
social mobilization campaigns, starting with the Three Antis and its
attack on intellectuals in 1951 and escalating through to the nadir of
these, the Cultural Revolution. The latter, presented even up to the
time of his death by Mao as one of his greatest achievements which
ranked alongside fighting in the war against the Japanese and unifying the country in 1949, was in reality a monument to ideological
and political bankruptcy. It proved to be unsustainable, a purge of
the Party elite dressed up in arrogant-sounding bombast, Daoist in
its encouragement of the yin of disharmony and the yang of conflict.
By the early 1970s, China was internally disordered and externally
isolated. As Deng Xiaoping reportedly reflected when in exile working
at a tractor factory in Jiangxi in 1971, this was not how the revolution
was meant to be.[20] People were still impoverished, and the country
was many decades away from industrializing fully and improving
the material condition most of the population lived in. When Mao's
death came, the Party was therefore having to deal with how to
criticize itself without bringing into disrepute its legitimacy and its
all-important narratives by which it justified its coming to power in
the first place. Reinventing itself was the sole option, but only in a
way that did not eschew this story about how righteous and proper

it was that it had come to power, and how in the end its stewardship of the country would be proved right. It needed to defend its moral narrative above all else and show that the problems before 1978 were honest mistakes, not inevitable products of its own unsustainable nature and approach to power. As Deng subsequently said, this task was a momentous one, because, were it mishandled, it could have spelt catastrophe for the CPC. It was the difference between perdition and salvation. However neat accounts of the era were afterwards, no one should ever underestimate the profound crisis the Party faced over this period.

Mao's emotional hold over the Chinese people, and his symbolic importance for the Party, meant it was not feasible to engineer a moment of brutal removal posthumously, as had happened to Stalin in 1956 when he had been denounced a few years after his death by his successor, Khrushchev. Instead, there needed to be a shuffling of the narrative landscape, a reorientation as it were, in which significant moments and events from the past were reappraised, relocated, and a new story structure was set in place. The approach was to downgrade the role of individual leadership and position the Party as a learning organization, one whose basic line had been sound, but which was faced with immense challenges that needed great effort to overcome:

> Our Party has made mistakes owing to its meagre experience in leading the cause of socialism and subjective errors in the Party leadership's analysis of the situation and its understanding of Chinese conditions. Before the 'cultural revolution' there were mistakes of enlarging the scope of class struggle and of impetuosity and rashness in economic construction. Later, there was the comprehensive, long-drawn-out and grave blunder of the 'cultural revolution'. All these errors prevented us from scoring the greater achievements of which we should have been capable. It is impermissible to overlook or whitewash mistakes, which in itself would be a mistake and would give rise to more and worse mistakes. But after all, our achievements in the past thirty-two years are the main thing. It would be a no less serious error to overlook or deny our achievements or our successful experiences in scoring these achievements. These achievements and successful experiences of ours are the product of the creative application of Marxism-Leninism by our Party and people, the manifestation of the superiority of the socialist system and the base from which the entire Party and people will continue to advance. 'Uphold truth and rectify error' – this is the basic stand of dialectical materialism our Party must take. It was by taking this stand that we saved our cause from danger and defeat and won victory in the past. By taking the same stand, we will certainly win still greater victories in the future.[21]

Strategically, the Party even in 1981 is aiming for justification deep into the future, when its achievements will allow it to look back at the arduous path of the early years and grant it the right to state that the ends justified the means.

That the Resolution was important, and that it proved hard to write, is testified to by a series of comments made by the emerging paramount leader, Deng Xiaoping, over 1980 and into 1981.[22] These were to Central Committee members, and occurred as a number of asides and critiques, shaping the numerous versions of the 1981 document before it was finalized. From the start, Deng urged that there needed to be an avoidance of a 'narrative' method, in order for it to be more succinct. 'It is better to write in broad outline and not go into too much detail,' he stated in March 1980. The aim after all was 'to encourage people to close ranks and look to the future'.[23] The main task was to affirm Mao's historical role, find ways of acknowledging his achievements, seeking the right framework to understand and recognize his faults, but above all to preserve the privileged place of Mao Zedong Thought. In effect, it was to downgrade Mao's person and his role, and to upgrade the influence of his ideas and political philosophy. 'On no account', Deng said on 25 October 1980, 'can we discard the banner of Mao Zedong Thought. To do so would, in fact, be to negate the glorious history of our party.'[24] One tactic by which to make sure this happened was to add a long preliminary section covering the era before 1949, one which had already been addressed in the 1945 Resolution, which recognized the centrality of Mao's contributions to the Party coming to power. There at least, the late Chairman's reputation was unassailable. The problems started once he had actually come to power! Another tactic was to carve out a space for Maoist thought, which had an existence so independent that even Mao himself failed to properly implement it. Discrediting Mao and Mao Zedong Thought in the end, Deng states, would be 'discrediting our party and state'.[25]

Despite Deng's strictures against it, the 1981 Resolution does provide a narrative structure. For the history prior to 1949, the emphasis was on the moral mission the Party had assumed, through the core role it believed it had in uniting China, in mobilizing the Chinese people, and in bringing about an end to their enslavement. It gave people mastery over their own situation, the document states. Since 1949, the Resolution then grows epically abstract. Rather than go down to level of detail about the Great Leap Forward of 1957, the backlashes against this, the devastating impact of the great famines from 1960, and then the various phases of the Cultural Revolution, the 1981 Resolution imposes what eventually becomes an apologia, a defensive

history guided along ideological tracks, with little observance of empirical happenings. The famines are simply not even mentioned. Instead,
three phases are outlined. The first, the seven years up to 1956, are
labelled the era of 'socialist transformation'. In these, the contradiction posited by Mao in particular between socialism and capitalism
was evinced in the clash between proletariats, farmers, and bourgeoisie
in Chinese society. State control was affirmed across the whole economy.
Land reform led to farmer empowerment. Industrial infrastructure
started to be reconstructed. The Communist Party set about revital-
izing the culture and intellectual level of the country. This was a phase
of material renaissance.

The next ten years, from 1956 to 1966, was labelled the period
for building socialism in all aspects. As a priority, agricultural industries were slowly replaced by light and then heavy industry. Human
capital and cultural levels were developed. The threat of leftism and
right opportunism was met by the introduction of the modernization
campaign, spearheaded by Zhou Enlai, the then Premier, but supported
by Deng, in which science, defence, industry, and agriculture (what
were later to be labelled the 'Four Modernizations') were all subject
to national plans for upgrading and improvement.

The real objective of the 1981 Resolution, and the period on which
it spends most time, was the decade from 1966 to Mao's death in
1976. This created the main conundrum. It was, the document's authors
admitted, the period when the Party made its greatest mistakes. These
were largely laid at the door of Mao. But the strictures from Deng
and the veteran cadres around him had to be observed. There was to
be no de-Maoization. Instead, a new kind of history was produced,
one staying faithful to the moral outlines of the old version (history
is always about progress, always leading to redemption and eventual
good outcomes) and which deployed the old traditions of blaming
aberrations and mistakes on the leftist enemies within from the past.
In the 1981 account, a fractious group of opportunists and radicals
around the 'Gang of Four' (the figures blamed for the excesses of the
Cultural Revolution after Mao's death), and then further leaders around
Lin Biao, a man originally marked as Mao's closest follower and most
likely successor from 1967 after the fall of Liu Shaoqi, occupied the
position of villains, saboteurs led by a variety of motives who wished
to steal the revolution away from Mao and contaminate it with their
own careerism and vested interests. That they used the verbal garb
of Maoist thought in order to subvert and undermine it only made
them more reprehensible.

Any subsequent history of the Cultural Revolution, either in English
or in Chinese, has needed to admit the immense complexity of its

causes and how it unfolded. From the comprehensive work of Roderick MacFarquhar on the origins of the Cultural Revolution, to histories by Yan Jiaqi and Gao Gao, and subsequently Frank Dikotter, Michael Schoenhals and others – all of these, along with many first-hand testimonies, support the notion that the movement was a many-headed beast, and that it had deep-seated and multiple causes.[26] The only commonality across all this material, even in revisionist material like that of Mobo Gao,[27] is that without Mao there would have been no such movement. And yet the 1981 Resolution was insistent on allocating much of the blame to figures around him who, it claimed, had manipulated and misled him. In this account, one of the most subtle, cunning, and strategic of modern political figures is painted to be gullible and naïve. This means that the 1981 Resolution is not about creating consensus on a thing called history, about events that actually happened, but about the political imperatives to preserve the Party's unique status and its monopoly on the right to interpret history. It was focussed on ensuring that the CPC's past did not undermine its present or future. It was in that sense a masterpiece of reinvention. And it showed the deep creative skills of the Party in telling its own story and maintaining control over how the story was told. Most importantly, it supported and sustained the moral narrative of the earlier Resolution. The Party was guided by the single mission of making sure China as a country was strong, powerful, and had justice restored to it. The Maoist excesses had been errors on the pathway of learning. But the path itself, and the endpoint, were not in question. The Resolution of 1981 was a proof of this, the organization sitting back, reflecting on its mistakes, and admitting it had got smaller things wrong, but the main, big thing right. It, and it alone, was able to deliver redemption to a China that had suffered, and now needed to be regenerated. That position has been maintained in the subsequent three decades, the period we will now shift our attention to.

2

Winning the Historic Mission
The Party under Xi

With the changes and events that have happened in China in the era
after 1978, some of which were referred to in the previous chapter,
it is unsurprising that there has been an accompanying sense of dis-
orientation. This has manifested itself in turbulent events like the
1989 uprising, but also in a series of crises about faith, ideology,
purpose, and direction within the Communist Party itself.[1] The very
personality of people had changed through this period of almost daily
transformation.[2] All of this will be attended to in more detail in the
following chapters. But the ways in which the Party has continued
to address these questions of its own history and the coherence of
that is important. There have been no subsequent resolutions produced
by the CPC since 1981, nor any sign that further ones are imminent.
In part this is a testament to the fact that over 1978 into the 1980s
there were issues of such fundamental importance which were changing that it would have been impossible not to have had a formal
appraisal to make sense of all of this. Since then, no similarly epic
political change has needed the sort of explanatory effort offered by
the 1981 Resolution.

Even so, the stark difference of China's economy, society, and the
CPC's role before and after 1978, and somehow providing a link
between the two, has remained a problem. China looked and felt a
different place the further into the Reform era it got. Cities acquired
skyscrapers. (Shanghai alone had 2,000 above twenty storeys by 2010
– not bad for a city built on marshy land!) Families dispersed across
the country through the phenomenon of migrant labouring. Foreign
companies became ubiquitous. The private sector started to account

for more than half of economic activity, up from 1 per cent or less prior to 1978. A whole raft of things like mobile phones, foreign travel, and the internet started to make a massive impact on the place some analysts called Deep China.[3] The old world, a world alive in many people's memories, grew more and more distant, with the only connection being that both places had a one-party system for its political rulers to operate in. It was natural enough to ask whether in fact even the Party itself had fundamentally changed, or, indeed, should reform as radically as other areas in society.

The tension between two such different eras threatened to create a schizophrenic identity for the CPC, dividing it into an entity that existed up to 1978 in one form and then another that existed in a different guise subsequently. But the 1981 Resolution made clear that there was no question of this happening. There would never be a wholesale repudiation of the period between 1949 and 1978. The Party now cannot say that the Party back then was incorrect, invalid, and can be jettisoned. The two remain one, with a common narrative thread running between them which is more than just fanciful. A solution to any possible hiatus was most strongly in evidence in the history of the Party produced in 2011 by the CPC Central Archives. After 1978, it asserted, there were still two fundamental pillars of legitimacy acquired from what is now called by some historians 'the era of high socialism' under Mao that mattered for the Party as it moved forward: these were, firstly, the ways in which Mao and his co-leaders took part in the Sino-Japanese War and the struggle against fascism and in alliance won this; and, secondly, how they unified the country after 1949. Those foundations for the CPC's right to rule were gained prior to 1978. They were not ones the Party post-1978 could repudiate without seeking a new source of legitimacy which had equally commanding and compelling power, one it would never be able to find. They were parts of its justificatory narrative, something that transcended the bounds of 1978. The Party was united, unified, and indivisible across this era because it stuck to the same grand story of history.

A formal resolution dealing with this particular conundrum of how to link the pre- and post-1978 story would have been too defensive, and its writing and issuance too potentially divisive. So despite the elapsing of over three decades since 1981, and the sense in which the distance between the Party and the society it was presiding over was increasing by the day, no formal attempt was made to reposition and rearticulate the Party's historic narrative. The 2011 history was a re-assertion that the CPC ruled because it still believed it was part of a common narrative, one reaching back prior to 1949, and one which justified it continuing to govern into the twenty-first century, decades after these events happened. The only new pillar of legitimacy that was added was the ways in which the Party had fulfilled the people's expectations for a better standard of life; its ability to pump out GDP growth and be economically successful. Economics involved, as we shall see in Chapters 3 and 4, buying people's bodily allegiance. History meant you had a chance of appealing to their souls, which is why the CPC could never relinquish this space.

The 2011 history is not the same kind of document as the 1945 and 1981 resolutions. It did not come through a process of stringent highest-level political vetting and patronage, was not authored or scrutinized by an elite leader (it was way too long for this, for a start), and did not figure as an important strategic document. Its importance is simply that it comes from a body within the Party formal apparatus itself – the historic archives group – and from this alone has a status and authority that makes it different from something produced even by a well-connected, well-informed professional historian within China. The four volumes which constitute the history, two for 1949 to 1978 and then two from 1978 to the current era, are over 2,000 pages in length. There is no named author or editorial board. This anonymity only adds to the impression that it is the Party which in the end is being presented as the author, acting collectively and presenting its corporate memory of what experiences it has been through as a governing rather than a revolutionary entity.

As a lengthy narrative history, it is presented as a work with the usual analytic framework of other standard histories produced in China about less prestigious and less sensitive subjects. Land reform in the 1950s; the setting in place of a planned economy model and the ways in which this impacted on the political economy of the country and on national development; the realization of socialism with Chinese characteristics and the gradual return of the PRC to a place of self-determination with agency and high status on the world stage – all are granted major roles binding this history together. The Cultural Revolution is written about as power grab by manipulators of Mao, along the lines of the 1981 Resolution, the most destructive impact of which was on the infrastructure of the Party, but which did allow for some economic benefits to be continued after 1978.

In this narrative history, at the foundation moment back during the genesis of the CPC, the Party gave itself two missions. The first was to use workers to overturn feudalism, imperialism, and bureaucratic capitalism in order to create new democratic socialism. The second was to bring about a socialist society within China.[4] In order to do this, the Party had allowed pride to return to China, passed the

first laws under the new regime, and produced a blueprint for economic planning to create industrialization. It had forged unity between
workers and farmers, and between different parts of China.[5] Through
the army, in the government, in society, it had been the force which
had instilled this unity.[6] The strongest statement was about the justice
and moral rectification that the Party had brought about:

> After the establishment of the PRC, this symbolized restoration of
> dignity and independence to the countless good people of the modern
> period, [the CPC] had completed the responsibility to victoriously achieve
> the basic historic liberation of the people, and from this had started
> bringing to reality the glorious strength and wealth of the country...this
> had deep and far-reaching meaning, above everything else.[7]

The themes apparent here had become staples of historiography for
the Party and the country over the period of late reform from the
1990s onwards. The keywords were 'liberation', 'people', and 'strength
and wealth of the country'. The last of these in particular had increasing resonance, and will occur when keywords from the Xi-era ideology
are discussed in Chapter 6. While terms associated with strength and
wealth enjoyed frequent usage throughout the period since the abor-
tive modernization reforms in the late Qing at the end of the nineteenth
century, the phrase was truly coming back into its own in an era in
which China visibly had more wealth and military might than ever
before. While being a strong and wealthy country was an aspiration
for any period up to the twenty-first century for the modern Chinese,
in this most recent period it had become a reality. That made a massive
difference to the deployment of this language and the way it was
received by audiences in China.

For much of the 2011 history, the emphasis is on the physical
rebuilding of this strength, even over the eras of internal turbulence
and crisis. In the 1950s, the Party had controlled inflation and avoided
economic implosion, despite the withdrawal of the USSR as an ally,
and with it its expert technological advisers.[8] It had built government
infrastructure, started to implement the first Five-Year Plan from 1953,
resurrected China's military capacity and its national defence posture,
and rebuilt agriculture.[9] The objective through the ups and downs of
this time-line remained unchanging: to guide China towards strength
under the unified leadership of a Party carrying out an historic mission.
This party was always a resiliently nationalist party, one which was
focussed on achieving the renaissance of the modern Chinese state
after the injustices and humiliations visited on it by colonial oppres-
sors since 1839. Such a history maintained the ethical framework

inherited from the 1945 and 1981 documents, with the sole difference that this element was much more strongly stated and evident in the earlier documents.

The 2011 document, for all its length, is underlined by one stark, simple message, refined and clarified from previous iterations: with no Communist Party, there would be no Chinese future. The country would have succumbed to the perpetual sickness of its past and been destroyed. Addressing the injustices this past contained created a foundation for a future where retribution and redemption would be possible. Such notions were remote in 1945, and still very distant in 1981. For the Communist Party in 2011, however, this promised future was just around the corner. The moment of realization of strength and power was imminent. This gave the Party story, and the telling of that story, even more piquancy and energy.

Telling the China Story: The Party as Hero

In the era of Xi Jinping, the standard accusation is that Xi's fixation on centralization of power and the cult of personality starting to emerge since 2012 makes him a Mao mark two.[10] Despite this, Mao remains a controversial figure within Chinese politics. The judgement of the 1981 Resolution still stands. There he figures as a leader with great achievements to his name, but also one who committed serious errors. As a sign of this, the fiftieth anniversary of the start of the Cultural Revolution of which he was so proud in May 2016 passed with only the smallest formal mention in the *People's Daily*, the official mouthpiece of the CPC, and that a critical and negative one. That the event that Mao stated was amongst his finest achievements has barely figured in the talk and public comments of the so-called 'quasi-Maoist' modern leaders needs explanation. It seems a bit like a British politician celebrating Churchill but ignoring his role in the Second World War. Maybe they are not so Maoist after all.

The more prosaic reason for their need to engage with Mao despite so many negatives about him is simply that even now he remains inescapable, and resists all the attempts to bury him. In terms of a charismatic style of politics which is viable in China, and the effective engagement with emotional narratives that really speak to many Chinese people's hearts, Mao's shadow looms large, because he was the one figure in modern times who achieved these things par excellence. One area in which this is truly striking is the use of storytelling, and the deployment of material from China's pre-modern past to utilize in contemporary political discourse. For the first, Mao's adept use of the tale of the foolish old man building a mountain (*yugong yishan* in Chinese) offers one of the most celebrated examples. This fable was used to instil qualities of endurance and fortitude into cadres and the Party faithful from the earliest era. It was deployed ad nauseum in the latter Maoist period. It is, in many ways, more informative for its phenomenal uptake and popularity and what reasons might lie behind this, rather than for what the story itself actually said.

The 1981 Resolution, with its rejection of overt 'narratives', marked a period in which the storytelling stopped, or simply became conveyed through outputs and facts, following technocratic strategies, with leaders filling speeches with statistics and figures rather than fables. If this told a story, it was an implicit rather than explicit one. Neither Deng, nor Jiang, and certainly not Hu, was a storyteller. They were administrators, interested in the business and detail of governance, avoiding the stirring stories that had mobilized publics in the past, and simply allowing the transformation of the physical landscape and the change in people's lives to speak for itself. Facts on the ground, not grand words or rhetoric, showed the resurrection to new life of a country that had suffered injustice and bullying and was now able to stand on its own feet. Reference is often made when discussing diplomatic issues to the so-called '24 Character' statement attributed to Deng from the 1990s: 'keep a low profile and bide your time, while also getting something accomplished' (*taoguang yanghui, yousuo zuowei*). But while this is taken as informative about China's international posture, in many ways China over the Deng and Jiang era was hiding its capacity and real aims as much from itself as from the outside world. These were decades where people adopted a humble demeanour, and where Chinese were busy travelling the world simply studying others. Everyone resisted getting fixated on the sort of grand utopian ideals that had caused such problems in the Mao era. Pragmatic 'seeking truth from facts', 'crossing the river by feeling the stones', or disregarding whether 'a cat is black or white as long as it catches mice' (other favoured Deng phrases) were the key conveyers of a new tale – neither dramatic, not really speaking much about what, in the Maoist phrase of the earlier era of storytelling, 'lay the other side of the river'. The focus was just on making sure China had a chance of getting there.

The Return of the Storytellers

Things under Xi are changing, however. The era of humility and reticence is over. In 2017, the People's Publishing House in Beijing produced a book simply called *Xi Jinping Telling Stories* (*Xi Jinping jiang gushi*). Its sponsoring department was the *People's Daily* Editorial Department. The book was neatly organized into two main sections: the stories for within China, and those for outside. The preamble to the book stated that since the era of Yan'an in the 1940s, storytelling had always been important to the Party. 'General Secretary Xi', it continued, 'is the teller of stories to everyone.' The various stories the book attributes to Xi, or gives attention to, range from the use of classical tales to Xi's dismissal of the American popular television series *House of Cards* as having any relevance to understanding the anti-corruption struggle in China. (The difference lay in the Chinese anti-corruption in Xi's words not being a 'power struggle'.[11])

Even Xi's life, in ways which simply was not true for that of Deng, Jiang, or Hu, became a source of new stories: of the man who had suffered in the Cultural Revolution, and then gone down to the countryside in Maoist fashion, working in primitive village surroundings before being summoned back to Beijing, continuing his education, and finally working his way up every level of government to reach the top. That the official Xinhua news agency produced a narrative of Xi's life soon after his elevation in 2012 was symbolic of a shift in leadership style. Nothing remotely like this happened in the era of the leader before, Hu, when the tenor had been against, rather than for, using a leader's personal story.[12] Larger narratives were equally important for Xi, however. The big story was making a comeback.

Part of this was derived from the way in which telling such stories promoted China's new interest since the 2000s of acquiring soft power, and of achieving this by getting the China story better understood in the outside world. Xi himself had chaired a Politburo meeting in 2013 in which, alongside a more proactive stance on foreign affairs, he had urged his fellow leaders to tell this China story, to gain the country a fairer and wider hearing and clean up some of the misunderstandings and misapprehensions surrounding it. Those fears by some in the outside world of China being a threat, an omnivorous, ominous usurper and disrupter needed to be confronted and answered. There needed to be a counter-narrative. Referring to the probably apocryphal comments attributed to Napoleon of China being like a 'sleeping lion', Xi skilfully tagged a new spin onto something widely known in the West: speaking in Paris in March 2014, he said that if China was a lion, it was a 'peaceful, lovely, civilized' one.[13] The immense efforts expended working on China's global image were evident in the establishment of Confucius Institutes, the expansion of media, the investment made in campaigns and image-bolstering work.[14] But the responsibility of Chinese leadership to take the lead was something explicitly recognized by the elite figures around Xi. He was telling stories not only that Chinese people needed to relate to, but also to support the soft-power efforts of the government. Observers of China understand the role of state-owned enterprises (SOEs) and their importance in the Chinese economy. These were state-owned stories. And as with SOEs in the economic and political realm, there were issues about how the outside world, with its different social attitudes and set of values, should best relate to them.

On top of this, however, there was an act of reconnecting to the earlier, more primitive, more raw and visceral approach of the Party, a period best exemplified by the 1945 Resolution. This was an era in which it had passed through immense challenges to survive, and in which its storytelling, through the mouth of Mao and others, and the ways in which it was able to relate to Chinese people's emotions, particularly those in the countryside, and create a tale, a *mythos*, which was meaningful, engaging and instilled hope, was crucial and had urgency and potency. That storytelling about the role of the Party, about the Party's meaning in liberating and directing people to a better future, was so vital for its ultimate political success was not in question. The main objective over seven decades on from becoming the governing party was to resurrect this skill at storytelling, and to ensure that in the stories the Party, with its complex, contradictory, often tumultuous history, maintained dominance of the centre stage.

Using the Past to Serve the Present

One of the main tasks was to address the thorny issue not just of how the Party in the twenty-first century related to its own past and created a coherent narrative about that, nor about what to make of events during the period since its foundation, but also how it then linked to the vaster and more diverse pasts of the country whose geographical territory it was now governing. This sort of challenge typifies the new kinds of problems for a country whose importance for itself and the outside world has enlarged as a result of the economic reforms over the last few decades. Xi's era is one of ambition. Its narratives are not parochial. They can afford to be, and must be, more expansive and all-encompassing or they risk sounding out of kilter and outmoded. The CPC, in the Maoist period, and for much of the time after the ending of this, dealt with this vast 'deep past' by simply condemning it as a feudal ghetto, a place of oppression which everyone had to get away from as soon as they could. History only properly started in 1921 with the founding of the CPC. In the area of narratives, and as the chapters on ideology, ethics, and aesthetics which follow will also show there too, this posture underwent profound change. The Party started seeking links in many areas in order to capitalize on and gain validity from the past of the nation. Under Xi it no longer condemns traditional culture and the imperial entities from which this emanated. On the contrary, it embraces what was once sniffily called feudal China, and at times also seeks to exploit it.

In Xi's China, the aim is not to deliver a 'rich, strong CPC' but a 'rich, strong China'. The Party is the enabler of this grand mission, its humble servant. The first Centenary Goal, which started to be mentioned in official discourse in around 2014, might be to mark the hundredth year of the Party's existence. But the real meaning of this moment will be to announce a key point on China's epic journey as a *country* towards modernity, and power and wealth. Not that the nationalist strand of CPC thinking was ever absent in earlier periods. But Xi's China has the means and the wherewithal to announce it much more assertively, and articulate it far more prominently.

One aspect of the ambitiousness of the CPC, something referred to in the Introduction, is the ways in which with its language, its rites, its elite leadership, and its history and doctrine, it often seems more like a religious organization than a purely political one. This permits the use of an example from theology to illustrate quite how the politics, administration, and country fit together. In many ways they are separate and yet figure as one indivisible whole akin to the idea of the Trinity in Christianity. The Party (politics), state (administration), and nation (China) have a mysterious symbiotic relationship with each other. Recent years have seen the nation and its fundamental importance outrank everything else, becoming like a divine fount from which all else flows. Of course, the nation would not function without governance, and the Party argues that it alone has the political skill and coherence (and legitimacy) to ensure its smooth running. But the nation and the appeal of national greatness and Chinese renaissance tower above everything else. This will be discussed in more detail in Chapter 6.

This had roots in the way in which, under Deng from the 1980s, while pragmatic engagement with other forms of modernity from the capitalist West gave the CPC new vitality, and, in some ways, saved it from oblivion, it also brought potential sources of threat, and demanded a spirit of compromise. One of the most extraordinary shrewd tactical concessions the CPC made was the accommodation of the country's own past, the decades, centuries, and millennium before it itself came into existence. This rehabilitation of the deep past, and the permission to start studying it again, referring to it, and having a feeling of pride and connection to it, is all the more remark-able when remembering the savage repudiation of that whole period in the Cultural Revolution. Modernization under the Communists after 1949 at best meant ambiguity and a feeling of distance and disappointment with the grand feudal period. But from 1966, the attitude was more akin to all-out war. While the Nationalist govern-ment still residing on the island of Taiwan could say that it preserved the traditional Chinese past, and honoured its memory (something that is still asserted to this day), in the PRC the objective was to shed this period, despite the paradox that Mao himself was still so evidently steeped in the ideas, themes, and world-view of the classical era (witness, for instance, the often conventional shape of his poetry). The acme of this was the 1966 campaign to 'Smash the Four Olds', which resulted in wholesale attacks on the country's historic cultural heritage, and the later 'Criticize Lin (Biao), Criticize Confucius' campaign of the early 1970s, in which Confucius took the brunt as the high priest of hierarchy, feudal oppression, the ideologue of a 2,000-year-old imperial legacy that finally needed ripping up. The savagery of this attack saw Confucian temples vandalized or destroyed, and scholars specializing in this area sent to Cadre Training Schools (a name for what were in effect concentration camps) and exposed to brutal re-education campaigns. When the onslaught died down after the death of Mao (he himself wearily admitting in an interview towards the end of his life that he had made little real difference to the thinking of Chinese people and their addiction to the vast burden of their own past), despite the initial burning interest in Edison, Einstein, and Western economists and scientists, gradually re-engagement with figures, events, and belief systems China itself had produced, and then a deep rising pride in these, came to the fore. The Chinese past had made a comeback.

How is it therefore that in the period of Chinese material enrich-ment and rising self-confidence the old imperial history, or a particular selection of its key moments and figures, has been able to make such a dramatic return? Why is it that the Party, equipped with a historic narrative of modernity and progress from its earliest days which painted this prior history as so problematic and negative, now presents 'tra-ditional Chinese culture and history' as an important resource, one which contributes to its legitimacy, and nourishes and supports its overall strategy to build a new modern China?

One explanation for this resurrection of the deep past is that it is profoundly pragmatic, and offers further evidence of a political entity (the CPC) so ruthlessly focussed on power that it is willing to wholly change its posture on an issue even as fundamental as this as long as it helps it maintain its dominance. But there is a better explanation. Deep down, the Communist movement in China was always different, always highly nationalistic and focussed on articulating a specific 'Chinese' movement. Marxism-Leninism had utility. It was useful in delivering modernity and therefore strength, dignity, autonomy, and pride. But as has been alluded to several times already, the moral narratives that the CPC deployed from the 1940s onwards, while Marxist-Leninist on the surface, were always servants of an underlying national, not Party, mission. This nation was one with a massive cultural and historic memory. Parts of that needed to be eschewed. But which parts and how was always a source of confusion. It was an issue that was never effectively and finally dealt with. The CPC loves China, it says, and its fundamental aim from Mao and Deng onwards has been to make China strong and powerful. But that China has as an inextricable part of its identity a specific set of histories, of cultural traditions and values, which at some points the CPC has critiqued and attacked, and at others (more recently) embraced and manipulated. It's complicated.

It might seem problematic that there are ancient narratives deeply embedded in Chinese language, culture, collective memory, landscape, and social behaviour which sometimes grate against the CPC's own vision of historic development. In some of the historiographies of the Chinese imperial pasts, there was a conviction about circularity, of history being a series of ups and downs, with no final resolution.[15] There is also a haunting message because of the immensity of this history about the inevitable limitations of human endeavour, and the imperfectability of all that people try to do. The CPC era from 1949 dwindles in this massive edifice down to a small footnote. The inference is easy to make. It, too, despite its claims to resolution, is pursuing a contingent historiography. It, too, will one day fail and fall. If that is one of the lessons that can be drawn by the Party from the sweep of imperial and pre-imperial histories, it is not one that seems to be dwelt on much. On the whole, the focus is on extracting as much symbolic capital and kudos from this era to use in the present, and bolster the sense that the Marxists-Leninists in the PRC are on a mission to give new life to this long history, and, dare it be said, bring it to its culmination.

In 2018, in the era of Xi Jinping the storyteller, the Party lives in a context where the sheer velocity of events means these unresolved underlying tensions can be tolerated. The crucial larger issue of a moral narrative in which the CPC is a vehicle pragmatically using Marxism-Leninism to deliver redemption, justice, and liberation to a wronged nation remains as intact now as it did in 1945. This links the CPC now to the CPC that existed pre-power, pre-PRC, pre-1978 and economic reform, and forms the great arch that combines Party, state, and nation. Within the starkly simple lines of this narrative structure there is space for much hybridity and diversity. Once this narrative is established and made sustainable, then other things can fall into place, from the ethical to the ideological to the aesthetic. It is to the first of these that we now turn, in order to understand better what a Party with moral narratives actually believes about its own moral vision.

3

Being a Good Chinese Communist
The Search for a Moral Narrative
in Xi's China

There is a moral narrative to the formal historiography of the CPC, as outlined in the key documents described in the previous two chapters. It is an organization which has delivered justice to and reawakened a country that has been victimized, subjugated, and brutalized in its modern history. The teleology of this history is towards a point of retribution and redemption, the resurrection of the powerful, strong, rich state, immanent in the first and second centenary goals articulated under the Xi Jinping leadership in the period after 2012. The first of these marks the hundredth anniversary of the foundation of the Party in 2021. The second marks the centenary of the PRC in 2049.

Such a moral history where the path is towards rectification of past hurts and wrongs is populated by moral actors and involves a play of forces where the good is ranged against the bad. This was true in the pre-1949 era, the time before liberation, in which the Nationalists (mostly bad), the imperial Japanese (always bad), the landlords, feudalists, and others were all ranged in a struggle against those on the side of the good: Communists, proletarians, farmers. There were also more ambiguous figures – intellectuals, for instance. But as the PRC started its own history from 1949 onwards, the struggle between good and bad continued, albeit in a different form and against different enemies. This battle was played out in propaganda, carried forward in mobilization campaigns, with fights against saboteurs and residual elements of the old society still lying underground. There were even new enemies who emerged: agents of the US, returned intellectuals whose loyalty was questionable, people like that. All of these were to figure in the greatest moral war of all, the Cultural Revolution, an elemental tussle played out like the Devil versus the angels of light in Milton's seventeenth-century epic *Paradise Lost*. A complex taxonomy of metaphorical labels for bad figures was created at this time: cow ghosts and snake spirits (generally indicating those accused of counter-revolution), revisionists (those too close to the USSR), the 'stinking ninth category' (intellectuals), and, perhaps worst of all, 'the enemy sleeping at our sides', the phrase finally directed at Liu Shaoqi and those around him, accused of being the opponents of Maoism and therefore of Mao. In a time when 'words were weapons', in the immortal slogan of Jiang Qing, Mao's wife and one of the radical leaders at the time, it was a 'struggle to touch the soul'. It is not surprising that being labelled as one of these morally condemned groups sometimes amounted to a death sentence.

In the reform era after 1978, the moral war was not so dramatic. Class struggle as sponsored by Mao and the cleansing and extirpation of enemies in society became unnecessary. Rectification campaigns rehabilitated most people, guided by Deng and his demand that past grievances needed to be forgiven and forgotten. He, after all, had the right to say this, through the suffering he had undergone, along with his family, in the period from 1966 onwards. His eldest son, Deng Pufang, had been crippled by being hurled from a window on the third floor of Peking University in 1968. Deng had the mandate to ask others to turn a new leaf. Communities that had once been riven by terrible division and conflict somehow had to cohere again.[1] Amnesia was the best balm, even for those who had lost their nearest and dearest.

But for the moral narrative of the Party, of course, the pre-1976 events under Mao did pose a problem. In the technocratic, administrative age from 1980 onwards, the CPC had to deal not just with the narrative caesura of before and after 1978, discussed in Chapters 1 and 2 of this book, but also with the very different moral postures of these two eras. Because it was pursuing a moral narrative, it had to come up not just with a policy and ideological justification for its deep involvement in failures like the great famines, the anti-rightist campaign (a campaign, after all, that Deng had been an enthusiastic director of), and the Cultural Revolution, but with one that was ethical too. Without abjectly asking for forgiveness, and running the risk of losing its mandate to rule, it had to make symbolic moves towards explanation and, most difficult of all for an entity that was always in the right, admitting failure.

Moral standing matters profoundly for the Party and figures as a part of its legitimacy, even though this is never spelt out. It is something implicit in the way it speaks about itself, the way it operates in society, and the view it clearly has of its right to rule. Aspiring to this moral position is a fundamental part of its identity and culture. But this issue is complicated by the slight matter of the Party's own past behaviour, a past where use of violence for political ends was regarded as legitimate and defensible, despite the terrible human suffering as an outcome (this figured in the 1945 Resolution). This need for moral standing and validation of this by outsiders is illustrated by the proclivity of Communist leaders, even in the era in which they were most flagrantly opposed to Confucian norms and influence before the 1980s, to aspire to the sort of authoritative, patriarchal superior position that the sage from the Warring States era (475–221 BC) insisted was the necessary role for rulers. The only adaptation is the ways that post-1949 leaders have attempted to argue that they are using Marxist-Leninist principles as the basis for their ethical standing.

As the Party draws its inspiration from two such different directions (classical Chinese philosophy and Marxism-Leninism), it is unsurprising that it has appeared inconsistent over what fundamental principles it uses to justify its actions and its rights to rule. Over the course of its history, it has therefore swayed between brute utilitarianism based in the inevitable, sometimes inhumane, forward movement of dialectics through history, where the ends ultimately justify the means, and a closer identification with the principles articulated by classical Chinese thinkers, where they are acting in accordance with a principle of order encoded in the world itself. This makes the identity of the CPC as an ethical actor complex, hybrid, and sometimes highly problematic. It lies at the heart of the confusion outside China towards an entity which one moment speaks the language of service, selflessness, and seeking good outcomes for all, and the next allows its agents to violate human rights norms, commit fundamental crimes, and be brazenly unashamed of belonging to a tradition tainted by immense moral failure (the famines, turbulence, and use of the military to quell civilian protestors). It is not hard to see why this is an area which is so difficult to address properly, and why it is so rarely written about.

Whatever the views about this contradictory posture historically for the Party, of one thing we can be certain. Ethical issues matter to the CPC in the twenty-first century as never before. It is seeking a more complex source of legitimacy than just raw production of material wealth. In the era of Xi Jinping, the anti-corruption struggle is the closest to what was, in the Maoist era, a mighty battle between the forces of good and bad. In its discourse something approaching an archetype of bad is presented: the cadre who has slipped from the right path and succumbed to temptation. That the Party does believe in a template of good behaviour in and for itself is shown in the way that cadres up to the highest level are incentivized. The simple expedient of paying officials competitively, as was used in Singapore and Hong Kong, to ensure that they do not start to seek personal gain from public money and projects has so far not been taken. Instead, Chinese officials, even up to Xi's level, are remunerated very modestly in view of their responsibilities. Xi himself, as the most senior official in the Chinese nomenklatura system, gets no more than US$1,200 a month. Despite this fundamental structural imperfection, officials are still expected to keep to tight strictures and meet high demands. In a country that since the 1990s has grown richer and more prosperous by the day, and in which cadres have some forms of power which are very significant, and in a cultural context in which networks, the famous issue of *renqing* (human connections and bonds), are so important and profoundly embedded, somehow Chinese leaders have to seek a form of motivation, an incentive, that transcends all this. They are offered an abstract notion of the 'good' that is worthy of pursuing in its own right, no matter what the material costs to that might be. Like the Catholic priesthood, celibate in a society drenched in sexual references and dealing with a crisis of belief and faith, Chinese cadres have to be economic eunuchs, self-sacrificing, presented daily with temptation, working within an ideological framework largely irrelevant to the world around them, and yet where they at least need to continue seeming to act in support of this.

The Fall of the Party Cadre: The Anti-Corruption Struggle

The ways in which leaders at the start of the Xi era focussed on the behaviour of officials and Party members in high positions in particular as being of significant concern is illustrative of the problem of the CPC's ethical belief system. In the fat years of Hu Jintao, the Party seemed to be populated by cadres who knew only the language of economic development and trade promotion, and who ministered the sacraments of material growth, infrastructure investment, and the creation of endless streams of renminbi (the Chinese currency). During that period, the entity that once conceptualized itself as the bringer of justice, dignity, and liberation to the Chinese people in the years before 1949, and which had maintained high standards of conduct faced with the rampant corruption and cruelty of the Nationalists in the Civil War from 1946 to 1949, was now the world's greatest money-making machine. Like Midas, all it touched turned to gold. It ran the risk of losing its own soul in this period of rampant growth, despite the warnings of figures like the Premier at the time, Wen Jiabao, who said that corruption was the greatest threat to the Party, and the issue that could truly bring it down.[2]

The Xi era can be partly interpreted as a corrective to this period of massive capitalist growth and the moral confusion to which it gave rise in the socialist Party. In essence the quandary faced by the Xi leadership has been how to marry the traditional socialist values the CPC still needs to adhere to with the completely different values that have driven the successful introduction of a market economy and enabled it to remain in power – the search for profit, for instance, and capital formation. It has two stark options. Either to try to sustain its own values and produce rhetoric defending these, while daily Chinese society seems to operate on completely different ones. That risks making it seem hypocritical and redundant. Or to jettison what it said it has believed in over the last ninety years, and transform to something like a social democratic party. Under Xi, there has been a categorical rejection of this option, which would mark such a wholesale change that it would spell the effective end of the Party. This is why its socialist values matter to it.

Meanwhile, as the Party (as will be seen later) fights over its moral position and tries to handle the tensions outlined above, in the real world of Chinese daily life, this lack of consensus over what people believe constitutes the basis for good action and honesty, integrity, and other virtues has created gaping spaces to be filled by individual agency. This is compounded by the fact that, because of China's highly networked and informal structure, corruption in the country is not a new issue. It existed profusely in the Nationalist era. The difference now is that since the Reform period, rising wealth has just created greater and greater opportunities for theft, larceny, and embezzlement. The 1980s saw the first signs of a novel kind of collusion, where state enterprises and state assets, latterly supplemented by non-state actors and the new temptations their work brought, were manipulated to create benefits not just for the Party, but also for pockets of vested interest within the political, business, and newly emerging social elite. This was only magnified by the lack of rule of law, transparency, and accountability. One of the principal causes of the 1989 uprising was this sort of corruption, where officials were seen as illicitly growing wealthy and arrogant as they created new business networks which paid them off and looked after them and their direct (and often indirect) associates. Despite sporadic clampdowns, in the 1990s and into the 2000s, as China's socialist market economy saw rising growth, and the development of non-state players who had to still work closely with government officials, things deteriorated.

According to scholars like Andrew Wedeman, the systemic causes of corruption in China, the ways in which Party officials were able to monetize their positions to bring illicit and direct gain for their networks, were an almost endemic problem.[3] With the CPC above the law, and with no other means apart from its own self-governance to hold it accountable, dealing with official larceny proved next to impossible. 'Strike Hard' campaigns throughout the last four decades only put a temporary halt on things but did nothing to address this fundamental problem of a lack of sources of transparency and effective regulation within the system itself.

When speaking as the Party Secretary on the first day of his elevation in November 2012, Xi Jinping explicitly mentioned the ways in which the CPC had lost touch with people precisely because of this problem. It was soon clear that fighting corruption was going to be one of the signature themes of his era. What was less expected was how long and drawn out this struggle would be. From 2013 to the time of writing (2018), over 88,000 officials have been tried, with figures drawn from across the various hierarchies of the party-state. Even Zhou Yongkang, a former member of the Standing Committee of the Politburo, has been indicted and imprisoned, the first time since 1949 someone at this level has been so treated.

Interpreting the political meaning of this extensive campaign (it has, in fact, in Chinese literature, been called a 'struggle') has proved problematic. This arises from the relationship the campaign has to Xi Jinping as the supreme elite leader, and to the CPC as an organization. The two are very closely related, but the ambiguity arises from whether the anti-corruption struggle is seen as serving Xi's direct political interests, or whether in fact it is part of a more profound movement by the Party itself to try to strengthen its internal institutions and become sustainable. The answer to this depends on the way in which one sees Xi as a leader: as an autonomous autocrat with high levels of agency, or as someone who works as a servant of the Party and gains his authority from that.

A further clue to answering this problem of whether the struggle is political or has some deeper purpose can be found in its genesis. It was, after all, not just Xi's idea. Even before Xi formally took up the main Party position, and before he had any sort of mandate, anti-corruption drives were already featuring in the elite leadership's minds. This bridged the Hu and Xi eras. The formidable economist Wang Qishan, a man who had skilfully guided the US–China Strategic and Economic Dialogue for a number of years, was appointed head of the Central Commission for Discipline Inspection (CCDI), the Party's dreaded anti-corruption enforcement agency, a little before the

Eighteenth Party Congress in 2012.[4] This indicated a cross-generational commitment in the Party elite that the problems arising from years of solid growth, and the role of the Party in delivering that, needed to be addressed.

Looking into Xi Jinping's background, we may not find searching, powerful, and highly specific declarations of ideological commitment. He is, like Deng, no theorist. He is a practising politician. Ideas have to have utility. (This is something that will be discussed in more detail in Chapters 5 and 6 on ideology.) They are there to serve a function. Of all the consistent and most coherent ideas Xi has been associated with, however, there is one that reaches back to his time in Fujian, the south-eastern province he was based in for fifteen years from the 1980s. In 1991, during an interview with Xinhua, he stated that cadres needed simply to manage and do political work. They needed to leave business to the entrepreneurs and state enterprise managers. And they needed to see their function as delivering a political strategy, not a commercial one. In essence, the Party was in the business of politics, not the business of business. It had to resist diversifying, and thereby betraying its culture and historic commitments and, by implication, the moral narratives these involved.

This was not a popular posture. Party figures, with their modest wages and small perks, were living in a society where each day they saw contracts they were awarding, or projects they had granted the go-ahead to, creating vast amounts of wealth. With the fading of the ideological commitment and the idealistic mission of the Party to create not just a strong, rich country (everyone wanted that) but a socialist one as well, so too were the barriers to temptation eroded. In the 1990s and into the 2000s, those visiting China would have been hard pressed to distinguish entrepreneurs and businesspeople from government figures. This even extended to the kind of luxurious cars both drove, the expensive colleges abroad to which they sent their children, and the costly five- or six-star hotels they stayed in.

Wang Xiaofang in *The Civil Servant's Notebook*, a novel from 2009, writes of this era of cadre enrichment and collusion.[5] He himself was the private secretary to a mayor in the north-eastern city of Shenyang in the late 1990s who was charged with embezzlement and jailed for thirteen years. At the most local level, lack of any restraints from an independent judiciary and protection for whistleblowers from rule of law, plus phenomenal growth, led to a position where the Party became like a mega-successful holding-company organization atop a myriad of subsidiary companies all paying dues to it. It was on this model that Richard McGregor described the CPC in his influential 2009 book *The Party*.[6] Policies it sponsored led, for instance, to the breakneck construction of the world's most extensive high-speed rail network, but also to the embezzlement of billions of renminbi from this alone led to the dismissal of the then Railway Minister in 2011. There was plenty of similar high-volume pilfering going on from construction, finance, telecoms, indeed practically any sector where there was heavy state involvement.

That Xi Jinping was associated with the reinvigoration of the idea that the Party was first and foremost a political entity and that its agents could no longer get away with this grand-scale theft, particularly at a time when the economy was tightening and there needed to be more efficiencies, was perhaps part of the reason for his final successful elevation. It was the attitude he had consistently held towards the Party, rather than anything about him as a person or his family background, that was the basis for his success. The fact was that he had largely observed the rule that politics had to take command, and that the Party needed to be situated only in a political space, not a quasi-commercial one. More importantly, through keeping his immediate family largely away from any province where he had been active, and making sure that his immediate networks were clean and not complicit in the most egregious corruption, he showed that this stance was more than just lip service. He seemed to actually believe it, something proved by the way he behaved. This was something of a rarity in China at this time. The question which is more interesting to address was what lay at the heart of this political disposition. The answer to that had to do with locating the CPC's most sustainable basis of power not in economic but in moral resources.

Understanding more clearly why corruption was such a focus for Xi, and what was so significant about addressing cadre behaviour, helps us to comprehend this issue better. This was not just an administrative matter about officials with their hands on the state cash bags succumbing to temptation. That is what made it different to the 'Strike Hard' campaigns of the past with their harsh, but limited and partial, impact. Xi's anti-corruption struggle was about operating within a far vaster framework, one where the behaviour of misbehaving officials was in essence an existential threat because it displayed a lack of faith in the CPC's vision of historic progress and its underpinning moral narratives by those who had to be loyal and believe in these. As discussed in the first two chapters, the Party always had two main pillars of legitimacy: unifying the country, and winning as part of the united front in the war against the Japanese. Since 1978 it has supplemented (but not supplanted) these with that of stimulating wealth creation and growth. This third area lacks the emotional power of the first two, but is far more effective in terms of practically getting

Chinese people on side, and, in the end, it is the tool most likely to create the conditions whereby China will be able to achieve the Great Nation status the CPC says it has always sought.

Indeed, since the 1980s, delivery of tangible economic results was asserted by leaders as the key source of their legitimacy and right to rule, seeming to overshadow any other source. Jiang Zemin and Hu Jintao at successive Party congresses made the CPC obligations here crystal clear: to raise living standards, feed and clothe people, and look after their wellbeing. There was, of course, a hard core of pragmatism in this. With no solid growth to give material incentives to people in society, the Party was vulnerable as older sources of appeal faded. It was also since 1991 highly cognizant of the mistakes that had led to the fall of the USSR, something attended to in more detail in Chapter 6. The main lesson drawn from this event was to ensure that while there was economic development at all costs, the Party needed to maintain its jealous hold on organized political power. Was this a tension the CPC would be able to manage more successfully than its Russian colleagues? Or was it, as everyone else said, a case of the CPC trying to square a circle?

Were the CPC to be solely an administrative entity, one whose legitimacy is judged on measurable outcomes which it can be seen to have failed or succeeded in, this would be fatal to its demand to have an existential right to the monopoly on power. In theory at least, other executive entities could come along with equally good pragmatic ideas to deliver outcomes. Competition would start. The CPC's dominating imperium would be over. At heart, the CPC operates as more than an executive entity. It is a faith community and one whose power is based on the emotional and moral power of its beliefs. When challenges to its privileged status in Chinese political life arise, it can therefore appeal to a higher level of reasoning and vision to defend itself. Economic growth is a means, not an end, in this framework. It does not justify the Party's power, just operates as an expediency, a point on the way to creating the primary state of socialism on which a great restored nation can be built, which is the real goal. As was made clear in Chapters 1 and 2, the Party believes, and has always believed, in a history which has purpose and a final positive outcome. Pragmatically using capitalist means at one point along this journey is fine, but they will one day necessarily have to be shifted aside. They are temporary stages along the path of faith.

That underlying narrative myth of the great positive progress of history and the ways in which in its grand sweep seemingly contradictory ideas can be engaged with had always been part of the mindset of elite Party leaders. It continues with Xi. It informs elite Party leaders' speeches and operates as a shadowy background to them. It figures as a grand assumption or article of faith much like the idea in America, for instance, that if someone works hard and strives, they will be successful because the world is a just place, or the notion in Europe that all people are equal and there is an intrinsic egalitarian order in the world. Under Hu Jintao, the catchphrase may well have been 'scientific development'. And the Party, with its technocratic leadership may have come across in Dutch Party scholar Frank Pieke's words as a meritocratic, technical organization, doing its government business in increasingly functional, almost mechanical ways.[7] But all of this was still driven by something that looks like an element of faith and vision: that socialism and its underpinning set of values will bring about utopian modernity in China, and that 'the China Dream', in Xi's words, will be a China which is industrialized, modernized, not beset by the fragmentations of its myriad of networks but held together by the Party, with its unifying, simple message of socialism with Chinese characteristics.

The Party's positive historic vision, and the way in which this lies at the heart of its politics, therefore are crucial things to understand. They are core assets. Western politics is beset by nostalgia for a past everyone is trying to regain – the Americans under Trump with their 'Make America Great Again', looking back to the fabled 1950s when everything was good, and society was booming. Or the British with their colonial daydreams and fondness for the immediate post-war era. For China, the vision is not a backward-looking one. The memory of much of its past is full of so much suffering and humiliation. Everything is geared to the future. China as a nation is not trying to revisit its modern golden age. It is heading there for the first time. This is an intoxicating vision, and a very dynamic one. The Party is the servant of this positive view of history, which will result in a powerful, strong country. That is the critical mission its officials are mandated with, above and far beyond their service to the CPC.

But how could such a vision be fulfilled when the officials tasked with bringing this about degraded themselves, jeopardizing their great responsibility by becoming servants of vested interest, prisoners of local networks, seeking benefits for themselves and their little worlds, rather than the great one they were meant to be constructing for everyone? Reports on Bloomberg.com and in the *New York Times* over 2011 in the lead-up to the Eighteenth Party Congress a year later showed how bad things had got. Figures not of tens or hundreds of millions, but billions of dollars of stolen cash were associated with the groups around Premier Wen Jiabao. Even Xi's family were connected with expensive property in Hong Kong. Kong Dongmei, granddaughter of the founding father of the regime, Mao Zedong, became China's 242nd richest person in 2013.[8] Such visible wealth had a huge impact on the moral image of Party officials and their standing in society. Trust surveys showed that local and national politicians were regarded with disdain.[9] Perceptions of corruption underlined the ways in which there was, to return to Xi's words – uttered on 15 November when he emerged as Party Secretary in 2012 – a division between the Party and the people. How was it that the CPC – object of the covenant before 1949, when it came to power, of delivering justice and liberation to the oppressed and humiliated Chinese people, defender of China's great vision to become a powerful, strong country again with its dignity and status restored – through ill fate, bad management, and the perversity of some of its members, could become the ultimate network of vested interest, solely defending and looking after itself? It had come to look like the 'mountain hold', as Mao's arresting metaphor from 1945 had put it, a rogue state within a state, parasitical on the world around it. Far from serving the people, it was serving itself.[10]

Moral Reboot: Going for Loyalty

The striking singularity of the many policy pronouncements made in the era since Xi came to power, from the raft of ideas at the Third Party Plenum in 2013 (one of the annual meetings of the Central Committee, a sort of management board for the CPC), to those around legal reform at the same kind of meeting a year later, and the proposals in the Thirteenth Five-Year Plan running from 2016, is the way in which the defence of the Party as a political organization, and the priority being placed on making its monopoly on power sustainable, have come to the fore. The articulation of grand projects like the delivery of the first and second centenary goals provides the outer garments to an all-encompassing political task: ensuring that the Party, with its unity, its consensus vision, and its positive view of historic development, prevails over evil forces from both within and outside China. This explains the huge efforts being put into attacking one of the most feared forces of opposition to the Party vision: Western universalism and democratic systems within the PRC. Under Xi, the message to the outside world that the one-party system and China as a nation are inextricably linked, and that there will be no tolerance of outsiders trying to contest or subvert this, has become clearer than ever before. Internal weaknesses from conflicts of interests, and dilution of purpose amongst elite cadres because of commitment to other networks, and the distraction these offer from deliverance of the Party's great goal, a strong nation under its wise tutelage and guidance, had to be dealt with. The Party in essence has undergone a restoration under Xi. It has been reconnected with the moral narrative from its early history. In the end, it is about delivering a moral vision based on justice, not wealth.

In this context, it is odd, therefore, that a lot of discussion in Western media and in some expert communities of Xi's anti-corruption struggle focusses on the ways in which it delivers power and influence to specific CPC factions, and in particular to those broadly assembled around the main leader. In this interpretation, it has been seen as a means of removing political threats and sources of opposition. According to this interpretation, what links the removal of Ling Jihua, for instance, the right-hand man of former Party leader Hu Jintao, taken down in 2015 despite sitting on the full Politburo, who were formerly seen as untouchable, or, at the other extreme, the fractious sons and daughters of former high-level leaders is their claimed links to power networks inimical to the Xi group. The *cause célèbre* of this antagonistic group was the trial and imprisonment of the already-mentioned Bo Xilai, charismatic, innovative as a local and national leader, highly ambitious, and someone who would have offered a real source of alternative ideas and power to Xi had he not been felled early in 2012 because of the involvement of his wife in the murder of British businessman Neil Heywood. His disappearance was an extraordinary piece of luck for Xi, removing a major source of distraction and the one person with the potential in the super-elite of the CPC to viably compete for public support.

The campaign ongoing since 2013 probably has been very useful as a means of clearing away potential, or actual, opponents. But this is only one way to understand it. It does not offer the full picture. The anti-corruption struggle far above and beyond this toughening up of some allegiances has been a major tool for the reformation of Party identity based on its primal foundational moral narrative, mentioned above. It has served in ways analogous to the Cultural Revolution of the past – but more as an 'intra-Party Cultural Revolution', a revolution without the horrible divisiveness and the widespread human costs of the first one. Its principal function has been to ensure that the primacy of the political vision and role of the Party is back in the forefront, based on its just historic mission and its corresponding right to rule. CPC members now need to be cognizant of the fact they are political players whose standing has to be based on moral posture. For an organization so mired in wealth creation and its repercussions, this seems counter-intuitive. It is for that reason that the anti-corruption struggle has proved more traumatizing than a simple act involving factional enhancement and strife.

We can see evidence for this broader strategic intent in the ways in which those who have been at the centre of the struggle seem to understand the meaning of what they are doing. Speaking to a group of Western scholars in 2015, Wang Qishan, the chief enforcer before he retired from the Standing Committee in 2017, made it clear that there were two core issues the campaign was trying to address. The first was inequity, the second inefficiency. China since the 2000s, he said, had become increasingly unequal. The resentments at this had reached deep into society. Contentiousness had risen. Party surveys had revealed the extent of the anger at officials and their privileges, and the backroom deals they were seen as involved in. Associated with this were inefficiencies in the real economy that derived from official malfeasance and collusion with the wrong networks. With falling GDP growth and tighter economic conditions, and while trying to navigate the treacherous period during which the country seemed exposed to the 'middle-income trap' (i.e. the threat of income stagnation), the Party needed all the social and public support it could get. Its leading figures could not, in this context, be seen as sources of difficulty. They had to return to the very idealistic image they had in works from the early history of the Communist movement – Liu Shaoqi's *How to Be a Good Communist*, for instance, which will be looked at in Chapter 4, being amongst the most seminal. They needed to show they were part of the solution, not part of the problem.

Strategically, there was also a pragmatic awareness that if every corrupt official were to be arrested, the country would soon have no one left to run it. There were no clear rules about how to behave in the new environment. The culture of the Party had gone awry. Codes of behaviour had not been internalized. For the anti-corruption struggle, something like a blitzkrieg of the spirit was utilized. Figures were arrested often arbitrarily to create an environment of uncertainty and apprehension. 'Shock and awe' local investigation tours were deployed, with the CCDI descending out of a clear blue sky on unsuspecting targets and undertaking investigations on them that were invasive, highly visible, and a warning to others of the treatment they might get if they did not start to toe the line and behave better. The simple fomentation of uncertainty and fear at all levels of officialdom served its purpose in that, at the very least, it curbed Party members' more excessive behaviour, causing them to become more careful and at least pause for thought before getting too immersed in illicit business.

All of this was supplemented by attempts to give more precision to the division between the Party and the commercial realm through legal reform. Changes to commercial law to provide greater clarity were introduced in 2014 at the Fourth Plenum. Court funding was reviewed so that money did not come from the same level of government but from higher up, to avoid conflicts of interest. Regulations and rules which had previously been unwritten and assumed started to be codified, with the Non-Government Organization law, introduced in 2015, causing particular consternation, despite the fact it seemed to be only spelling out what was already widespread practice.

In addition to this, there was a clear understanding that at the very top of the Party there needed to be no ambiguity or doubts about where this group's loyalties really lay. People were not there, as Zhou Yongkang or Bo Xilai were claimed to have been, to promote themselves, feather the nests of their networks and enrich them. They were there to serve the corporate interests of the Party. For this group, therefore, the enforcement of loyalty through heavy ideological training, tests, and the deployment of the sort of highly publicized symbolic cases mentioned above to show that no one is safe has been highly effective. Loyalty for senior cadres, who might number no more than 3,000 in the whole system, and members of the People's Liberation Army (PLA) was not requested but demanded. For other groups in society, the Xi leadership has calibrated the same message. On his visit to China Central Television (CCTV) in early 2016, Xi told media people to be 'responsible'. The great middle class, emerging in the cities, who are so key to China's future economic growth, have been appealed to through the nationalistic message already mentioned: tying the sustainability of the Party to the delivery of a rich, strong nation. Once, getting rich and material gain were the universal currency by which to incentivize people. Now, things are more nuanced and complicated. Different messages are aimed at different groups in different ways. But the purest and harshest of those are directed at the Party elite.

Critics of the anti-corruption campaign have pointed out that were this struggle really intended to deal with the issue of combatting larceny and official misbehaviour, it would need to make fundamental structural changes, introducing proper divisions of administrative and political responsibility, greater openness and accountability, and allowing the judiciary to hold the executive to account. None of this has happened in China. On the contrary, the primacy of the CPC has never looked stronger and starker. This proves that the anti-corruption struggle has a predominantly political function, but one that is deeper than simply ensuring Xi's hold on power. It is a fundamental tool to deliver one-party sustainable rule through the creation of loyal, faithful, and unified top-level officials. The question is whether, in the long term, it will work. Can the CPC once again prove it is able to buck the trend, and be exceptional, undergoing none of the structural reforms everyone else has used to fight corruption, but achieving a unique arrangement where commitment to the great vision of national regeneration through the CPC enforces the need for clean behaviour? To understand the issues around sustainability, we need to have a clearer idea both of the CPC's articulation of its own ethical views from its earlier history, and of the depth of the moral malaise and confusion that afflicted Chinese society in the era of fast enrichment. It is to those issues that we now turn.

4

Back to Basics
The Roots of the Party's Moral Crisis

While the epic events around anti-corruption from 2013 onwards focussed interest on the CPC elite leaders and their internal relations, that was a side-show. The real problem was much deeper. The CPC's legitimacy was often talked of in terms of its basis in ideology or politics. But the key question was its moral rights. What right did it have to use certain privileged vocabularies and occupy the specific space in society that it did? This question nagged away at the Party leadership like a memento mori, a ceaseless reminder of its own mortality. Was it, like the USSR, living on borrowed time? And was its inevitable moment of meeting with fate only a little way down the line? To add to the problems, the CPC was using a moral historiography: the belief of a history directed towards a future with a good outcome which it had been mandated with command over. In this history it was on the side of the righteous and the right. And yet it was seen as acting venally and despicably, and its values were either not recognized or at odds with the wider society around it. Reform since 1978 had created many new issues through pragmatic engagement with capitalist economic methods. What was it that the CPC believed after all this change and transformation? What were its core values, or did it, in the end, have none at all? Was it a dying faith?

A way of focussing on this issue is to return to the foundation documents of the Party, and in particular perhaps the most important manual for cadre behaviour, the short piece by one of the founding members of the CPC, Liu Shaoqi. His *How to Be a Good Communist*, written in 1939 in the era of existential struggle during the Sino-Japanese War, is a work about the ways in which cadres have to live up to standards set by the Party. At its heart is a project of self-annihilation, or self-abnegation. This element of sacrifice for the collective good was to be a mainstay, sometimes explicit, sometimes implicit, for the Party for the next seven decades. It is the spirit of this self-abnegation that the Xi leadership is trying to reignite.

Liu starts his piece by saying that he will 'discuss how members of the Communist Party should cultivate and temper themselves'.[1] Humanity, he goes on to state is 'in process of historical development'. This is a struggle in which 'men change nature, change society and at the same time change themselves'.[2] Struggle is key: '[T]hrough such struggles [cadres] must seek to make progress and must enhance their revolutionary quality. An immature revolutionary has to go through a long process of revolutionary tempering and self-cultivation, a long process of remoulding, before he can become a mature and seasoned revolutionary who can grasp and skilfully apply the laws of revolution.'[3] While following the principles of Marxism-Leninism, a cadre for the CPC, living in the practical reality of Chinese society, 'will give no thought whatsoever to his own position or fame in the Party'.[4] Looking back to classical times, to one of the feudal philosophers, Zeng Zi, Liu implores his readers to practise self-examination. They should 'resolutely oppose and thoroughly eradicate one of the worst vices bequeathed to us by the old society in the field of education and study, namely the separation of theory from practice'.[5] They must be living exemplars, applying Marxism in the light of China's specific characteristics: 'We Communists must not separate our study of theory from our ideological self-cultivation.'[6] This fundamental remoulding must not come through book learning, but through life and daily practice.

At the heart of this daily practice of Marxism-Leninism is one simple objective, drawn from the logic of dialectical materialism and the development of history: the ultimate elimination of all individualism.[7] For Liu, the Party's teleological vision of history comes down to the level of reforming and changing individuals, where the end point will be a time when 'all humanity will consist of unselfish, intelligent, highly cultured and skilled communist workers'.[8] Part of this will be achieved by constructing a new Communist morality. 'We Communist Party members must have the highest goals in our struggle and the highest ideals.' The cause of supporting the Party and the Communist movement and its objectives allows no space for individual preference or maverick behaviour. Cadres are servants of an impersonal ideal. 'Throughout our lives, our every activity is exclusively devoted to it and to nothing else.'[9] According to Liu, 'a Party member's personal interests must be unconditionally subordinated to the interest of the

Party'.[10] At no time, he states, 'and in no circumstances should a Communist place his personal interest first'. Liu spells this out further:

> Unhesitating readiness to sacrifice personal interests and even one's life, for the Party and the proletariat and the emancipation of the nation and all mankind – this is the one expression of what we usually describe as 'Party spirit,' 'Party sense' or 'sense of organization.' It is the highest expression of communist morality.[11]

Cadres embrace hardship, put others first, and are motivated by service. Their morality is founded on the scientific laws of Communism. They constantly fight against individualism. In an adaptation of the Kantian view that morality is based on the principle of universalizing actions so that only those that can be applied in every situation and across every context are sustainable and rational, the cadre operates as a personality-free agent, someone without appetite, passion, or aims beyond those the Party corporately hands to him.

Liu was developing and echoing what had been stated elsewhere. Mao Zedong in 1929 had written about mistaken ideas in the Party, particularly in the context of its militarization and the creation of the Red Army (the forefather of the PLA), when he had listed a number of crimes and problems, from ultra-bureaucracy, to subjectivism, and absolute egalitarianism. Individualism was one of this list of deadly sins. Components included pleasure seeking, passivity, the desire to leave the army, and 'the employee mentality'. 'The method of correction is primarily to strengthen education so as to rectify individualism ideologically,' Mao argued.[12] In 1937 he had returned to this theme of the crucial importance of having cadres who were exemplary in their lack of ego and selflessness. 'A great revolution requires a great party and many first-rate cadres to guide it,' he stated. 'Such cadres must be free from selfishness, from individualistic heroism, ostentation, sloth, passivity, and sectarian arrogance, and they must be selfless national and class heroes.'[13]

This campaign against individualism and selfishness was an easy thing to support rhetorically, but a hard thing to put into practice. Despite saying that Chinese Communism was growing from the roots of local society, and adapted to the realities of local daily life, what Liu and Mao were up against in their struggle to create a new morality was the issue that Fei Xiaotong, the great sociologist, referred to a few years later as the 'most serious shortcoming of country people': selfishness. The problems of selfishness in China, Fei went on, 'is really more common than the problem of ignorance or illness'.[14] In Chinese society, on his analysis, the most important relationship was kinship. This was 'similar to the concentric circles formed when a stone is thrown into a lake'. Around this were spread circles of relationships and interlinked bonds, sometimes vast in their extent. 'Despite this vastness,' however, 'each network is like a spider's web in the sense that it centers on itself.' Social relationships in society 'possess a self-centered quality'.[15] The self sits at the heart of all of this complexity: 'The path runs from the self to the family, from the family to the state, and from the state to the whole world.'[16] The most radical proposal of the imported ideology and practice of Marx and Lenin, as interpreted by Mao and Liu, was to contradict, or subvert, this self-centredness in traditional Chinese social structure, and to replace the morality of the world centred on the self by that centred on a collective organization.

From 1949, there were in fact two revolutions unfolding in Chinese society under the Communists. The first was the attempts to industrialize and create a new economic model according to state planning. The second was to remake the very nature of people within themselves, the mission, in the discourse of the era, to create 'the new person'. Rebuilding the infrastructure of the self, remaking the intimate life of the nation, was a truly radical and disruptive experiment. It focussed on systematically attacking the institutes of the family and clan system, and ripping up the Chinese educational structure. In the spiritual remodelling of China, the Cultural Revolution was the apogee, the supreme moment of undermining the sovereignty of the individual self.

Remaking People: Maoist Morality and the Great Cultural Revolution

For those looking at the photographs taken by reporter Li Zhengsheng during the Cultural Revolution in the north-east of China in the late 1960s, many questions will rush through their mind.[17] How was power so subverted and upturned, for instance, that formerly authoritative figures like local Party Secretaries or governors could be paraded in dunce's caps, or placed on stage and violently attacked, largely by groups of the young? What was the central leadership's underlying intention, and in particular Mao, about the aims and objectives of this event? And why did the Party's founding leadership, people who had been working in concert with each other through thick and thin for decades, turn against each other so violently.

Beyond these questions are less often asked ones. As Li's extraordinary photographic record testifies, the Cultural Revolution across the country, for all its local idiosyncrasies, had a specific grammar of physical drama, a drama enacted on an epic scale, with quite unique stage directions. Under the spectacle or performance of chaos there were signs of organization and management, leading to a theatre of well-ordered disorder. This was something that was common nation-wide, where struggle sessions, use of the aeroplane position to torture victims publicly (i.e. with head hanging down and arms pointing upwards), placing heavy placards around their necks with their names crossed out, putting them in places euphemistically called 'cow sheds' between public humiliation sessions, happened with a choreography that was not the product of pure chance. Quite how these common national phenomena arose has been the subject of considerable debate. Mao himself, in one of his earliest essays, the 'Report on an Investigation of the Peasant Movement in Hunan' from March 1927, referred to the use of placing dunce's hats on rich landlords, and holding what in hindsight were clearly prototypes of the struggle sessions that became so common across all areas of China from 1966.[18] If these were innovations, they took on in Chinese society with great success, and without too much tutelage.

The CPC after 1949 used these methods of struggle as a part of self-reformation much more systematically. It did so in order to aid an inner revolution, a revolution guiding society away from the tribal and networked alignments of the old world and the focus on the selfish individual at the heart of this to an ethos of selflessness and self-sacrifice. This was for the corporate good of the Party–state–nation trinity referred to earlier. Deploying radical tactics like that of searing self-criticisms, first written, then escalating to the level of large public gatherings focussed on tearing down the defences and self-respect of individuals, served this revolutionary purpose of remaking the inner person. The ambition of the Maoist revolution was shown in this way to go far beyond changing the outward environment, and aiming to remake the core of the self.

The Cultural Revolution was the final act of this psycho-drama. It developed processes and techniques of thought reform perfected over the previous decade. Some of these were documented at the time by the American psychologist Robert Jay Lifton. Based on his research on Western and Chinese survivors from prisons and other entities in the 1950s and 1960s who had managed to make it out of the PRC, he outlined what was clearly a highly deliberate and guided common process of self-reform. This consisted of an assault on personal identity, the establishment of guilt, encouragement of self-betrayal, self-fragmentation, and then lengthy, harrowing, and often intricate processes of confession, running either towards annihilation (through execution or other forms of maltreatment) or towards resurrection and rehabilitation as a newly reformed person.[19] In a subsequent book specifically on the Cultural Revolution, Lifton described thought reform at that time as 'a carrot-and-stick application of power for the purposes of controlling behavior, using various kinds of coercion and threat, together with a promise that those properly reformed will merge with and partake deeply of the invincible revolutionary force'. But he also offered an alternative framework: 'a method of individual purification which, by means of detailed self-examination, provides benefits akin to those of psychotherapy and spiritual enlightenment'.[20] The incentive for this in Lifton's analysis was for an individual to partake of 'revolutionary immortality' through complete and total service to the Communist Party under Mao and its spiritual message, Mao Zedong Thought:

> The total revolutionary … is 'ready to sacrifice his life' and is (in paraphrase of Mao's own words) 'not … afraid of wolves ahead and tigers behind … determined to change heaven and earth, fight the enemy, stick to the truth.' Such dedication and courage are indeed possible insofar as one can genuinely worship Mao's thoughts along lines suggested by still another passage, which could well be viewed as the epitome of the immortalization of the world and all who embrace is: 'The thought of Mao Tse-Tung is the sun in our hearts, is the root of our life, is the source of all our strength. Through this, man becomes unselfish, daring, intelligent, able to do everything: he is not conquered by any difficulty and can conquer every enemy.'[21]

There were plenty of people who resisted this process and fought for the maintenance of their selfhood and self-integrity. A good case was that of the Sanskrit scholar Ji Xianlin, whose memoir produced long after the Cultural Revolution had ended described a thought reform process which, far from purifying those who endured it and making them into more perfect revolutionary models, was brutal and crude and ended up only destroying. 'The rats grew bold', he wrote of his time in the 'cowshed', a metaphor for internal incarceration,

> and scuttled about in broad daylight. I found them gnawing in a dried steamed bun I had brought from home, and when I tried to chase them away, they glared at me with their little eyes and hid on the windowsill. Perhaps even the rats had realised that the building was inhabited not by ordinary human beings but by blackguards whom they could bully if they felt like it.[22]

Being made to feel subhuman was a common theme of recollections of this period. The writer Yang Jiang and her husband Qian Zhongshu were to be sent down in the late 1960s to a May 7th School, one of the cadre concentration camps established after the eponymous directive demanding reformation of CPC members' inner lives. Husband and wife offered particular challenges to their interrogators. They were both multi-lingual, had resided abroad for a number of years before 1949, and were the epitome of the 'stinking number nine-category', intellectuals, with their complexity and their ambiguity towards the party they had ostensibly returned to serve. While targets of savage cleansing campaigns through the 1950s, unlike Hu Feng, an associate of Lu Xun, another celebrated cultural figure from the pre-1949 time who ended up being imprisoned for a quarter of a century after 1957, they had maintained their liberty till the most complex period of the vast Cultural Revolution movement. In her brief but searing memoir published in the early 1980s, Yang referred to her husband being reduced to such a dishevelled, emaciated condition in the late 1960s that only a dog was able to recognize him by his smell.[23]

Critics like George Orwell and Arnold Koestler had written of Communist systems generally that the way they made participants servants of a vision of a forward-directed logic of history resulted in outcomes which were inhumane.[24] Everyone was seen as an actor in a mission of abstract progress. The person did not figure in this march forward except as a tool, not an agent. The Maoist post-1949 approach with its purity and simplicity fits particularly well into this framework. Achieving collective identity was so all-important in China because it operated as a corrective to the selfish 'spider's web' of relationships around the person in traditional Chinese society as seen by Fei Xiaotong. This attribute was the most significant impediment to modernization. It was a curse that needed to be broken at all costs, even to the extent that it entailed in its realization going through terrible human tragedy and suffering. All of this was a price worth paying for achieving the final great goal, the logic went. The ends truly justified the means. While there had been events in the imperial history of China like the epic Taiping Rebellion from 1850 to 1864, or the Boxer Rebellion in 1900, which offered similarly searing experiences of physical social turbulence and unrest, the Cultural Revolution was cataclysmic in its impact on the inner lives of people. It aimed to eradicate these. That made it uniquely harrowing and profound in its impact, because it was, in the words of the writer Ba Jin, a spiritual holocaust.[25]

1978: The Moral Impact of the Reform Era

In most accounts, reform and opening up from 1978 is seen as having impacts which were largely economic. What is less attended to is the very profound impact the changes from this period had on the psychology of the nation. Ideas, processes, and a whole world-view were allowed space that subverted the selflessness and self-sacrifice in service of the CPC and elite leadership around Mao which had reached their peak in the Cultural Revolution. Propaganda messages from the early 1960s from figures like Lei Feng to 'serve the people' and give no regard to the self were replaced by a set of new, more permissive strictures which seemed to be totally opposed to what had been stated before, like 'getting rich is glorious', a common 1980s slogan. 'Socialism with Chinese characteristics', the ideology under Deng, led to the reinstatement of attitudes and a society that reinforced the Chinese self, and its 'spider's web' of networks, allowing the return of its self-interest. Entrepreneurs, as American political scientist Yasheng Huang's work makes clear, were amongst the most prominent in their enjoyment of a whole new era of freedom.[26] They were able to openly and unapologetically return to an era which had existed before 1949 of building personal links, creating business associations, and constructing a world beyond the state.

In an article from 2002, the Hong Kong-based academic Xiaoying Wang wrote of the 'social and political changes that hastened the collapse of the "communist" moral order of the Maoist era and with it the personality structure that was an integral part of that order'.[27] This was not an outer transformation. Changes in that China had been well documented by, amongst others, the architect Rem Koolhaas and his co-editors in their spectacular and breathless description of physical change, *Great Leap Forward*.[28] Skyscrapers were being thrown up at such a pace in the southern city of Shenzhen they were able to add a floor to a building a day. In this nation of energy and purpose, where everything was propelled towards some great developmental divine future, a village one year became a city the next. But in the other China, the place in people's inner lives ('Deep China', as it came to be referred to), changes were less easy to detect. In this hidden world, the collectivist values of the era of high socialism were clearly being demolished as epically as the old-style edifices in the outer place. 'The reforms in China...presided over by the Communist Party is linked with the equally important facts', as Wang went on to state, 'that the reforms have largely been limited to the economic domain, and that they have been conceptualized or publicly characterized in terms of socialism.'[29] This introduction of elements of capitalism into the economic model in China had created one particular paradox: '[T]hose in charge of reforms have a vested interest in pushing a moral and ideological program that is often at odds with the market reform agenda.' The language of 'serving the people' referred to above, lifted straight from Mao, and of standing by collective identity where the self was subordinated was maintained by the CPC. Throughout the 1980s, this moral posture defending selflessness was promoted by campaigns waged against 'bourgeois rightism' and 'spiritual pollution' (in other words, hedonism), all this at a time when economically privatization and entrepreneurialism seemed to actively encourage such behaviour. These mismatches 'within Chinese official moral culture point to a deep crisis of society and of self'.[30] That was the much more hidden, but much more profound, impact of the post-1978 new order.

Using the work of American sociologist and political scientist Daniel Bell (referred to in the Introduction), Wang characterizes advanced capitalism in the moral sphere as a shift from Weberian asceticism to hedonism, a hedonism best exemplified by the consumer society with the relentless demand of people to gratify their needs immediately, with the creation of impulses and desires that need constant servicing. This creates a persistent tension. The individual is forever feasting, and yet forever hungry. China in the 1980s was to become in many ways a society increasingly dominated by this sort of behaviour: market competition, rising inequality, the fetishization of the future (because people always want better, bigger, bolder things to be happening, and are forever fleeing the dissatisfying present), and what Bell called the 'institutionalism of envy', which was a mark of late capitalism.[31] In China, however, after its recent searing experience of selfless Maoist rapture, and with the Party still standing by its moral vocabularies condemning self-centred behaviour, even as it jettisoned most of its economic and political discourse from pre-1978, something new had arisen: a post-Communist personality that needed a new language which was not so easy to create. Wang described this figure as 'a new type of person', but the antithesis of the new person dreamed of during the struggle process and the transformations aimed for in the Cultural Revolution. Instead, this was a 'communist turned nihilist, a nihilist turned hedonist'.[32]

Let free in the superficially liberal terrain of marketizing China, those with the post-Communist-type personality could indulge themselves in the karaoke bars and nightclubs springing up across the country. The idealism of the Maoist era, now so thoroughly discredited, haunted people as strong passions once they die often do, leading to a collapse in public faith, and high levels of cynicism. 'We see the post-communist personality in action everywhere and every day,' Wang stated:

> in things big and small; from habitual littering of public spaces to massive, knowingly perpetrated pollution of the environment, from

wining and dining at public expense to bribery and embezzlement of epidemic proportions, from routine disregard of rules of social order and co-operation to extraordinary indifferences at scenes of rape and murder committed in broad daylight, from prostitution to the de facto revival of concubinage on a national scale, from the issuing of all manners of fake certificates to the manufacturing of fake products.[33]

These outward manifestations of the inward fact that, as Wang states, 'the post-Mao Communist Party has not been able to develop a comprehensive, internally consistent ideology to go with its program of economic reforms'[34] were complicated by a number of other features: the nostalgic memory in society (because, after all, the Maoist period had been relatively brief) of another Chinese culture prior to all of this of great sophistication, delicacy, and diversity, which writers like the late Simon Leys (the pseudonym of Pierre Ryckmans) had focussed on so eloquently.[35] The Communists had, with their anti-feudal zeal, attacked this culture savagely, but they had found nothing to replace it. On top of this, with the onset of the internet in China from the late 1990s, and, even more importantly, the rise of smart phones, things grew rapidly more contentious. Citizens were able to film cadres doing, saying, and acting inappropriately, so that what had largely been hidden behaviour before that era was now all too easy to bring into the light. 'Flesh searches' was the term used to describe this process, with many famous incidents, like one where an official sitting scoffing the expensive delicacy of hairy crabs while moaning about the poor quality of Chinese people and their base nature was caught on video in the north-east of the country, or another of an official from Kunming, a city in the south-west, who became so incensed when he missed his plane that he trashed the departure lounge at the airport.

To complicate things further, there was another kind of nostalgia. For all its instability, the Maoist era came quite quickly to be regarded with some longing by many for its assertion of simple values, and the more equal society and at least a unified public morality, albeit a puritanical, ascetic one, that had existed then. At the heart of it all sat the issue of the hollowing out of Marxism as a public belief system. In the era after 1978, Wang explains,

Marxism, or communism for that matter, has become a synonym of everything that resonates with the political rhetoric of collective solidarity, equality, social justice, and the giving of special consideration to the underprivileged. All such left-sounding values have been discredited by contagion to one degree or the other.[36]

Those with the post-Communist personality in post-Maoist China, 'hedonistic to the core', were almost anarchic in their disregard for rules and parameters on their behaviour. The gap between rulers and ruled, rich and poor, west and east in the country widened rapidly. The Party's technique to deal with this was a 'spiritual civilization' project, trying to rein in individualism and resurrect the notion of selflessness that Liu Shaoqi had spoken of in 1939. 'Strike Hard' campaigns, referred to in the previous chapter, instilling sporadic fear in cadres and other associates, were waged to combat corruption. Intellectuals were slapped down from time to time, perhaps the most famous being Fang Lizhe, the astrophysicist, who eventually had to leave the country after being expelled from the Party and fleeing for refuge to the US embassy during the 1989 uprising. But these measures were limited in their success. They were akin to treating cancer with an aspirin, half-hearted superficial exercises which did not attend to the core problem, which was the complete lack of a new, revised set of values and moral standards for the CPC in order to face these changes happening in society that had been brought about by reform.

Liu Xiaobo and the Moral Critique of Contemporary China

The indictment of author, academic, and critic Liu Xiaobo for state subversion in 2009 was mostly attributed at the time to his close involvement in the Charter 08 document issued after the Beijing Olympics the previous year. This had argued for more political and civil freedoms in China. The demands for more human rights, equality, democracy, and constitutional rule formed a menu of the kinds of pernicious threats to the stable governance of the one-party system the Communists most resisted and feared. 'Our political system continues to produce human rights disasters and social crises, thereby not only constricting China's own development but also limiting the progress of all human civilization,' Charter 08 declared.[37] In fact, the calls in this document were by no means the most trenchant that Liu had made over his writing career. His main criticisms had been along the lines of those made by Xiaoying Wang quoted above. Liu therefore stands as the most prominent critic of the moral life of the PRC under the CPC who still operated within the country. That gives his words a particular authenticity and integrity in this space.

Liu called the post-reform period the 'age of cynicism', one in which 'people no longer believe anything and in which their words do not match their actions, as they say one thing and mean another'.[38]

Those in power 'want desperately to hold on to their dictatorial system'. But they are faced with a society which 'no longer approves of such a system of dictatorship'. Those brought up in this system, particularly since the Tiananmen uprising of 1989, are 'not interested in things like deep thought, noble character, incorruptible and well-ordered government, human values or transcendent moral concerns'. They are principally post-Maoist machines for consumption. In such a society, there is a 'split consciousness' where people speak one language, and actually believe in and live their lives using another. Publicly, all adhere to the mantras of the party-state and its authority. Privately, they live in a chaotic, largely values-free 'carnival world'. The net result of this is to produce not just an age of cynicism but one of sarcasm[39] where the only strategy to preserve sanity is to deploy a loaded irony in which every word, every sentence, carries a double meaning. People don't want clarity and honesty. The costs are too high. They live in the shadows of ambiguity and irony.

It is unsurprising that the idea of 'carnival', borrowed from the great Soviet philosopher and critic of society Mikhail Bakhtin, is one that attracted Liu. 'Carnival, according to Bakhtin, has two sides: it is fraudulent, heartless and vulgar; but it also expresses authentic feelings, feeds real creativity, and brings rebirth and renewal,' Liu states. 'When "carnival" comes along,' he continues,

> the people at the grassroots, accustomed to their place at the receiving end of scoldings, suddenly become fearless. They produce a spontaneous logical inversion of the base and noble, of up and down. They use parody, mockery, ridicule and insolence – sarcasm of several forms – to vent their sentiments.[40]

These are manifested in the literature, films, art, and music of contemporary China, which are often loaded with double meaning, or outright nihilism.

There are three points at which Liu's critique of the moral malaise of post-reform China and the Party ruling it differs markedly from that of Wang. The first is that he sees the whole era under Mao prior to 1978 not as one prompting nostalgia for a simpler, more straightforward age, but as a time at least as morally bankrupt as the current 'quasi-capitalist' era. Far from being a period of selflessness, the pre-1978 period enjoyed its own distinctive form of venality:

> The roots of [the current] cynicism and moral vacuity must be traced to the Mao era. It was then (an era that 'leftist' nostalgia today presents as one of moral purity) that the nation's spirit suffered its worst devastation. During the Cultural Revolution people 'handed their reddest

hearts to Chairman Mao'.... The cruel 'struggle' that Mao's tyranny infused through society caused people to scramble to sell their souls; hate your spouse, denounce your father, betray your friend, pile on a helpless victim, say anything in order to remain 'correct'.[41]

In other words, do anything to save your own skin, even if it meant betraying those closest and dearest to you. This was a form of selfishness beyond anything seen after 1978. The changes to the 'post-communist person' after that time were not because of the collapse of one moral system, therefore, and the failure to replace it by another, as Wang's diagnosis seems to suggest. They were simply the continuation in a different form of a moral degeneration and crisis.

The second difference is the ways in which this almost unbearable tension within the inner ethical lives of Chinese people under socialism with Chinese characteristics also offered a possibility for creative outcomes and liberation. For once, the Party had seemingly run out of answers. The completeness of its offer, and the totality of public belief under Mao, had gone. Mao's extremes had relieved people of the need to have naïve belief. They were in a strange way liberated. They had the freedom in a world largely devoid of meaningful public values to find their own way and think on their own terms. This lay behind the revival of religion seen in some areas of the country from the early 1980s.

A third difference, in terms of the focus rather than the content of his argument, is Liu's use of the sexualization of Chinese society after 1978 during the era of commodification and commercialization as a key area for criticism. His main point seems quite prurient: that Chinese society after the collapse of selfless values in the Mao era and the retreat into hedonistic individualism was pervaded by what he describes as an 'erotic carnival'. His descriptions of this phenomenon are lurid and compelling. After all, enjoying Eros, as he puts it, showed the ways in which 'in the nineties, popular culture came increasingly to be dominated and controlled by the market, and this spelled the end of its utility in undermining Party culture'.[42] It did at least serve some kind of subversive agenda. But the burgeoning of sex in society went far beyond the sort of confines of cadre narcissism alluded to by Wang:

> Outside of film, in the real world, and taking advantage of the new fungibility of power and money that pervaded our society, the sex industry has burgeoned. Across the country, in rural and urban areas alike, streets are lined with shabby barbershops, foot massage parlours, Karaoke clubs, video parlours, small hotels, little restaurants, and motels – many offering sexual services on the side. In the big cities, high-class

hotels, nightclubs, bars and social clubs provide nights of sex for rich and influential men. Vacation getaways and seaside cities offer 'mistress villages' and 'lovers' gardens'. Prostitution remains illegal in China, but rough estimates put the number of prostitutes in the country somewhere above six million, making us number one in the world. Commercial competition and the fungibility of money and power have created a category of women who are packaged mainly as gifts for clients: lover secretaries, hired 'public relations' consultants, and banquet escorts.[43]

The physical terrain of the 'Great Leap Forward' in post-reform China outlined by Koolhaas and his co-editors in their book of the same name, with its vast infrastructural transformations and immense housing and industrial projects, exemplified perpetual restlessness, energy, and change. But there was a further, much more secret, subtler map one could superimpose on the landscape from 1980, populated by places where desire was sought and satisfied. Shenzhen may have been the Special Economic Zone launched by Deng and his co-leaders to spearhead the manufacturing revolution. But it was also the home of a suburb in which mistresses lived in flats waiting for the early evening visits by their Hong Kong-based lovers who kept them. In this light, it was more akin to a Special *Erogenous* Zone. Dongguan in Guangdong province may have been the world's greatest source of manufactured microwaves and socks, but it was also the home to the largest constellation of brothels and prostitutes nationally. The country was industrializing, but also eroticizing. Nor did this sexual revolution confine itself to standard forms of venality. For Liu, it even infiltrated the discourse deployed about nationalism, meaning that Japan was regarded as a 'whore', making the clothes women wore if they were suggestive of Japanese connections fair game for attack and slander in order to protect the virginal purity of a China so often violated in the past.[44]

This even figured in the relations between ethnic minorities and the dominant Han. Cambridge scholar Uradyn Bulag addresses this theme in work on the Inner Mongolian region, one which suffered badly in the Cultural Revolution, predominantly through treatment of ethnic Mongolian cadres on charges they were enemies within, trying to agitate for their own independent country. Dealing with the case of the ancient Han dynasty figure Wang Zhaojun from 2,000 years before who had been married to a member of the Xiongnu tribe native in the region to forge political unity and concord, Bulag noted the ways in which in contemporary Chinese historiography this forced act of matrimony was presented as a great romance. In iconography, Wang figured in an almost semi-erotic way, with her sweeping silk clothes and youthful demeanour, offering herself passively to the fierce, savage potential invaders.[45] Those who visit any of the shows celebrating China's ethnic minorities and their unity with the majority Han will be familiar with this process of eroticization of minority groups through stressing their subservience and disempowerment and caricaturing their identity.

The disappearance of the Maoist focus on selflessness and total service to the Party in Liu's probing critique had created a space for exposure and revelation. In the end, the CPC, for all its talk of ethics and the need for good behaviour, had been an entity focussed purely and simply on power. 'In my view,' Liu stated, 'to attribute China's spiritual and moral emptiness to marketization and globalization is superficial.... It ignores the obvious fact that China's system itself is anti-humane and antimoral. The biggest and most destructive shamelessness in China today is political shamelessness.' Sexual shamelessness is merely a symptom of this, unimportant in its own right. The tactic that the party-state apparatus in its ideological and administrative modes of behaviour had adopted to handle this tension was one of highly adept hypocrisy:

> In its public stance, the regime calls itself a 'representative of advanced culture'.... Meanwhile, at the personal level, no one actually cares about ethics. Just as in matters of revolution, political power, fame, profit and many other things, in matters of sex, too, the end always justifies the means.[46]

Once more, pre- and post-1978 are not separate. For Liu, they belong to the same continuum, but not in ways the Party would be happy to recognize: 'The extreme political hypocrisy of the Mao years has blossomed, in post-Mao times, into a bouquet of hypocrisies in the several spheres of public life.'[47] The Party, in all of this, was the problem, not simply a part of the issue. It lay at the root of the moral vacuum, for Liu, because its continuation of being in control, uncontested and monopolizing, was the most dominant expression of an ethos of power for power's sake with no underlying intellectual or ethical justification. It was for this key point, one fundamentally attacking the legitimacy of the Party, that Liu was rewarded with an eleven-year prison sentence on Christmas Day 2009, a punishment that was to be terminated by his own tragic death from cancer in July 2017.

The Fat Years: China Out of Control

The Fat Years, the novel by Canadian writer Chen Koonchung, typified the Hu era and its heady atmosphere of rapid growth and perpetual hedonism.[48] Set ironically only a little after its publication date in English in 2011, it stated that the year 2013 would be one of unending self-satisfaction and pleasure in which Chinese would be so overwhelmed by feelings of superiority and nationalist pride that they would literally be falling ill with happiness. Chen's sarcastic, spirited style captured the zeitgeist well. At the time, five-star hotels were accommodating tribes of the sort of cadres Xiaoying Wang and Liu Xiaobo wrote about, maxing out on the best food, the best massages, the best wines imported from abroad, and anything else that they could consume most conspicuously. Chen is in some senses one of their chroniclers.

The group in society that most typified this heedless, freewheeling behaviour were the sons and daughters of elite political leaders or Party dynasties. Zhu Rongji, the much-respected Premier in the late 1990s who had done so much to restructure state enterprise and prepare the country for entry to the WTO, had a son heavily involved in the finance sector. Jiang Zemin had sons and nephews who controlled a large part of the telecoms sector. Li Peng, infamously Premier during the Tiananmen Square uprising in 1989, had a daughter and son involved in the state energy sector and provincial leadership, respectively. The list went on. The *fu er dai* (second generation of the fortunate) or the *gao ganzi* (princelings) with their excellent elite political and business networks acted with a sense of entitlement and impunity which was breathtaking. Around most of the elite in the Politburo swirled stories of the bad behaviour and venality of their children. Typifying precisely the kind of patronage links and family networked system that Mao Zedong had done so much to wipe out, it seemed of all the networks that proved hard to control and most irresistible that based on blood relations was the strongest and most prominent. Telling this group to serve the people and practise self-sacrifice was regarded as pointless. It never worked.

The years 2011 to 2012 will go down perhaps as the period which saw the nadir of this sort of elite misbehaviour, a time when the clash between the excess of the Hu years and the loss of any kind of cultural or moral values in Chinese society became most starkly evident. In November 2011, as already referred to in Chapter 3, the dead body of British businessman Neil Heywood was found in a hotel in the suburbs of Chongqing in South-West China. He was originally believed to have died of alcoholic poisoning, but this account unravelled the next year during an extraordinary sequence of events which started with Wang Lejun, the head of security for the municipal-sized city, fleeing to the American consulate in neighbouring Chengdu. He took with him a stash of top-secret documents. These seemed to prove that the real reason for Heywood's death had been covered up. He had been murdered. To compound matters, his death had happened at the hands of Gu Kailai, the wife of the most powerful official in the city, Politburo member Bo Xilai. Wang was eventually enticed out of the consulate, and ended up indicted for corruption. But his testimony ensured that Bo himself, soon after the convening of the annual parliament, the National People's Congress, in March 2012, was removed from office.

Rumours circulated around about why Gu had murdered Heywood, and what Bo's involvement had been. Despite the trial of Gu in August that year (and her inevitable conviction and sentencing for life), and of Bo for corruption a little later, the information seemed disarmingly simple. Gu had slaughtered Heywood over disputed monies he claimed were owed to him for help he had given with some of her interests abroad, most of which were not permitted for a public official's closest relatives. Fearing blackmail, she had taken events into her own hands and silenced him (reportedly by pouring cyanide down his throat). Bo had not been directly involved in this, but he had seemingly helped her in the cover-up. For the public, the story typified an elite acting without restraint on their behaviour for whom even murder was acceptable.[49] This image was reinforced when the son of another Politburo member, Ling Jihua, who, as we noted in Chapter 3, was regarded as Hu Jintao's most important aide and right-hand man, was killed in a car crash along the sixth ring road in Beijing. The tragedy of the event itself was overshadowed by the fact that the offspring of an official nominally earning only a few thousand renminbi a month was driving a state-of-the art Ferrari car worth perhaps US$400,000. Even worse, the two survivors of the crash were two young naked Tibetan women. If ever an event was grimly symbolic of the depths to which parts of the elite and their networks had reached, this was it.

The ways in which the Xi leadership had to create a radically new narrative not just about the story of the country and its relationship with the rest of the world, but about the Party and its relationship with society has been referred in the previous chapter. It was the cumulative impact of this sort of behaviour and the way it indicated a moral rot in the CPC that gave force to Xi's words about the imperative to reduce the gap between the Party and the people, issues he spoke about from the moment his elevation was made public. When things had got this bad, there was a need to go back to basics, and restore the CPC's moral sheen and its own ethical image and health. This was the sort of crisis Politburo member Liu Yunshan referred to during the meeting with foreign scholars in 2010 described in the Introduction when he talked of a country afflicted by daily change over the era from 1978 which had no means of keeping up with itself. The CPC's economic narrative was understood well. But its moral one was lost, particularly because its highest leaders were themselves often conveying a message through their actions which indicated a hedonism, selfishness, and parochialism utterly at odds with the self-sacrificing ethos of 'serve the people' that the CPC still said so strenuously it adhered to.

The Party Rescues Itself

Liu Xiaobo's forensic critique of the Party's lack of a convincing moral framework and the ways in which this impacted negatively not only on its own officials but on the wider society contributed to earning him a lengthy jail sentence. But ironically statements given by senior Party leaders after 2012 and the transition to Xi's leadership showed they appreciated as much as him that this was a serious problem, even if they didn't accept the interpretive framework he offered explaining why this situation had come about. The most significant difference with Liu was that they believed that the issue was one that could be fixed (betraying their perpetual optimism and their belief in the positive direction of history) and the CPC was the body that could achieve this. At the heart of this lay addressing the problem of the inner lives of cadres and the motivations that operated for them.

A good example of this thinking is an article written by Wang Qishan, the director of the anti-corruption struggle between 2012 and 2017. Issued in the official *People's Daily* on 17 July 2017, this statement from the most authoritative of sources and in the most prestigious of outlets outlined the new approach to making sure that cadres were steady and stayed onside.[50] Unsurprisingly, in this discourse there was little space for consideration of what causes might lie behind the confused, chaotic collapse in the country's public and private moral standards. And the CPC was certainly not identified as one of the key culprits, as it had been for Liu. The main assumption was that the whole situation was the result of slack observance of norms that had been there all along, and that all that was needed were procedures to bring people back into line. This was an administrative, not a cultural, issue, and demanded administrative, not cultural, remedies. That, at least, was the message on the surface.

The help of everyone was enlisted here, from their being involved in surveillance mechanisms on others, to using an online whistleblowing helpline to report on suspected wrongdoing. All of this was to clear up the cancer of corruption. Wang's analysis of the whole problem was simple: 'The source of problems found by inspection is a weak central authority and lack of ideological commitment.' In order to address this, 'the core is to maintain Party leadership, this most essential feature of socialism with Chinese characteristics'. Referring almost constantly to the importance of 'Xi Jinping Thought', Wang explained the techniques of rooting out those who had erred: full coverage (across Party structures, regions, levels of government, and institutions), and a programme of 'looking backwards', 'tracing previous inspections'. This was the 'above the ground' approach, dealing with symptoms. It asserted that the Party on its own could manage and address its own governance and self-discipline, dismissing criticisms of it being both judge and jury in one entity and the scepticism about this being possible. There was no need for extra-Party forms of inspection and accountability, and a rejection of any urgings to adopt a Western 'division of powers' model with all the threats and complexities that entailed. This quandary would be circumvented by disaggregating decision-making within the Party between its component parts, so that it had a balance of surveillance and accountability internally. Hypothetically, this was a viable option in such a vast organization. But what was much more difficult was the issue that Wang finished his essay talking about: self-vigilance, the development of an effective institutionalization of pre-emptive self-criticism, one which could detect problems and correct mistakes before they reached a critical level in the individual.

It was on this final point that a deeper intention can be divined, and one starts to dive under the surface. Wang's proposal involved a reversion to the ambitious idea of a reform of the self which had been present in the Maoist era. But remaking people's inner worlds in the new cultural revolution could not involve the sort of oppressive thought control and brutal methods of the past. It had to be done with more dexterity and sophistication, and some recognition, unlike in the Maoist period, that even officials, after four decades of quasi-capitalism, had agency and a level of sovereignty. It was good that there was some assistance for the great aim of cleaning up official behaviour from new forms of technology like smart phones, which were used to film misbehaving cadres, footage of which could then be put online. But all that served to do was to create shame and a sense of unworthiness in the targets once the bad actions captured came to light. This was not enough: a negative process of dealing with the symptoms rather than the root causes, creating people who behaved well through fear rather than genuine commitment. Under Xi, the desire was for a transformation of attitude and heart, changing the way that cadres regarded their own behaviour and actions so that even in private, on their own, they behaved well. To achieve this, Wang's words make clear, there needed to be a return to the ideals and self-sacrificing ethos of the Party in an earlier, more idealistic age, and an upgrading and adaptation of these. Contemporary officials had to see themselves once more as servants of the CPC in its moral mission to bring about a great nation, just as they had in the period of their most pure ardour in the 1940s and 1950s. Only that way would ensure that their good posture was sustainable, and that they had become worthy warriors for the cause of national regeneration. These days, however, they could not be coerced into doing this. They had to do it willingly, with consent and a good heart.

This was an historic shift. The Party since 1978 had increasingly adopted a complacent position on these matters. Under Mao, the attitude had been that the private self was a problematic entity that needed to be battered down and wiped out. In reform China, things went to the other extreme. The inner person of the cadre, the soul of officials, was mostly just ignored. The CPC was distracted, busy building the physical infrastructure of a new world. It lacked a moral language and refused to recognize how problematic it had been for modern cadres, while this world was being rapidly thrown up, to deal with the sea of temptation that they had been abandoned in without any clear understanding of what the CPC's ethical posture was or the values that it represented beyond the economic. Liu Xiaobo's explanation for this predicament was profoundly critical. The CPC was, and would always be, a power entity. Power was all it understood. All it knew was how to dictate. This even applied to how it tried to speak to the inner person. Cadres had to display obedience, knowing that there were imposed restrictive boundaries within which they operated, the trespassing of which could involve vicious recriminations. There was no discussion about where these boundaries were put and why they were there. Their location and existence were just taken as a given. And incentives to not violate their limits were negative – fear and shame. There was little sense of embracing of Party values and implementation of them flowing from positive inner conviction and belief. For the rest of society, individualism and pursuit of personal aims and profits were side-effects that had to be tolerated by the CPC as the economic superstructure was being constructed. But for Party officials, they had to stick to the old morality, no matter how unfit for purpose and anachronistic it seemed. No one had thought of any resolution to this problem, because in the early years, as the situation in the country changed so much, it was hard to really see what the problem was. It is not surprising that in this confusion, observance of the CPC's outmoded self-sacrificing norms was so lax, and that so many were willing to take the risk of violating them in the hope they would never be found out. In this way, ill-discipline became almost endemic.

Under Xi, this challenge of mobilizing the inner person of the CPC's officials and reigniting the spirit of self-sacrifice in an updated form was dealt with by reinforcing the core identity of the Party as one involving a moral narrative, one guided by redemption, delivery of justice, and a renaissance of the nation. This was an aim officials who loved their country had to believe in, even if they regarded Marxism-Leninism only as a means towards that end rather than having any truth in and of itself. Being well behaved and obedient in Xi's China, and curbing rampant self-centred behaviour, is therefore part of the duty to contribute to the great nationalistic mission. Self-sacrifice and self-abnegation in this new guise flows from allegiance not to the CPC as such, but to the nation that its work is trying to construct. To have this good new China, they have to be good Chinese Communists, because these are the only people in a practical position to bring this vision about.

In this task, the presentation of the character and leadership style claimed for Xi in officially sanctioned propaganda and imagery plays a significant role. He was clearly used from 2012 to embody leadership standards that stood as a corrective to the imperfect, flawed ones of the recent past. In particular, attention was draw to the ways in which Xi's persona (i.e. his publicly presented character) illustrated how the gap could be bridged between CPC officials and the people. Thus the visits in his early period in power to humble eateries, and scenes of him walking amongst smiling farmers, in a return to the sort of iconography popular during the Maoist era. Thus the stress in his own story on the hardships he had been through, and the price he had paid to be where he now was. All of this conveyed, in an intricately managed and highly considered way, the archetype of the selfless leader, someone for others to emulate. This was the behaviour the CPC now wanted to see from its chief foot soldiers, the message went.

Assisting in this programme to rediscover and then cleanse the socialist souls of CPC cadres was the fact that the incentive to do so was not abstract and remote, but concrete and immanent. It was true that they believed they were servants of the impersonal, scientific laws of history governing human development, but these laws were about to see the achievement of something incredible: the modernized, strong, confident China of 2021. This was a phenomenon cadres, like all of the population, could emotionally relate to, not just cognitively understand. And they could take pride in and derive confidence from their crucial role in its delivery, as long as they remained well behaved. The anti-corruption campaign, with the clear objective to reconfigure and change not just the surface of official behaviour but the workings of the inner self underneath, showed the CPC's ambitions to reach beyond the material country that people physically moved around and lived in, into a place far less easily understood and more mysterious: Deep China. Officials in their self-reformation were implicitly admitting that they too were members of this place which existed under the daily flux of events, the realm, as Liu Yunshan had said, of people's hearts, which they, and only they on their own, could see. This was a world that Liu Xiaobo had suspected the Party would never be able to speak to and conquer, but which it was now clearly trying hard to.

Welcome to Deep China

The critique of the moral crisis of contemporary Chinese by Liu Xiaobo, and the connected issue of the appearance of post-Communist-type cadres and their confusion and dilemmas, alert us to the rise in understanding of this other country, Deep China. This is a place which is so neglected and misunderstood because of the large assumption that the cultural reality of the PRC, and of China historically, is one of collectivist principles, and the attendant underestimation of the forces of individualism and selfdom this brings. For the CPC, too, Deep China matters. As shown above, in its mission of moral self-reformation, the CPC officialdom have had to become adept at speaking not just as rulers, but as members of this place, the China of inner lives and individual narratives and life stories which stands in opposition to the physical realm, which we can call Real China, over which they rule. They have had to recognize that they are part of this place, and it is part of them. Real China and Deep China exist in the same place and time. It is just that they do so on different levels.

Deep China is now so important to understand because it has been dramatically energized by the opportunities arising from a country undergoing quasi-capitalist reforms. This is not a place to which one can buy a train ticket, nor where a visitor can be accompanied by a tour guide, as though they were travelling along the Great Wall. It is a place which has always been there, however, despite the problems in seeing it clearly. In the Maoist era, as Simon Leys pointed out in the 1980s, the proclivity of outside observers was to see the country buried under the absolutism of the CPC messages and its attendant anti-individualism. This was a terrible mistake. Those who listened could always, even in the years of starkest repression, hear voices from Deep China. 'A certain type of "instant Sinology",' he wrote,

> was indeed based on the assumption that the Chinese were as different to us in their fundamental assumptions, and as unable to communicate with us, as the inhabitants of the oceanic depths; and when they eventually rose to the surface and began to cry out sufficiently loudly and clearly for their message to get through to the general public, there was much general consternation.[51]

Historian Zheng Wang, writing over three decades later, also testified to the elusiveness of this China story beyond the headline statistics and the bold narratives of growth. 'The reason China is still a mystery', he wrote,

> is not a lack of data of statistics. Even if the Chinese government could adequately address people's complaints about its lack of transparency, the mystery of China could remain because the roots of these questions [about China's possible futures] lie in the lack of understanding about the inner world of the Chinese people.[52]

But failure to get a grip on Deep China, by outsiders and insiders, is increasingly less permissible. The Chinese are no longer unknowable. This is especially so with the lifting of travel restraints in and out of China, and the immense connectivity between the country and the outside world. The voices of Deep China are in fact not hard to hear now. They are a cacophony. The question is how to interpret and understand them best, something which is proving as challenging for the CPC as for the outside world.

The phrase 'Deep China' is most fully explained in a book of the same name by American- and Chinese-based anthropologists, medical professionals, and sociologists which appeared in 2011. Modernity with Chinese characteristics since 1978 in particular, they argue, has involved the 'remaking of a moral person', the key inhabitant of this place. What is new now, they say, is 'the emergence of a new and original Chinese bourgeois culture that centres itself on the outer and inner furnishings of a new Chinese self'. Rising levels of wealth have bought material opportunities that have had an impact on the world of the spirit. New freedoms have arisen. 'It is our belief that this is one of the great historical pivots in Chinese society.'[53] But this has brought as many challenges as spaces for liberation. The reality of this country manifests itself in areas like the sexual revolution underway since 1980, the rise in depression, and the incidences of other psychological and mental health issues commonly found in the

West, but until the 1980s unadmitted and unrecognized in China. Depoliticization in Chinese society since 1978 and the removal of many of the main forces of repression have also led, for the authors of this book, to the creation of an unleashing of emotions:

> Since 1978, Chinese society has continued to change profoundly and at high speed. The 1980s was a period for many local communities to recover from collective trauma and to resurrect their heritage. ... Albeit selective, the retreat of the Party State has facilitated a dramatic reconfiguration of the material and psychological life of the people of China.[54]

Deep China is an emotional China, a place where people can seek self-expression and spaces to validate their agency. There is no privileged space for politics, or the Party, or ideology in this place, as opposed to Real China. But for the CPC, the particular challenge of the rise of Deep China is that it is here that people now predominantly seek meaning and fulfilment, rather than in the public sphere, which is pervaded by issues of lack of trust and disengagement because of its overt politicization. Deep China is the terrain of the real new cultural revolution. 'This quest for happiness is a common narrative in interviews with ordinary Chinese,' one of the contributors to the 2011 study states. 'It is a narrative that regards the current political reality as acceptable because it has made possible the opportunity to have a good life.'[55] But that is pragmatic tolerance, with clear boundaries and restraints on CPC fiat. It is not acceptance of or surrender to the Party.

Deep China is where people try to answer the fundamental questions of meaning, faith, and ultimate belief in their lives. As British sinologist Mark Elvin points out, Chinese Communism, at least in the era of high Maoism around the Cultural Revolution from the late 1960s, was a living faith, 'not just a discredited shell', and dared to speak to these questions. It did 'provide people with a story by which to live. With its current disintegration they [Chinese people] face the loss not of one but of two systems of belief and life orientation within a single century', that of imperial Confucian traditional values and Marxism-Leninism.[56] After 1978, the stories by which Chinese came to live their lives were mostly relevant to Real China: material enrichment, scientific progress, physical reconstruction. For the authors of *Deep China*, this created a crisis of meaning and a 'divided self'. This concept 'is a still valid depiction of the human condition in China'. They go on:

> The divided self (or double consciousness) of the Chinese turns on the unsettling realization that things can get worse (much worse) in a hurry and that the moral context in Chinese society can be and frequently is

divided against the moral person. The state that has been so successful
at creating prosperity ... is also repressive and can be dangerously so.
The moral text created by the party-state is as much a place of collusion and collaboration with ruthless pragmatic power as it is a place
of aspiration.[57]

Failure to speak to these concerns, or speaking in the wrong way,
only using the tactics of repression and coercion, creates resentment
at the Party, and disengagement from it. This quandary is precisely
the same as the one the CPC faced when dealing with its own cadres
referred to in the section above. How to reach them, how to mobilize
and incentivize them in ways which were about more than just enforcement, the issuing of imperatives and coercion. In its dealings with the
more individuated, morally more liberated, less beholden members
of society who have arisen since the great economic transformation
from 1978, the CPC in reform China has appeared in two guises: as
the provider and giver of the spaces for this liberation and freedom
but also as the enforcer of rules and restraints. It is an entity that
presents itself as the new people's best bet for a better life, and a
richer, more satisfying future, and yet at the same time talks of enforced
self-sacrifice and abnegation of the individual self. This is a complicated message to convey.

It is particularly problematic because of the new Chinese social
contract that has been created since 1978. The CPC in this era needs
the people more than the people might need it. The depth and extent
of its repressive powers in both Real and Deep China are circumscribed
and limited in ways which grow more complicated by the day. Its
ideological potency, as will be seen in the next chapter, is fatally
weakened. Its moral hold, because of this mismatch between demands
for self-sacrifice in the face of a society of unbridled self-satisfaction,
is undergoing urgent renovation, as was made clear above, and needing
to seek new sources of replenishment. In Deep China, the Party figures
as a target of Liu Xiaobo's coruscating wit, an object of subliminal,
but easily detectable, public sarcasm and double-speak. Worst of all,
it often dwindles to such an extent it is almost invisible. In this place,
it has a dilemma of relevance.

And yet this is a place that the CPC has to find a way to speak to.
The compact from 1978 onwards was to tolerate Deep China and
accept that its revivified forms of individualism existed, but ensure
it remained behind well-understood boundaries and barricades. Real
and Deep China were parallel worlds with an uneasy, but workable,
truce between the two. As the CPC faced its own crisis of faith and
legitimacy, its need to reassert its moral narrative and the underlying
belief in a vision of positive historic progress entailed acknowledgement that a fundamental part of this involved seeking to mobilize

people's emotions. In this realm, Deep China matters. This process has reached its climax in Xi's China. There the CPC is increasingly seeking to get the people's emotional engagement rather than their tacit physical consent. Its sustainability in power demands allegiance from their whole selves, not just their material bodies, because reliance on the latter will always run the high risk that the CPC will go the same direction as the USSR, and be expendable. Only conquest of Deep China will lead to the absolute victory of perpetual CPC rule. This is the frontier that needs to be crossed, by officials who have first won the battle within themselves to placate and recruit from this place. This is an immense challenge. It appears almost an insurmountable one. But while critics like Liu Xiaobo, for all the nobility of their purpose, understood well the appetite the CPC had for power, they underestimated how creative it could be in ensuring that it achieved this goal. And there was one area it could deploy in the battle to conquer Deep China: an appeal to traditional Chinese culture. Thus came about one of the greatest armistices in modern history.

This armistice was made more urgent by the rise of a new form of competition for the spiritual loyalty of Deep China, and a new source of ordering values in people's lives: religion. Although faith under the Nationalists had been tolerated in the five forms Sun Yatsen had first tabulated – Buddhism, Daoism, Islam, Catholicism, and Protestantism (note no Confucianism here) – the CPC on coming to power had adopted an atheistic stance and outlawed all organized expressions of belief. Since 1982, and the issuance that year of an official government document in Beijing mandating more freedom for religious practice, Buddhism and Daoism have made a comeback (with perhaps 200 million followers), followed by Islam (25 million), and the various forms of Christianity (up to 70 million). This is not taking into account folk religions and other forms of faith, which might number up to 170 million observers. As Beijing-based journalist Ian Johnson has shown, the challenges of a society undergoing such widespread change have resulted in people asking questions about the meaning of their lives and the purpose guiding them which have ended up in conversions, or adoptions of forms of faith.[58] But the CPC has ensured that these take a 'patriotic' form and that they do not threaten to compete with its own attempts to speak to the souls of the new China.

Deep China and the Deep Past

In the summer of 1973, the 'Pi-Lin Pi-Kong' (Criticize Lin, Criticize Confucius) campaign rolled out from Beijing. Partly it was a direct response to the shocking news released the previous year that Mao's erstwhile chosen successor and second in command, Lin Biao, had died in a plane crash in the depths of Outer Mongolia. He was on his way to the Soviet Union, reports stated, after what was claimed was an attempt at an armed putsch. But the 1973 campaign had also been linked to attacks by the radical 'Gang of Four' leadership against the long-serving Premier Zhou Enlai. The spirit of these times meant that even the most obvious things had to be conveyed in indirect and metaphorical ways. That, it was claimed, was the case here.

The other target, Confucius, had been in the sights of the revolutionary Party leaders for a long time. Mao, the son of a rich farmer and landowner, had complained bitterly about the influence of the ancient sage on his own traditional upbringing in the central Hunan province countryside. Throughout the 1920s and 1930s, Confucianism was regarded as symptomatic of a culture mired in hierarchy, the legacy of an ossified past and a weighty imperial history that needed to be shifted. In the trenchant words of Lu Xun, the greatest writer from this era, 'Confucius owes his exalted position in China to the wielders of power. He is the sage of the wielders of power or those who would be wielders of power.'[59] From 1949, this process of bringing down the figure nicknamed 'the tireless nagger' by Lu gained momentum. The Cultural Revolution, from the day it started in mid-1966, was the acme of this, with the destruction of the Qufu temple, Confucius's reputed birthplace in Shandong province, in the winter of that year. In 1973, however, the movement intensified, with Mao reportedly stating that summer that 'Confucius has to be criticized.' *The People's Daily* ran articles like 'Confucius, A Thinker Who Stubbornly Upheld the Slave System'. In this piece, produced by a professor at Zhejiang University, the argument was brutal: 'The fundamental principle of Confucius had been to restore the disappearing slave-owning society and to suppress the new things emerging in feudal society.'[60] Linked to the 'Smash the Four Olds' campaign of a few years before, this was part of a concerted effort to undermine and root out the influence of the old society. But it was also linked to contemporary political events, with the claim that in his heart Lin Biao (and, by implication, Zhou and his supporters) had been an admirer of the ancient thinkers, and possessed works by not only Confucius but also Mencius and others.

The campaign continued into the next year. But then the focus moved on to other targets, from Legalists in the pre-Qin era to the First Emperor himself, set up as a figure of despotism and misrule. After the death of Mao, these overt attempts to purge China of traditional thinking and culture petered out. Interest shifted in the era of early hot and rapid reform to importing as many ideas from the outside world as possible. A more liberal atmosphere meant there was tolerance for the restoration of Confucius and others to public discourse, but no active pursuit of them or their meaning in Chinese society. In some ways, their influence was swamped by the exciting reacquaintance with ideas from the outside world. It was only in the late 1990s that there were the first real attempts to see in 'traditional Chinese culture' a resource that the Party might use and benefit from. Its first appearance was somewhat prosaic, in the dense use of the mantra of '5,000 years of history' which came to appear frequently in Chinese leaders' speeches. This long history which once figured as such a burden suddenly became a source of pride and esteem.

The most significant subsequent development of this process of the rehabilitation of traditional Chinese culture was the explicit reference to an inspiration from ancient Chinese thinking in the new slogans of Party leaders like Hu Jintao in the middle part of the 2000s. This was at a time when Chinese society domestically was becoming increasingly fractious. 'There were 8,000 "mass incidents" in 1993, according to China's Ministry of Public Security,' Guobin Yang writes in a study of the internet and its links to public protests.

> This number rose to 32,000 in 1999, 38,000 in 2003, and 87,000 in 2005. Accompanying the alarming ascendance of social conflicts in recent years is the appearance of an official rhetoric of building a 'harmonious society'. Perhaps more than anything else, this new discourse indicates that Chinese society has entered an age of contention.[61]

By 2010, according to some statistics issued by the Chinese Academy of Social Sciences (CASS), this was to get even worse, with as many as 200,000 such incidents.

'Harmonious society' (*hexie shehui*) was an idea related to another of Hu's core slogans: 'taking people as the base'. This linked to notions from a near contemporary of Confucius, the great thinker Mencius, who had made the pronouncement *yiren weiben* ('take people as the foundation'). The allusion was to a form of Chinese humanism spreading back far beyond the limits of modern history. The Party, after its era of conflict with the imperial past and the philosophy and thinking associated with some parts of it, was now introducing terms and ideas that emanated from this once forbidden zone. It was also starting to use these ideas derived from ancient sources to address the issue of how, despite its history of commitment to collectivism and the ethics of self-sacrifice, there were ways in which it could speak to people directly as individuals, and demonstrate that it was on their side. In the classical thinkers, the CPC found a language it could use by which to talk authentically to Deep China. 'Taking people as the base' was a key part of Hu Jintao's speech to the Seventeenth Party Congress in 2007, the one which had seen Xi Jinping introduced into the Standing Committee of the Politburo as his most likely successor.[62]

'Taking people as the base' occurred as one of a suite of ideas lifted from the classical past which the Party was now seeking to apply to contemporary China as compatible with its own vision of moral standing and positive historic progress based on authentic, deeply rooted Chinese values. Harmony in this discourse referred to a balance between nature and humanity, between different forces in society, and to the overall idea of a universe of equity and stable, counter-poised forces. Ideas recurred of the 'order under heaven' (*tianxia*) in governance, and in the way in which China related to the outside world. This was indeed a post-Communist Communist-style pragmatic solution: to use the past for the sake of the present, and to fill the huge gap in the Party's armoury of values and its lack of a language that appealed to the larger public with something that had historic traction and linked to the nationalism, the promotion of a strong, resilient, enduring culture, and the mission to create a 'strong, rich China' which lay at the basis of the Party's new claim for legitimacy.

The CPC's pact with what is posited as the country's long imperial past has turned into a major strategic relationship under Xi. In the collection of speeches published by him in 2013, *The Governance of China*, along with a second volume in 2017, Tang and Song Dynasty poets and Warring States thinkers are mentioned more than the works of Mao, Marx, or Lenin. The Confucius Institutes which started to dot the world in the Hu era have increased, along with the fractious welcome given them in some countries because of suspicion about their real intentions. The Party had become interested in the merits of using soft-power instruments to create a more sympathetic, benign reception for its message in Hu's era. But this too has been a process that has intensified, as it becomes clear that China has limited chances of winning a fair hearing while it still has a one-party regime. Its most significant source of appeal to the wider world is through reference to the great past as a civilization – a past lamentably little appreciated in the outside world, but one which at least gave some distractions from the less palatable aspects of China's recent history, and the role the Party has played in that.

There are many questions about the complexity of this past, and the multiple levels of histories that it is constituted by. China itself as a unified cultural and historic entity is a highly contested idea. Its shape, identity, and contours have radically changed over the course of the last two millenniums. On top of this, there are a diversity of cultures and intellectual traditions within these strands that constitute Chinese histories. But in this diversity and flexibility lies a great opportunity for the Party, which since 1978 has attached itself increasingly to the idea of a specific Chinese way of doing things, and an exceptional Chinese approach to problems. The historian of imperial China the late F.W. Mote wrote of this great difference between the European and Chinese intellectual traditions in terms of resistance to unified, prescriptive models in the latter. 'The notion of "exclusive truth" was absent from East Asian mentality,' he stated, when referring to the differences between Buddhism, Confucianism, and Daoism. '[E]ven when the jealous God of monotheism was imported with Judaism, Nestorian Christianity and Islam during these centuries, it was most difficult to maintain that idea in the prevailing atmosphere of Asian religions' mutual compatibility.'[63] As with the Roman Empire before the adoption of Christianity as the state religion in AD 315, imperial China from the pre-Han era right up to the twentieth century was a place where syncretic traditions could exist. The scholar of Chinese literature C.T. Hsia referred to Buddhism, Confucianism, and Daoism as the 'three teachings', which 'enjoyed government support and popular reverence'.[64] Within this marketplace of different belief systems, people were able to operate freely, moving between each one of the great three, not needing to make any particular choice, shifting from one framework to another.

It is ironic that the Communists after 1949 attempted to reject this hybrid belief system, and as part of their project of modernity introduced the idea that there was a unique form of truth, and that at its heart lay the Marxist-Leninist view of the world. The Cultural Revolution has already been described as one of the few moments in Chinese histories where something approaching a unifying religious fervour overwhelmed society. But the experience was not a positive one. China effectively returned to syncretism in the 1980s, allowing practice of the five religions recognized in the state constitution: Buddhism, Protestantism, Catholicism, Islam, and Confucianism. All of these offered believers a set of ethical principles and rules by which to conduct their daily lives. It is a remarkable moment, therefore, to see China in the era of Xi Jinping not just tolerate but positively embrace this diverse, syncretic tradition as a strength. But in this act, it has found a bridge with which to finally talk to that place so long eluding it: Deep China. Because here, pride at China's culture and its epic longevity is high. And wearing the garb of traditional Chinese culture, the Party can steal its way in.

That was the theory. What about the practice? How did the
CPC create a new model army with which to conquer Deep China?
How did the exemplary messages presented through Xi's leader-
ship persona impact on the daily lives of cadres? Speaking in 2013,
Xi stated:

> If you don't be strict with yourself, how can you discipline others? The
> comrades of military commission are in high position, all the army
> officers, soldiers and people are looking at us. They want to know if
> we are decent and clean or not? This is the issue concerning the Party
> and military's image. We should play an exemplary role in front of the
> entire army, then we have the confidence to improve the army's working
> style. If we are associated with misconduct and are unclean, people
> will criticize us behind our backs, then how should we discipline others?
> It's impossible and useless.[65]

The tools to achieve this reformation of cadre behaviour were Maoist
in their outward form, even if the underlying reasons for them and
their outcomes were very different. Self-criticisms targeted at cadres
made a comeback as part of the new moral training added on to the
technological training of the previous era. In Shaoyang Zhang and
Derek McGhee's book *China's Ethical Revolution and Regaining
Legitimacy*, based on field research undertaken amongst officials in
Xi's brave new moral China, there is the idea of encouraging cadres
to retreat and 'watch themselves then they are on their own'. The
Party's responsibilities need to be internalized.

Cadres are encouraged in these activities of self-examination to
divide the 'small self' (the private self with its private networks and
interests and aims) and the 'great self'. For Zhang and McGhee, the
Party defines a *telos*, an overarching objective, which transcends the
small self, and leads cadres irresistibly towards the larger one, where
interests are defined in terms of service to country, and to the greater,
more noble good of the Party. In Maoist China, there was no inner
hierarchy tolerated between the smaller and larger self. The former
died so the latter could live. In Xi's China, the two can exist, but
there is an hierarchy. 'To be a good leader, we must have the following characteristics: loyalty to the Party and its political character,
personal cleanness is the official line, professional qualifications are
political criteria.'[66] This is achieved through a system of sessions involving criticism and feedback from others. Acceptance in these of the
tenets of Marxism-Leninism is not about their truth function, but
about laying oneself open to obedience and discipline. The larger self
is not there to argue, but to accept. It is seeking not financial capital,
as had happened under the corrupt practices of the past, but much

more precious moral capital. The question under Xi was whether these regimes of self-cultivation addressing seemingly intractable old issues – personal networks, mountainism (i.e. factionalism), the challenges of *renqing* (human relations), and the issues of prioritizing the personal over the collective – would actually work. Remember, this was not about achieving this through fear and coercion, but getting the active engagement and belief of cadres so they could undertake their mission. Here, there were major questions and huge anomalies in the way the CPC went about its business, pointing to profound structural faultlines in its modern persona.

Written on Water: The Sustainability of the CPC's Moral Fightback

One of the idiosyncrasies of modern Beijing is that the more significant the powers associated with a building, the less likely it is to have any signage on its front indicating what precisely it is. While the bombast of the Great Hall of the People seems to shriek importance and status, the real pulsing heart of political Beijing is in the anonymous group of buildings concealed behind a stark red wall on the opposite side of the road: the Zhongnanhai leadership compound.

Of all the most important, feared organizations, none is more dreaded than the CCDI. In the north-west of the city, beside one of the very anonymous-looking major boulevards, it has a standard gated entrance manned by impassive soldiers in the standard olive-green uniforms of the PLA, and a Soviet-era-style façade. There is no indication of what the building houses except for the hammer and sickle symbol of the Party stuck prominently on the front.

In this structure, the files indicating cases of malfeasance arrive for their investigation and adjudication. The 1,000 personnel of the CCDI have immense powers, above and beyond anything allowed in civil law. Once instructed, they can swoop down on any locality, on any official, or on any organization. When they do come, no protests are permitted, nor any recourse to legal action. And once they start to tear away at a specific area, their actions can be similar to that of locusts visiting on a summer's day. The leave nothing in their wake. This was particularly the case under their formidable leader from 2012 to 2017, Wang Qishan.

At the back of the building is a lecture theatre. It is here that groups are able to come and hear some of the public-facing work that the CCDI does. It, too, is in the business of crafting narratives, to allow the wider world to understand, inside and outside the PRC, what specifically it does. It wants to be sympathized with and better known, if only because this helps it with its work.

Sitting in this theatre hearing high-ranking officials explain their work is a disorientating experience. Their language is surprisingly dramatic. They are 'holding the sword of Damocles' over the heads of those accused of being impure or incorrect. They have to adopt 'innovative investigation methods', applying creativity to ferreting out their key targets. Their main weapon, it becomes clear, is surprise, and lack of transparency. They wish to engage finally in a casino game where they hold all the cards, and have all the advantages, and where those who dare to play against them know they are engaged in a contest where there is only ever one winner.

Maoist China lives on in the processes of the CCDI. The only correct response when the investigators come is complete and absolute submission, and admission of total guilt. No punishment is too serious for those caught in the organization's grasp. The sterile theatre atmosphere and the silence of the audience in the room is not a good indication of what the auditors might be feeling as they hear this strategy outlined. The CCDI exists like the ultimate dispenser of justice, and decider of fate. But no explanation is given that day, or on any other for that matter, about how decisions are made for targets, and why. These are the most secret of CPC secrets.

It is the way in which the CCDI operates which most merits attention. For all the talk of the creation of new standards of behaviour and correct moral posture, it operates as a bridge, a very tangible link, to another age. Here is the Leninist Party in its purest essence: an expression of pure power, arbitrary, self-defining, operating according to its own principles, in a privileged space above every other entity in society. It is the final acknowledgement that for all the change and transformation in society and the ways in which the Party has reflected this, its culture remains the same: secretive, controlling, willing to use violence and coercion to get its way. Coming up for a moral justification for this falls back on the same utilitarian ethics of the Maoist past. The ends justify the means. People are the servants of the greater narrative of history. And the self, for all the new negotiations, is subservient to the higher agency of the Party and the collective. The CCDI is proof, in the flesh, that the Party four decades after his death still lives in the shadow of Mao Zedong.

Practice was regarded as the ultimate test for an ideological and theoretical posture from the time of Mao onwards. Marxism-Leninism with Chinese characteristics was pragmatic. The CPC was and remains an executive organization. It does things. The rise of Deep China and the complexity this has resulted in within society has created significant challenges. The CPC in 1978 unleashed a process it did not know the outcomes of. One of the most important of these has been this creation of a world beyond the confines of the state and public discourse, a world of private agency, private needs and dreams, which seems to cut across all of the self-sacrificing, collectivist language the CPC was founded on and is ostensibly still using. In the 1980s to the 2000s, a laissez-faire attitude led to tolerance of these two realities in China: the CPC busy attending to the infrastructure of the material world, building the primary stage of socialism, and undertaking sporadic but largely limited campaigns to tie in the other China, where people increasingly did as they pleased and reverted to old modes of behaviour centred on personal networks, private interest, service to what Fei Xiaotong called the selfish heart of traditional Chinese society.

The rise (or return and rejuvenation) of this kind of Chinese self which had validated space for individuation impacted on the CPC itself. Its cadres became as good at assembling a private world and living in private space as anyone else. In doing so, they violated the self-sacrificing codes the CPC had been based on. Even worse, they betrayed the ethos of serving the people. This eroded the identity and mission of the Party.

From the era of Hu Jintao, and increasingly under Xi, the aim has been to restore CPC involvement in and control of this space called Deep China. This has been undertaken by two moves. One has been to purge the CPC cadres, and particularly the leadership, so that their actions restore the idea that they believe in service and a mission that transcends their selves and can therefore occupy an exemplary role in society. The main means to achieve this is through self-criticism and struggle sessions, which mean that even when they are on their own they are reformed and observe the CPC norms. The production of more loyal, faithful, and upright cadres in this way means they will be able to speak to and operate in the spaces of Deep China. The other method has been use by the CPC of a richer moral vocabulary, using ideas and forms of words from the classical past, appealing to a sense of fundamental Chinese cultural identity arising from Confucianism and other thought forms which have traction to this day.

All of this is motivated by a link with the narratives of the CPC in the end being moral ones, and the ways in which these gear to the creation of a strong, powerful nation. Nation building, not CPC building, despite the public language, is the goal. In Deep China, people's sense of security, identity, and emotional pride is linked to an idea of being Chinese, and being part of a civilization and nation they can now be proud of. It is here that the CPC has space to make a deeper appeal as part of that message, as the entity that states it has a monopoly, not on power, but on the ability and right to deliver justice for a nation wronged in its modern history and now in the right place to have redemption. These are practical aims, but they are at heart spiritual. The link is sought between Deep and Real China for the CPC here.

But it is in practice that issues arise. What the CPC says it wants to do is one thing, but critics like Liu Xiaobo have always been adept at finding large gaps between the rhetoric and the reality. In the practical attempt to create of CPC cadres moral actors able to infiltrate and have appeal in the Deep China space, there are immense structural flaws. In the end, the CPC through the work of the CCDI is attempting to achieve this through processes that appeal to fear, that coerce and that operate only in the realm of force and punishment. These are authentically Maoist methods, but are incongruous in an era where the onus is on softer, more consensual modes of action where the aim is to have willing, free consent.

All of this indicates a new kind of unsustainability, and one it is hard to find an answer to. The CPC has a moral code based on self-sacrifice and self-abnegation, on collectivist goals. It has sought to update this since 1978 by maintaining the underlying principles of this code, but giving it a nationalist dimension, talking of commitment to creation of the great nation-state. All of that relies on its being inextricably linked to this mission. Once the great nation-state has been achieved, however, the thing that Chinese people really believe in, what role for the CPC then? Surely it should simply disappear, having achieved its task. And how can it operate coherently when it assumes the position of being able to engage with the Deep China of individuation and personal agency, and yet with its own cadres it uses discipline regimes that, through their use of fear and force, seem to undercut this, not recognizing agency and personal power? Similar problems of structural inconsistency are found in the related realm of ideology, to which we now turn.

5

The Drama of Ideas
The Party and Ideology

For anyone wanting to visually encapsulate the greatest paradoxes of China today, then standing opposite the Bund waterfront buildings in Shanghai by the Huangpu River while dusk is falling offers the most dramatic and visually stimulating way to do so. Here in a country ostensibly run on socialist rules with a Communist Party still maintaining a monopoly on power is a sight that would make most capitalist societies proud. Across the river heaving with boat traffic there stands the mighty modern landscape of Pudong district. An assemblage of warehouses, small farm holdings, and dirt tracks only three decades before, in 2018 it hosts hundreds of skyscrapers. One, the Shanghai Tower, is the world's second tallest building, so tall it is often wrapped in low-lying clouds. The other, immediately next to it, the Jinmao Building, was once the world's highest hotel. The Oriental Television Tower over to the east stands beside a myriad of shopping malls, atop a subterraneous museum. The whole magnificent gleaming, glassy frontage is lit up at night with adverts, colourful montages, displays, beaming across at the swarms of domestic and international travellers who have come to the true epicentre of the modern in China. This indeed is socialism with Chinese characteristics.

To feel disorientated and awestruck is not unusual for visitors to Shanghai, particularly for those coming to the city for the first time. It would be odd not to be powerfully impressed as much by the sight spread before one as by the fact that this exists in a socialist country. How can a one-party state achieve the kind of dynamism usually associated with capitalism? Political economist Yasheng Huang in his book *Capitalism with Chinese Characteristics* has a chapter simply entitled 'What is Wrong with Shanghai?' In it he refers to Indian businesspeople and officials flocking to the city and looking with envy at its uber-modern urban centre, its massive, brand-new subway system (already the world's second largest), and the high-speed Maglev train racing people at over 450 kilometres an hour into the city centre from Pudong airport. For them, with the creaky infrastructure in their own country, it often seems like they have arrived at the model for what they might do back at home.

Huang, however, makes some powerful points about how what they are looking at is in many ways a mirage. Firstly, for all its entrepreneurial, freewheeling veneer, Shanghai, despite a history of being the capitalist hub of China (in the 1920s and 1930s, it hosted the Communists because it was the only place with anything approaching a national urban proletariat), is to this day overwhelmingly an economy under state control. Huang quotes Chen Liangyu, Party Secretary boss of the city in the mid-2000s: '"If I am not mistaken," Chen proudly stated, "in our country private businesses contribute 40 per cent of GDP. In our Shanghai, SOEs create nearly 80 per cent of Shanghai's GDP. Who upholds socialism most rigorously? Who else if not Shanghai?"'[1] Chen's words are not so often quoted in China these days because he was removed for corruption in 2007. But that does not stop them being accurate. The Pudong area with its mighty modern buildings was, as Huang continued, 'a massive taking of rural land, huge government investments and subsidization of [Foreign Direct Investment]'.[2] 'Shanghai', Huang concludes, 'is a classic industrial-policy state' with 'a highly interventionist government', and one with 'a lot of power'.[3] Chen Yun, a senior leader in and highly influential (but very conservative) economist of the 1980s, referred famously to the Chinese version of the market economy being like a 'bird in a cage'. Shanghai's form of capitalism exemplifies this. How can we make sense of a phenomenon like Shanghai with its combination of ostensibly wholly contradictory elements?

At the heart of this is the role of ideology and what the CPC having an ideological position means in contemporary China. The complete dominance of the one-party model over the last seven decades in the PRC, with its associated vocabularies, constitutions, documents, and articulations of unified belief systems, tends to support the notion that ideology has, and still should have, a role. We see threads of this commitment to an ideological posture in the power structure, in the way leaders speak, in the documents they issue even in 2018. In this vast corpus of material, we can seek evidence for their adherence to, or (occasionally) signs of dissent from, an extensive but often elusive belief system that leaves its shadow everywhere, but whose role and social importance prove hard to describe. What do Chinese leaders believe about the role of ideology in the current market socialist context? Are they hypocrites, saying one thing they don't truly adhere to while practising another? Are they nihilists, people who engage in the theatre and rhetoric of ideology for its form's sake and in the end believe nothing at all, or true believers in some underlying set of ideas and principles which matter deeply to them? Or are they pragmatists, stuck with a set of beliefs from another age and time which matter to their identity and history, but which have little resonance today?

China's current political model where the CPC has a monopoly on power makes this issue of the status of ideology, and the relationship between it and elite leaders, even more prominent. In Western multi-party systems, there are an openly admitted range of ideological positions and competition between these. That gives choice in terms of which ideology is dominant, and which politicians want to use. Sometimes it is conservative, sometimes more liberal, depending on the party in power. In China, there is none of this flexibility. One party has perpetual power. It has Ideology with a capital 'I', which presents itself as something which is not contingent, but almost along the lines of dogma or doctrine in a religious context. This 'Ideology' has a unique status as 'truth' and presents itself in a far more prominent way than in Western political ideologies. Its demands on politicians to believe in it, adhere to it, and do something with it are also much more stringent.

Ideology as a genus of revealed truth figures as a fundamental part of the identity and culture of the CPC from the earliest period to today. The Party was founded as a vehicle for a specific ideology. Fights over how that core ideological offer was best interpreted and understood in the context of China have taken up much time and energy throughout its development. As Beijing academic Wang Hui has stated, 'a central element of the [CPC's] history' is that 'every great political battle was inextricably linked to serious theoretical considerations and policy debate'.[4] These were about ideological principles and development. On a practical level, were ideology not to matter there would not be 2,000 Party Schools across the country teaching cadres what they must believe.[5] Nor would ideology figure so heavily in the education of school children and university students, as it still does. And nor would it be conveyed through so many large public events, and through so many forms of media.

Even in post-1978 market China, the country remains a place where ideology is hard to avoid. It figures as far more than just a form of words associated with a belief system. British critic and academic Terry Eagleton said of ideology in general that it was a set of practices,

behaviours, a cultural standpoint. 'The term "ideology",' Eagleton
states, 'has a whole range of useful meanings, not all of which are
compatible with each other.' He continues: 'The word "ideology" is
a text, woven of a whole tissue of different conceptual strands.'[6] It
can be linked to producing symbols, signs, and values in social life,
a body of ideas characteristic of a particular group of class, ideas
which help to legitimize a dominant political power. In this sense, the
CPC clearly does have ideology.

This chapter makes two principal arguments. The first is that just
as there is an historic moral narrative moulding the Party together,
so is there an ideological narrative underlining and supporting this.
The second it that as the historic and moral realms have been afflicted
by deep structural challenges in the last forty years, so too in ideology
there has been a massive underlying set of readjustments and challenges. The lazy response is to dismiss this and say that China is a
post-Communist society and therefore a post-ideological one. This
ignores the fact that, as Eagleton makes clear, all societies have ideologies. The issue in China is whether 'Ideology' with a unified façade
will remain an integral part of the CPC's claims on power. As in the
areas of moral narrative missions and ethical reform, therefore, the
question is whether the Communist Party can win this battle and
create a sustainable role for its beliefs and ideas.

The Ideological Narrative: The Origins of Plenitude in Contradiction

In the beginning, Marxism seeped into China via Japanese translations
of the great German thinker's main works. The first, *The Communist
Manifesto*, appeared in the 1890s, with parts of *Capital* following
afterwards. Their audience was miniscule, however. The godfathers
of modernity in the late Qing, figures like Kang Youwei, Liang Qichao,
and even Sun Yatsen, were largely unaware of, or indifferent to, their
contents. Their modernity was more associated with adapting Western
industrial models to Chinese traditions. This was the great hunt for
a viable Chinese form of modernity, on its own terms, in its own way.
Kang and his contemporaries did not feel Marxism offered a relevant
and workable way of doing this.

To what was initially a tiny set of believers, however, Marxism
offered a group of concepts and ideas which they did feel spoke to
the need for progress and change. In the work of Cambridge scholar
of modern Chinese history Hans van de Ven we can plot the slow
growth of this weak, marginal movement from the central province
of Hunan, where most of its early members were located, outwards

to other places.[7] For them, Marxism-Leninism offered a set of useful conceptual tools by which to understand the benighted predicament of their country and try to find a path out of this. Left-wing intellectuals during this period embraced the liberating notion that were Chinese history seen as a working out of dialectical forces, this gave a scientific way to show how it could lead to a positive future. For Mao and those present at the dawn of the Communist movement in the country, these ideas made sense and offered a way forward.

As stated previously, one of Mao's greatest organizational contributions was to shift the centre of revolutionary focus from the cities to the countryside, creating an indigenous Chinese form of Marxist action. As made clear in the 1945 Resolution, analysed in Chapter 1 – and in many other places in his work – he was also aware of the need for accepting the utility of violence as a tool. But while he was not a major theoretical thinker, there was one immense tactical achievement that can be attributed to him. In his 1937 essay 'On Contradictions', he achieved two things. He managed to marry one strand of ancient Chinese thinking – the Daoist love of counterbalancing opposing forces – with the new modernizing Marxist world-view. The famous Yin and Yang Daoist dialectic spoke from a deep and authentic strand of Chinese thinking, and made the unfamiliar Marxist version, dialectical materialism, at least a little easier to relate to. But he also created a liberating space where seemingly different thought systems and truths might co-exist. The dislike throughout Chinese history of commitment to a notion of singular exclusive truth, noted in the previous chapter, could thus be side-stepped in this way. Truth lay in different places in different ways. It was a case of wandering between these in a happy state of non-commitment.

Throughout his political practice, Mao proved the master of simultaneously holding opposing ideas in balance, creating immense tensions. In the Cultural Revolution, this resulted in a grotesque carnival of celebrating ignorance ('better red than expert'), praising what was judged to be political correctness at the time over all other forms of knowledge, and upturning society so that he could state approvingly in the late 1960s 'There is chaos under heaven – the situation is excellent.' In 'On Contradictions', his 1937 essay, he had presented his most extensive and celebrated defence of this posture. There he had written that unification of opposites sat at the heart of understanding and nature. 'The law of contradictions in things, that is, the law of the unity of opposites, is the basic law of materialistic dialectics.'[8] He went on:

[T]he universality or absoluteness of contradiction has a twofold meaning. One is that contradiction exists in the process of development of all things, and the other is that in the process of development of each thing a movement of opposites exists from beginning to end.[9]

'The law of contradictions in things,' he concluded, 'is the fundamental law of nature and of society and therefore also the fundamental law of thought.'[10] This stance justified a Maoist view of a community contaminated by struggle between opposing classes, mandating the need to cleanse society by pitting one of these groups against the others. Embracing perpetual conflict in this way was, unsurprisingly, to prove costly and hard to sustain.

The Maoist love of contradictions did not go away when Mao died. The 1978 reforms introduced ideas as inherently contradictory as any that Mao had ever championed. Some aspects of this have already been explored. But one idea in particular encapsulated this continuation of seeking for and celebrating contradictions: that of 'market socialism', the overarching new ideological position adopted from the 1980s onwards. In an essay by Mihai Craciun, he scanned the daily changing landscape of Shenzhen in the years when it was afire with reformist zeal, and divined there something of the contradiction-celebrating energy that still lingered from the Maoist era, trying to harmoniously marry the very disharmonious notions of market and Marxism. The aim was to create, in an imperfect world, a kind of utopia. 'Communists throughout modern history have inherited a Utopian ideology that mandates belief in an ideal history.'[11] Shenzhen was realization of that ideal for Chinese Communists, the city built from fields and wasteland embodying progress and a perfect future. For Craciun, this utopianism was, under Mao, delivered through the working out of contradictions, but by regimes of coercion and control, accepting the inevitable tidal flow of history. This allowed for the construction, often with no consent, of bold new cities built in the Soviet style atop ancient ones, their communities swept away.

With the Dengist pragmatic engagement with marketization after 1978, a whole new set of parameters were created which on the surface looked like they eschewed the Maoist embracing of contradictions and the attempt to create heaven on earth. In fact, though, the root convictions of the CPC had not changed:

> The [Special Economic Zones] are the cradle of contradictions. The consumerism sanctioned by the Party in exchange for modernisation and participation in the global economy is in contrast to the Communist regime itself. ... In [these zones] the syncretism socialism-capitalism – an expression of hybrid ideology – sustains a fragile ecology of juxtapositions.[12]

These zones are 'pragmatic constructions', laboratories that bring together contradictory world-views and ideologies, mixing Eastern culture with Western manufacturing processes, taking locally made products to a global market, combining socialist planning with capitalist economics. The reformation of the ideological space to accommodate places like Special Economic Zones was not so radical. It just involved invoking the need to use contradictions sanctioned by Mao decades before. In this framework, anything went. Maoist celebration of contradiction may have provided the opportunity for this volte-face after 1978, but the roots reached far back into China's culturally syncretic past. Maoism was a system of thought attuned to much more enduring and rooted modes of belief and understanding. The combination of these created the opportunities for a radical realignment from 1978 onwards. This is perhaps the main reason why leaders still stand by the statement that without Mao Zedong there would have been no China as it is today. It is a statement of fact. And encoding tolerance for contradictions in the deep structure of the Party's ideology from the very beginning was the main reason for that.

Putting Ideas into Practice: Ideology, Action, and the Maoist System

Contradictions might have supplied the philosophical basis for the CPC's ideology. But another attribute of the system from its earliest days was that all ideology needed to be linked to practice. The late American scholar John Wilson Lewis wrote in 1963 that while 'the prevailing intellectual climate of Communist China blends extremes of philosophy, sophistication and emotion',[13] Communist ideology at this time was 'an effective instrument of training', an 'educational process which elevates the system of training above simple discipline'.[14] 'For training the cadre and party member, Chinese Communist theory...provides a comprehensive theory or learning to ensure the thorough remoulding of each individual' (reverting back to the notion of abnegating the self).[15] The attributes that Lewis goes on to outline result in a personality type who can make a 'quick appraisal of situations and people. There is a correct niche for everything.' There is an 'unrelenting search for contradictions'. 'Ceaselessly criticizing others, the cadres and party members are reared in a climate of sin.' Here 'ideology warns that behind the mask of overt obedience lurks the contraction of latent deviation'.[16] Ideology therefore links to the issue of morality, covered in the previous chapters, but also to the

fundamental importance in the Maoist world-view of practice. 'Ideology provides the cadre with ready explanations and a vast inventory
of techniques, slogans and labels.'[17] As Wang Hui noted over four
decades later, in a different time and place, 'An outstanding characteristic of twentieth-century China's revolutionary transformations...has
been the continuous and intimate connection between theoretical
debate and political practice.'[18]

That connection is testified to in the work of scholars looking at
China around the same time as Lewis. For A. Doak Barnett writing
about party-state organization in the early 1960s, 'society has been
politicized to an unprecedented degree'. This served as a tool of control,
creating common standards of behaviour and a common notion of
what actions needed to result from all of this.

> Dedicated to the aim of controlling and changing the totality of a
> society, the regime has had to build new institutions to enable the
> nation's leaders not only to police the entire society but to manage the
> economy as a whole and indoctrinate the mass of the population in
> Marxism-Leninism and the 'thought of Mao Tse-Tung'.[19]

Franz Schurmann in his epic treatment of ideology from 1966 reinforced this idea of a clear link between ideology and practice: 'Although
Mao has not created a pure ideology, he has again been credited with
having created a practical ideology.'[20] Barnett's work looked in detail
at the elements of daily life that came to be informed by ideological
intention, structured because of a particular commitment to a world-
view shared across the organization. This manifested itself in internal
structures within the Party, from its committees to its leading small
groups, departments, and bureaus, to the hierarchy of leadership,
from central, high-level leaders down to local officials working in
village committees, to the activities they filled each day with – delivering, writing or reading reports, attending training sessions or (at least
in one of the many mass campaigns Mao's China was afflicted by
from 1949) struggle sessions, engaging in administrative activities,
involving themselves in rectification movements. This complex new
ecology of meetings, contents, movements, styles of work, and a whole
gamut of other identifying elements was driven by a commitment to
the belief in a unified thought system, even if the articulation of that
system remained elusive. It was therefore a predominantly ideological
structure, one where observance of, acceptance of, a belief in a unified
ideology mattered and had an impact on the structure of careers, the
way in which daily life was carried out, and the whole direction of
society.

Schurmann's work acknowledges a key way in which this 'ideological conquest' of Chinese life and its impact on action happened: through language:

> The Chinese communists have developed a rich vocabulary, which has in many ways changed the Chinese language. Ideas and terms have come into popular usage which never existed before.... One of the major contributions of the practical ideology of the Chinese communists has been the generation of these many new and useful categories and language.

This was no small matter. It gave the Chinese 'a new manner of thinking'.[21] That was an epistemic revolution guided by ideology, rather than a moral or political one guided by economic or political change. It shows the comprehensive nature of what Communists aimed to achieve after 1949.

In a contemporary context, however, all of this raises a question. Society in the Maoist era was regimented in ways unimaginable today. The mass media, such as it existed, was wholly under Party control. People were increasingly organized into state communes, with a command economic model prevailing over everything. The work unit system (*danwei*) prescribed what could and couldn't be done in even the most private areas of life, from whom one could marry to where one worked and if one could attend college or university. In market socialist China, this structure, supportive of an ideological position (upholding the mass line), has disappeared. People find their own marriage partners, find their own work, find their own houses. The state has vanished from most aspects of life. The Party operates like a backdrop, something people are aware of, but barely take much notice of. Ideological education, at least for 99.9 per cent of contemporary Chinese, operates like Religious Education in schools in the UK, a mandatory part of the curriculum, and yet one that rarely captures the interest or attention of those attending. In this new organizational context where the rationale and the support system for ideology which once existed are largely gone, or going, what real role does ideology still play in China, and why does the Party place such emphasis on it? Once more, the cause of this relates to questions about identity, moral narratives, and their links to cultural practices.

The Narratives of Chinese Communist Ideology

As the CPC today has a narrative of its own history which has been shifting and rebalancing itself since 1945 but which is committed to a specific moral teleology and a belief in ultimate positive outcomes, so too a major part of this is the supporting narrative it has about its ideological progress and development. When elite central leaders stand up to make major addresses, such as political reports at Party Congresses, or during Plenums, then they are duty bound to run through the various iterations of ideological development that the Party has experienced over the last nine decades. This gives even the most gifted orator in Chinese major issues. They must first recognize Mao Zedong Thought, then Deng Xiaoping Theory, then the Three Represents and Scientific Development. Each of these acknowledges the ideological imprint of a former elite leader, from the era of Mao down to that of Hu Jintao. This is an ongoing process. In 2017, at the Nineteenth Party Congress, a new formulation appeared which will now need to be accommodated: 'modernizing socialism with Chinese characteristics'. Before a leader can even start to say something, they have to give this run-through of their organization's own ideological narrative. It occurs like a mantra, said without thinking.

What is the meaning of each of these different formulations, however, and how do they combine, in the twenty-first century, to make a coherent ideological story? First, we need to look at what might be the core content behind each thought label. What, in the end, do these ideas actually mean? And what is their function and utility in the context of the modern party and its culture and identity? Before we even start, we also need to know that even in the realm of the abstract, there is a hierarchy, with 'thought' (*sixiang*) accorded the highest status, then 'theory' (*lilun*), then 'important thinking' (*zhongyao sixiang*), and finally 'viewpoint' (*guandian*).

Mao Zedong Thought

Mao Zedong may have been cut down to size in the 1981 Resolution referred to in Chapter 1. But the wording of that document is very careful about how this issue is handled. Mao the man made many mistakes. But Mao Zedong Thought remains valid and true. This strange bifurcation between a person of flesh and blood and his or her abstract intellectual contribution solved a major problem. Part of Mao, after the disasters of his final years, could live on and remain influential. Elements of Mao Zedong Thought have been referred to throughout this book so far. Maoism is practical theory – ideas not for the sake of ideas, but to be carried into the real world. That gives it its punch. Class struggle and striving for utopian goals were some of the early aims. These have become less important in recent years. There were other elements in its more native, primitive state that are not so popular now: a commitment to atheism; the need to overthrow the status quo and abolish all forms of non-state ownership; and then a raft of ideas linked to the specific historic circumstances in which Mao Zedong Thought came into existence.

Other key elements which are less palatable today are the conviction that 'political power grows out of the barrel of a gun'. This was theoretically informed by the Marxist view of politics as a power struggle; and practically useful to justify deployment of force in revolution (the root of the early PLA's loyalty to and ownership by the Party) and of a specific kind of Chinese Communist aesthetics linked to glorifying the people's struggle and being a tool of the revolution – something that will be covered in more detail in the final chapter. Lastly there is the Theory of Continued Revolution, something post-dating the PRC. In this theory, even after the proletariat establishes power, the capitalists will still fight back, from outside, or when Communists are corrupted into 'capitalist roaders', necessitating continual vigilance and struggle. This was an idea heavily used in the Cultural Revolution.

With so much abandoned detritus, how is it that the Party today stands by an ideological system which seems in most respects to have been superseded? From a theoretical point of view, a deconstruction of the more ludicrous aspects of Mao Zedong Thought would be an easy enough task. But as was already made clear, ideology is about more than mere ideas. It is about a set of practices, symbols, habits, and the whole cultural infrastructure supporting this. And Maoism is seen as contributing to the success that the Party enjoys today. Therefore, as an act of historic respect it cannot be abandoned. More importantly, it contributes towards the Party's sense of itself. Li Junru, the former deputy of the Central Party School in Beijing, wrote in a book explaining the CPC to the outside world that Mao Zedong was 'a great thinker. His thoughts, especially those of "serving the people" and "seeking truth from facts", are rules for our everyday living. They are useful,' he concludes, 'and eternal.'[22] But in the narrative of the ideological story of the Party, Mao Zedong's thinking was crucial because it achieved the 'sinification' of Marxism, and became therefore an irreplaceable tool of nationalism and patriotic performance. 'Mao Zedong Thought became the first achievement of the sinicization of Marxism, which was created by the Chinese communists closely associated with the Chinese nation for the purpose of reviving the Chinese nation.'[23] This means that it can no more be discarded than someone can ask to have their heart, brain, head, and spine replaced and still be the same person. Mao Zedong Thought is part of the life-blood of the Party, even to this day.

Deng Xiaoping Theory

Deng Xiaoping's history of subliminal heresy even in the hottest years of Maoism has been well documented. It is a miracle in some ways that he survived at all. Associated with the fierce attacks on rightists in the 1950s, he became a key ally of the then President Liu Shaoqi in the brief era of pragmatism in the 1960s, when the Four Modernizations in agriculture, industry, science, and technology and defence were first mooted. These had been announced by Zhou Enlai, another masterful practitioner of impenetrable ambiguity. After the tragic débâcle of the Great Leap Forward (1957), and then the famines that followed (1959–61), the need for stabilization was key. The priority was to strengthen the core areas covered by the Four Modernizations. The attempt was a bold but ill-fated one. By 1966, the onset of the Cultural Revolution meant Deng was felled and sent out of the capital to languish in the provinces till his recall in the early 1970s.

Deng was no theorist, as his slender volume of writings makes clear. He had little shame about this, once simply declaring that Marxism-Leninism was the plain truth and that it did not need to be learned from books. Unlike Mao, neither did he have a hinterland populated by close study of classical texts. Those who managed to penetrate the inner sanctum of Mao's study in the central compound were always impressed by the masses of books around him. Deng seldom referred to anything except what experience taught him.

Deng's essential contribution to Mao Zedong Thought and the Party's ideological narrative was the simple proposition that 'socialism with Chinese characteristics' was a paradox that could work. Beyond this, phrases associated with Deng promoted a pragmatic 'seek truth through facts' approach, mandating experimentation at lower levels of administration which could then be adopted higher up. For example, once they proved themselves successful, revolutionizing productivity in the countryside, the unsanctioned, experimental changes known as the household responsibility system were adopted more widely, even to the point where they eventually became national policy.

Deng's pronouncement that 'It doesn't matter whether a cat is black or white as long as it catches mice' has become the most celebrated of his phrases. There is a debate about when he used such a phrase, and indeed if he ever did so, and what the colour of the cat was, but the sentiments behind the words were what counted, and the way these allowed scope to simply row back from the harsh dialectical battles of extremes in the recent past. Ideological truth was created, not pre-known. Deng's approach was different to Mao's: it was less about aiming to achieve utopia in the long-term future, and more about attending to the here and now. It was also strongly anti-dogmatic.

This anti-dogmatic, practice-orientated ideology perhaps explains why so much of Deng's 'theory' comes via these epigrammatic statements which cut things down to bare essentials. They were easy to memorize, and, to an extent, copied Mao's own gift for nailing issues important to him with simple slogans. On economic reform, for instance, Dengism can simply be reduced to the slogan 'crossing the river by feeling the stones'. Allowing 'some to get rich quick' mandated embracing economic growth at differing rates to bring everyone up to the same level eventually. On foreign policy, peaceful, independent, and proactive diplomacy with foreign powers matched this domestic pragmatism. Opening up China to the world could be done, indeed had to be done, but only on China's terms. No more victimization. Now everything had to be geared to serving China's interests. If that meant keeping within clear boundaries and not seeking a high-profile role, that was fine. This attitude was captured by the famous '24 Character' statement about China's international position: 'keep a low profile and bide your time, while also getting something accomplished' (taoguang yanghui, yousuo zuowei).[24] Deng also effectively solved the puzzle for Chinese of how to have Hong Kong revert to Chinese sovereignty in 1997 after over a century under the British with his gnomic formulation 'One country, two systems'.

The underlying impulse of Deng Xiaoping Theory, however, was to take the two keywords 'reform' and 'modernize', and to revivify the abandoned idea of the Four Modernizations from an earlier age. Deng Xiaoping Theory's anti-theoretical bent pushed the spaces for action in China way beyond anything that had existed before. It was, in many ways, an admission of the failure of one particular line of thought or approach once believed to be universally applicable across a whole vast and complex country, that of support for class struggle and aiming for long-term utopian goals. But it was also an acceptance that the alternative options of no theory, or multiple competing ideologies, were not permissible either. There needed to be a Daoist great unity, with counter-balancing forces holding each other in check. To the Yin of Mao was added the Yang of Deng.[25]

Jiang Zemin's Three Represents

Dengist pragmatism had repercussions. He himself had used the apprehensive phrase of 'letting a few flies in' when the windows of reform were opened. The 1980s, a period Yasheng Huang said was the most liberal and free spirited in modern Chinese history, came to a shuddering halt with the 1989 uprising.[26] Attempts by the Party to keep a tight rein on non-state businesspeople springing up everywhere, and efforts to keep officials onside, caused immense social dislocation, as was discussed previously. The Party nearly got swept away as a result of these and other forces in the events over the summer of that year.

The response, as a result of Deng's famous Southern Tour in the early part of 1992, was not to retrench on pragmatic reform, but to ensure that the Party had a far stronger and clearer strategic role. There was no question of returning to the past. In the words of Deng, 'without reform there is only one road – to perdition'.[27] From 1992, the need to revitalize 'socialism with Chinese characteristics' at a time when the Communist parties of the Soviet Union and elsewhere were failing and then falling led to a new social compact: more reform, more privatization, more changes to the SOEs under the zealous and effective Premier from 1997, Zhu Rongji, and a clear aim to enter the WTO. As Deng said, during his tours in the winter of 1991:

> If we did not…implement the policies of reform and opening to the outside world, develop the economy and raise living standards, we would find ourselves in a blind alley. We should adhere to the basic line for a hundred years, with no vacillation. That is the only way to win the trust and support of the people.[28]

Jiang Zemin, Party boss from 1989 to 2002, was the great dark horse of modern Chinese politics. Son of martyrs for the revolution, and Soviet-educated, he had pursued a career in the state sector since the 1950s, before moving across to politics and becoming, eventually, Party boss of Shanghai. His ability to avoid bloodshed there during the uprising in 1989 meant he attracted support in Beijing, and became Deng's final choice as Party leader nationally. This was a surprise. He was largely regarded as a buffoon, keen to parade his foreign-language skills, and burst out into singing karaoke whenever he had the chance. (During the State Visit to the UK in 1999 he famously serenaded the Queen with a rendition of 'My Darling Clementine'.) But looking back on his era, his skills were impressive. He stabilized China after 1989, re-embraced the reform programme with Deng's help after two rocky years of economic trauma in 1992, allowed reforms of state entities, got Hong Kong's reversion of sovereignty to China successfully finalized, and secured the Olympics and WTO entry for the country. These were real achievements. He had clearly learned the key lesson of succession politics in China: the aim was not to be the most liked, but the least disliked.

Throughout the second era of reform in China from 1992 and Deng's re-energizing Southern Tour, the non-state sector started to play an increasingly important role. Larger numbers of people simply left state enterprises, or, if they were younger, went direct into what were notionally private companies. As Yasheng Huang showed, however, the state enterprises still received the best treatment in terms of capital and resources. There was the manifestation of what he called a 'political pecking order' where the default was always to support the commanding heights of the economy, even as they went through reform and restructuring under Zhu Rongji's premiership. By 2001, when China entered the WTO, the non-state sector accounted for almost a third of GDP. This was to slowly rise, so that a report by the Organization for Economic Co-operation and Development in its first major study of the Chinese economy in 2005 saw the non-state as critical partners in half the whole economy.[29]

By the latter part of Jiang Zemin's period as Party leader, the issue of what to do about entrepreneurs was becoming more pressing. Since 1989, they had been associated with potential agents for pushing for political reform and democratization. As the work of Bruce Dickson and Jie Chen makes clear, some businesspeople had been highly supportive of the student protesters.[30] They had moulded themselves after the reformist, liberal business constituency in the Soviet Union who had been so important in the coalition to enforce political change. The Chinese government therefore had a choice either to repress this group (which carried potentially significant economic costs, in view of the size of their contribution in terms of jobs and growth), or to find ways of enfranchising them. Around 1998, an ideological campaign proposing the 'Three Speaks' kicked off. This evolved into the 'Three Represents' which were to represent the developmental needs of China's production force as an advanced society, the forward direction of China's advanced culture and civilization, and the essential interests of the broadest spectrum of Chinese citizens.

The idea was initially met with scepticism by commentators inside and outside China. However, it figured more meaningfully as a tactical move to finally enfranchise a crucial group within the Party, allowing entrepreneurs to join in 2002 after over a decade and a half of being excluded. The symbolism alone was immense. The CPC was avoiding creating a new group of oligarchs like those emerging in the former Soviet Union by co-opting them into a new United Front, the grand coalition of Party and non-Party forces first assembled in the late 1940s to reconstruct China after the foundation of the PRC. Through the consultative body established by the Communists earlier in their history, the Chinese People's Political Consultative Conference (CPPCC), entrepreneurs as Party members could have a voice. Zhang Ruimin, for instance, CEO of the Haier electronics goods company based in the north-east of the country, was able to sit as a full member of the Sixteenth Central Committee from 2002, and as an alternate member from 2007 till 2017. Liu Chunze, founder of the computer company Legend, renamed Lenova in the 2000s and one of the earliest technology companies to make acquisitions abroad, was also involved in the CPPCC. In ways like this, China's emerging super-wealthy were given a political role which was controlled, through the implementation of the Three Represents and its recognition of the new social structure of society.

Hu Jintao's Scientific Development

Hu Jintao became Party Secretary in late 2002. Reportedly handpicked by Deng Xiaoping many years earlier, he had spent his career mostly in the less developed provinces: in Gansu in the far west, then Guizhou down in the south-west, then Tibet (a three-year stint around the Tiananmen Square incident blighted by his own absence physically in the region owing to reportedly suffering from high-altitude sickness), till finally ending up in Beijing. His decade has been criticized as the ten lost years. And yet it had one immense achievement: rapid, huge surges in GDP growth, despite exogenous negative factors like the global financial crisis from 2007.

As American scholar Theresa Wright made clear in her study of the new class structure in China, the most problematic group after over three decades of reform remained people in rural areas.[31] Farmers constituted a large proportion of those protesting each year, usually rebelling because of the poor compensation given for their land when it was requisitioned to be developed or what they regarded as unfair tax burdens. For the Hu leadership, while businesspeople had been successfully enfranchised and posed no significant immediate threat to the Party's monopoly on power, the countryside was never a place to be complacent about. Around 2005, the notion of a harmonious society became heavily used. China's rise was a peaceful one, and the countryside, where half the population lived, also had to be stable, a place, in the language of the time, of happy rural socialism. As those focussing on protests there saw, however, the dense usage of this term 'harmony' (*hexie* in Chinese, a homonym for 'water crabs' to the delight of satirists) was only indicative of how troubled things were across the country. Those travelling around China in the middle part of the decade did not have to look very hard to see stark inequalities and evidence of deep contention. Massive uprisings were common, with provincial leaders like Zhang Dejiang in Guangdong using brutal repression to clamp down on them in the early part of the decade. Leaders across the country were judged on their ability to 'preserve stability', with an extensive apparatus of state security which started to cost more than national defence. Everyone seemed to be perpetually at war with everyone else. As revealed in an exposé by Chen Guidi and Wu Chuntao, two journalists from the central province of Anhui, in villages local officials were regarded as the enemy, meting out extortion, violence, and summary justice on local people.[32] Their work was almost immediately banned, testifying in the eyes of many to its accuracy.

A better deal for farmers was crucial. Most of the policies since 1978 had been pro-urban. The countryside had received village democracy and some greater autonomy,[33] but it was still a place most young wanted to get away from, where healthcare and public goods were poorly developed, and where there were huge inequalities in terms of gender balance and wealth levels. One of the greatest complaints was about tax burdens on farmers, something that was addressed by the central government in 2007 when the then Premier Wen Jiabao abolished these. Attempts were made at the Seventeenth Party Congress the same year to create a comprehensive framework to deal with these issues through the notion of Scientific Development (*kexue fazhan*). Taking a concept from classical philosophy (particularly the works of Confucius's near contemporary, Mencius), where citizens were taken as the base, the Party mission was to serve the interests of all of the people. More specifically, this meant continuing to increase standards of living, protecting human rights in politics, economics, and culture, and continuing to raise people's intellectual, cultural and scientific, and health quality (*suzhi*). The second core idea was of a 'comprehensive, flexible, sustainable growth' model. This was in answer to the four structural challenges Wen Jiabao had mentioned in 2008: that the Chinese economy was 'unstable, uncoordinated, unsustainable and unbalanced'. Six areas of coordination were proposed: urban and rural growth; regional growth; economic society growth; environmentally friendly growth; domestic growth with regard to international trade; and the two arenas of domestic and foreign relations.

Scientific Development was exhaustively promoted after the Seventeenth Congress, but it was regarded with high levels of cynicism because of its lack of concrete content, and its highly abstract sound. That was probably testimony to the fact that while entrepreneurs were a relatively easy group to keep on board, simply by giving them more chances to make money and grow rich, farmers and those living in rural areas were a far harder constituency to please, even while their numbers were falling. The CPC was in good company in finding this group challenging to satisfy. Practically every Chinese administration over the last two and a half millennia had tried. To some degree each had failed.

These were the core iterations of an ideological stream running from the foundation stage of the CPC to its era in power. They bridged the 1978 divide, and continued to figure as part of the Party's core identity into the twenty-first century. It is obvious that each different formulation was aimed at addressing specific questions about the country's development, and the role of the CPC in trying to answer these. Remaining relevant and in control was key. Some ideologies were disruptive, seeking to encourage social movements and attitudes that upturned existing conventions and habits (Mao Zedong Thought is pre-eminent here). Deng Xiaoping Theory was more hybrid, a subtle rejection of some of the more muscular elements of Maoism, but an attempt to develop and adapt the more positive, practical aspects in order to remain in power and honour the historic moral narrative the CPC believed it was following. The ideologies after this were more local in their effects, attempts to make sense of and ideologically enfranchise changes Party policy action had brought about which needed fuller and better explanation. For the CPC in the era of Xi, however, the question was whether this complex, sometimes clunky, and often contradictory ideological narrative had become too diffuse, and too variegated. Was there need for a process of simplification here? This will be attended to in the next chapter.

6

The Ideological Fightback under Xi

Contradictions in the Maoist account, and dialectics in general, necessarily need two sides, negative and positive, thesis and antithesis. For the Party's ideological narrative over the last nine decades, there had always been a counter-narrative it was arguing against beyond the arguments it was having within itself. Sometimes this was very openly expressed by groups which opposed the CPC's rise to power. In the era before 1949, these had been landlords, small-scale capitalists, and the constellation of forces around the Nationalists mapping out a contesting vision of the nation and how it might develop in the future. From 1949, most counter-ideologies were eradicated or went underground. But in the discourse of the Party, whatever the reality of the continuing viability and influence of these ideas, fear of their potential remained a major influence on it. This figured in the CPC's attack on those who were accused of having divided allegiances, the 'enemy sleeping at our side', and became more prominent in the 1960s when those labelled as Soviet revisionists and Nationalist lackeys took central stage amongst a rich menagerie of villains, smashed down by the relentless and coruscating rhetoric of the Cultural Revolution. As the great tragedy of this era meandered to its conclusion, there were more nuanced counter-ideologies. An example is that presented by the three authors going under the name Li Yizhe who put up a big character poster in Guangzhou in 1974 with the title 'On Socialist Democracy and the Chinese Legal System'.[1] They were rewarded with incarceration, but their arguments for a replacement of rule by man (*renzhi*) with rule by law (*fazhi*) continued with the Democracy Wall movement over 1978 to 1980.[2] That, too, was closed down by Deng

Xiaoping's leadership. One of the movement's central arguments, articulated by the former electrician at Beijing Zoo, Wei Jingsheng, was that the Four Modernizations mentioned in the previous chapter needed a fifth – democracy. He was to be jailed for over two decades before being exiled to the United States as a punishment for saying this. Amongst a whole generation of activists radicalized by the Cultural Revolution and its memory of idealistic politics, many responded by pouring their energies into delivering the sort of democracy they felt had been promised with the new opening up. They had miscalculated the real intentions of the Party elite, however. By 1981, Democracy Wall was fast becoming just a memory.

Within the Party through the 1980s and into the 1990s there were ideological counter-narratives that proved harder to manage. These spoke directly to the compact that Deng Xiaoping Theory had made with the market and with foreign capital, entrepreneurialism, and capitalist methods of development. For holders of this viewpoint, what mattered most was not whether the cat busily trying to catch mice was black or white, but that it was red. Loyalty to the Chairman ran very deep. His appeal was not so easy to eradicate even with the 1981 Resolution on history, which was exhaustively devised after many drafts and redrafts trying to achieve this. One of the most representative figures from this school was Deng Liqun, who remained an irritating, persistent defender of residual leftism right up to the twenty-first century.

Deng Liqun, no relative of the much more powerful paramount leader then in the ascendant, only occupied positions in the senior leadership of the Party very briefly in the era after 1978. He was elected to the Secretariat of the Central Committee in 1982, and then involved in propaganda work in the middle part of the decade, directing the 'spiritual pollution campaign', a kind of CPC-style inquisition to root out those categorized as subversives. While lacking the epic, savage qualities of similar kinds of campaigns in the Maoist era, these were a sharp reminder that the Party, despite all the other changes in society, did not intend to betray its Leninist, power-monopolizing roots. After Deng's dismissal in 1985, subsequent attempts to lobby to have him join the Politburo failed. His main means of influence was as the chief spokesperson for a highly critical attitude towards the kind of hybrid system that Deng Xiaoping Theory was allowing to establish itself in China. Tiananmen Square in 1989 was an event that he capitalized on fully, showing that it indicated what could happen in Chinese society if it deviated too far from Mao Zedong Thought. Relentlessly negative about the capitalist models prevailing in the US and Europe, Deng argued that these would cause a spiritual collapse if introduced into the PRC. His fundamental point was that Liu Shaoqi's vision from 1939 of selfless moral behaviour needed to be adhered to. The people were God, and the Party represented the people, so all ambitions, desires, and impulses needed to direct themselves towards serving it. Engaging in a form of economic development that saw the rise of individualism and the old curse of self-centred networks riddling Chinese society was unsustainable, and a betrayal of all the great achievements of the CPC in the past.

Deng's critique, where it focussed on rising levels of inequality in Chinese society and a return to some of the evils of the bad old days – crime, prostitution, hedonism, corruption amongst cadres – had traction. And while never a popular figure, he did pose the question which had also been asked by the Democracy Wall activists: what was the future path for Mao Zedong Thought? His answer was simply that Mao Zedong Thought should continue, and that Chinese society needed to remain Communist, with a stress on the collective. This primitivism was to remain appealing to at least a small group even after his death, at the grand age of 100, in 2015.[3]

The counterbalancing existence of this alternative, more loyalist, ideology did mean that the arguments over the role of the state and where the boundaries between it and the free market lay never went away. Liberalization was always occurring after 1992 within very set parameters. The Party ceded space, but made sure that it kept control of the things that mattered for it: state ownership of key industries; no tolerance for organized political opposition; and tight control on non-governmental organizations or civil society groups. In the early era of entry to the WTO, therefore, with the implementation of the Three Represents and the admission of non-state entrepreneurs into the Party, there was an expectation that SOEs would be increasingly exposed to market forces, and their subsidies in terms of utilities, land, and labour removed. Whatever hopes of this happening quickly dissipated in the period after 2007 when there was a spirted defence of the state sector and its crucial importance by the then number two in the Politburo, Wu Bangguo. Around this time, books like the *Six Noes* started to appear, arguing against any introduction of governance systems into China that mirrored those prevailing in capitalist countries. There were to be no bicameral parliamentary systems, no multi-party democracy, no division of powers, no constitutionalism or federalism. The market under the Three Represents and then Scientific Development existed as a political tool to preserve the one-party state as it sought legitimacy through economic success. It was not to become an autonomous entity in its own right, dictating the way that China's politics and its development should go. The quest was for balance, for the sort of 'bird in a cage' Chen Yun had referred to in the 1980s (see Chapter 5) – a market system at the service of the party-state and operating within the limits allowed to it.

The more extreme counter-ideological position towards the Three Represents and Scientific Development was that they lacked all content and had no real meaning. They were doomed to ineffectiveness because they were irrelevant. This was a particularly damning indictment for an organization that had stressed from the very start the practical orientation of its position. A representative of this posture was the argument of Chinese economic and Marxist academic Su Shaozhi when in 2000 he issued a stinging critique on the BBC website.[4] 'What is the "Three Represents?"', Su asked at the head of the article. 'Jiang Zemin hasn't really said this clearly.' Scientific Development sounded even more complicated and devoid of content. How could it relate to the practice and lives of Party members, let alone the larger public? For the Hu era, there was the issue not so much of a counter-ideology facing them but of no ideology whatsoever to oppose that of the Party beyond cynicism, nihilism, and, perhaps worst of all, indifference. This was the net result of the CPC driving all potential opposition underground. It was the broad critique of Liu Xiaobo and other dissidents discussed earlier. Obviously the CPC didn't want organized opposition. That was clear from everything it had done in the previous six decades in power. But it did now need a set of intellectual tools to accompany the task of its emotional and moral struggle in conquering Deep China.

The Great Warning: The Collapse of the Soviet Union

A factor behind the widespread cynicism towards the key ideological contributions of Jiang and Hu when they appeared, and the anxiety of the CPC in response, was a general collapse of faith in the whole belief system of the Party. This has partly been discussed in the previous chapter. The cadres Liu Xiaobo castigated for their moral laxness were not just people mired in a self-centred, hedonistic quagmire. They were symptomatic of a much deeper crisis: believers meant to believe something, but exposed as having no convictions at all. Their moral failings flowed from their lack of intellectual conviction in a set of principles and fidelity to this. For Deng Liqun, his greatest complaint was about the ways in which market socialist China was becoming a place with no faith. Faith was important for the Party. The collapse in this was a catastrophe because in the end the Party was as much a faith entity as anything, and losing that meant it became something completely different. It changed its identity.

If the Party was in crisis, then the terrible spectre of history returned. Without a unified political entity in charge with a unified belief system and adherence to this, the claim went, there would be a reversion to the bad old days, the nightmare of the past when the country was disunited, weak, and poor. This crisis reached its peak in the 1989 revolt. Even Party members joined in the protests. The head of the CPC itself at the time, Zhao Ziyang, showed his own wavering when he went out in late May to meet the students, weeping before them, an act of betrayal in the eyes of the leftists that was to seal his fate when the hardliners around Deng assembled to decide what to do. Zhao was removed from power days later and spent the next decade and a half till his death under house arrest.

Saving the Party in 1989 meant first of all using the Maoist gun to ensure there was discipline. The students were cleared from the central square by loyalist crack troops. A clampdown immediately afterwards targeted the workers, academics, and officials who had been as uncommitted as Zhao. Deng himself had admitted that events outside of China had contributed to the sense of confusion and threat when he met with troops on 9 June to thank them for their actions. But these events foreshadowing the fate of Communist parties were only to grow more ominous by the end of the year. The Berlin Wall fell in November, leading to the quick demise of the one-party system in socialist East Germany. The long-term Communist dictator of Romania, and frequent visitor to China, Nicolae Ceauşescu was booed at a major rally in Bucharest on 21 December and then executed on Christmas Day. Poland, Czechoslovakia, and other countries once behind the iron curtain broke free. The greatest shock occurred two years later. In mid-1991, the Communist Party of the Soviet Union collapsed. A seventy-four-year-old project to build socialism disappeared almost overnight. For observers in China, it was akin to being like Europeans watching the fall of Rome fifteen centuries before. Something eternal had been snuffed out without a real fight. It had simply vanished, as though it had never really existed in the first place.

While the US and its allies celebrated, for the CPC the implosion of the Soviet Union was an unequivocally bad thing. This was despite the complex and often fractious history between the two countries since 1949. Mao had been no easy bedfellow of Stalin. He and his style of indigenous socialism had risen to power often despite, not because of, support from Moscow. Moscow's perpetual interference in the Party's affairs in China left a deep memory stain, from the time of the twenty-eight Bolsheviks around Soviet loyalist Wang Ming who had nearly taken over the Party in the early 1930s, to the massive fall-out with the Soviet Union in 1957 over de-Stalinization. The relationship had gone through peaks and troughs. In the earliest era, the CPC only survived because of tactical and financial support from the USSR. A Dutch Comintern activist had been in attendance at the First Congress, in July 1921. Stalin had advised that the Chinese Communists align with the Nationalists in their struggle against the Japanese during the 1930s, something they eventually did. But underneath this was a growing residual distrust, something that came to the fore the closer Mao's party came to power. By the early 1950s, the two seemed to be pragmatically engaged with each other again. But tensions remained, flaring up in spectacular fashion at the end of the decade when thousands of Soviet technical advisers and specialists were withdrawn. In the Cultural Revolution, Soviet revisionism became amongst the main targets. Those who were most reviled were labelled 'China's Khrushchev'. Things deteriorated to such an extent that in 1969 the USSR and China experienced a major military clash on the north-eastern border, resulting in hundreds of casualties on both sides. All-out war was avoided, but the shock was sufficient to start Mao on his rapprochement with the US. He calculated (rightly as it happened) that even the capitalist West was a better ally than the vast fellow socialist country across the northern border.

In view of this strained history, 1991 might well have figured as a moment of *schadenfreude* and celebration in Beijing. But the response was the opposite. For China it was the collapse of an ideological ally, a country that at least in name belonged to the same camp as it. Its demise made the PRC a lonelier nation. It threatened to show that the set of ideas China had underpinning it were doomed to end in the same place. What subsequently transpired was somewhat more complex. Chinese in the 1990s watched as under Yeltsin Russia's economy faltered and then collapsed, human development metrics fell, and the empire that had been existing under the umbrella of the USSR disintegrated, creating a series of new states across Central Asia, and around China's border, that added to levels of uncertainty. In many ways, things were worse under reform than when the socialist system still existed in the USSR. This reinforced the conviction in Beijing that it was not Marxism that was at fault, but the imperfect implementation of it by the Russians. The Chinese would be smarter. They would get it right.

As the work of American CPC expert David Shambaugh and British scholar Neil Munro has made clear, this was the reception of the collapse of the Soviet Union within China and the gradual internalization of its message.⁵ For Chinese analysts at think-tanks like the Academy of Social Sciences in Beijing and elsewhere, the issue was to learn from the mistakes of their imploding northern neighbour, and make sure that nothing similar could happen to them. There was a long list of lessons to be learned. Making sure that control was exercised over the military and that they did not become an autonomous actor in their own right was one. Placing economic reforms before political ones was another. But perhaps the most important of these was ensuring that ideology continued to receive attention and did not just become pro-forma rhetoric. Ideology was not the cause of the fall of the party in the USSR. It was precisely the opposite. Lack of ideology, or, more precisely, lack of conviction and faith in this ideology, was their undoing.

The elite in the CPC articulated this message of the importance of ideology in the language of reform, stressing flexible, pragmatic adaptation of the core ideology, not a relinquishing of it. Long after leaving office in 2009, Jiang Zemin reportedly asked scholars to discuss the real reasons for the Soviet Union's collapse.⁶ (One of those present was Shen Zhihua, one of China's most eminent experts on the Cold War era.) In the words of a former Ministry of Foreign Affairs official, and writer, Yang Hengjun, after the meeting:

> The reason China has a future and hasn't followed the USSR's disastrous road, the reason the [CPC] is still in power today, is because of reform. It's because China has chosen the road of marketization. It's because, in the fields of society, culture, and even some political areas, China has appropriately opened up space for diversity. It's because China has 'opened up' and taken great pains to keep up with the global mainstream. It's because China is resolutely fighting corruption, and because China is bravely admitting the mistakes made during the Cultural Revolution. China has kept up with the times, putting forward the 'three represents' theory and reforming the ruling party, always holding fast to the goal of deepening reforms.⁷

Despite this assertion that the CPC would learn from what happened in the USSR, ensure ideology was supported, and that it succeeded where others had failed, the spectre of the Soviet Union's failure did cast a long shadow. Even in the China of Xi, with its confidence and increasing sense it had won the battle of making Marxism-Leninism sustainable (with Chinese characteristics), the nagging feeling that what happened in the Soviet Union portends the Chinese version's own mortality means vigilance is ever-present and ever-necessary. While the USSR system sustained itself for seventy-four years, that is still, as of 2018, five years longer than the reign of the CPC. Looking at the Soviet Union and the fate of the party there raises all sorts of insecurities for the CPC in Beijing. Perhaps these systems and their guiding ideology are generically simply not sustainable? Perhaps they are fated to last only a few decades and then be washed away by other historic forces. The answer by the CPC to this has been on stressing its exceptionalism and on following a unique path (deployment of contradictions again – following a global ideal in a unique way). But this only goes so far towards defending against these fears. The simple fact is that, as of 2018, no Communist one-party system had proved sustainable. The Chinese are the only ones in a position to try to buck this trend on a scale and with a significance approaching that of their erstwhile partners. This gave the endeavour to achieve precisely this under Xi even more import. It was attempting to do something unprecedented.

The Resurrection of Party Building, Culture, and Belief: The Years of Xi Jinping

Just as in social and moral behaviour, the assumption was increasingly made in the era of reform China from 1978 that faith in sinified Marxism was dead, and that the Party's sole function now was simply to be an enabling body, helping Chinese people grow rich and prosperous. The natural expectation in 2012, when the Eighteenth Party Congress marked a generational change in elite political leadership, was that a pragmatic line-up would appear, and that the theme of ideological diffidence that had been evident under Hu Jintao would continue.

The first real indication that this was not the way things would be was the brief speech Xi made when he emerged after several days of tense haggling at the head of a new, tighter, more consolidated line-up, as the new Party Secretary. For those who remembered the largely emotionless, anonymous addresses of Hu Jintao, Xi's directness was a surprise. But in hindsight, for all its brevity, the speech marked the start of a Party fightback. There were three key elements that in the ensuing years have become important. The first was the stress on the Party's moral narrative:

> Our responsibility is to unite and lead people of the entire party and of all ethnic groups around the country while accepting the baton of history and continuing to work for realising the great revival of the Chinese nation in order to let the Chinese nation stand more firmly and powerfully among all nations around the world and make a greater contribution to mankind.[8]

The second was the notion of service, of the Party still abiding by the ethos from the Maoist era of being a servant of the Chinese people, and implicitly subscribing to a self-sacrificing, collectivist ethos:

> This great responsibility is the responsibility to the people.... Our people love life and expect better education, more stable jobs, better income, more reliable social security, medical care of a higher standard, more comfortable living conditions, and a more beautiful environment.

The notion of the Party serving the expectations of the Chinese people was only new in the sense that as China had become wealthier, so demands had climbed. In the past, as leaders were fond of saying, the main objective was to just have food and clothing. But now there was a complex set of different demands to fulfil, from good healthcare, to education provision, foreign travel, housing, and a clean environment. The list was endless. Service to these aims was no longer a game of avoiding the worst. It was more about the struggle to manage sky-high expectations.

Thirdly, there was the issue of what the Party's function was in all of this. It was, as Xi made clear, a 'political' party. It had a belief system. That belief system was a fundamental part of how it operated, how it viewed itself, how it related to people, and what it was:

> Our responsibility is to work with all comrades in the party to be resolute in ensuring that the party supervises its own conduct; enforces strict discipline; effectively deals with the prominent issues within the party; earnestly improves the party's work style and maintains close ties with the people. So that our party will always be the firm leadership core for advancing the cause of socialism with Chinese characteristics.

These words were soon to transform from simple rhetoric to real action. That was consistent with the tradition of ideology being practical in its orientation that reached back to the Maoist era. By 2013, the anti-corruption struggle was in full swing, taking down former Politburo Standing Committee members, and thousands of lower-level targets guilty of moral deviance arising from failure of belief. The issue of how much this was political rather than a simple cleaning up of excess within the Party has been discussed above. But the key point here is that the words the new Party Secretary used, whatever their tone or style, did start to unfold in a way that hinted more and more strongly at the Xi period becoming one where the Party was reinvigorated, and that involved taking its ideology and the impact of that on practice seriously.

All of this was surprising. The common assumption before they were reinstated under Xi was that the methods of the past, of the mass line, party building, and ideological campaigns, were increasingly remote from a diverse, complex, highly aspirational society. And yet from 2012, the new Party mode of operation became one of relentless refocus on these things, a return to the founding vision of the Party as a 'city on the hill' which shone its exemplary light on the world around it, setting itself up as a model. Observing the mass line – the line of the Chinese people and their collective aspirations – was a strongly Maoist term. Party building was also another borrowing from the Mao and then Deng eras. Heavy ideological indoctrination involved even more retro phenomena like the use of mild self-criticism sessions in the think-tank, university, and military sectors. The PLA was exposed to heavy doses of training. In all of this ideology, the need to believe in it and to observe it was central.

The framework for this ideological renaissance under Xi was provided by the Four Comprehensives. These were to build a moderately prosperous society, deepen reform, advance the rule by law, and strictly govern the CPC. Issued in 2014, they harked back to the Four Modernizations of an earlier era, and what was called the Four Cardinal Virtues of the Deng period.[9] As Perry Link has shown, Chinese slogan creators love numerical figures.[10] And four always seems to have traction, even though in Chinese it is a homonym for 'death'. There was also a phenomenon of ideological inflation. If Jiang had his Three Represents, Xi needed to go one better. But there was also a strategic enforcement and logic in this set of ideas, and a claim on their all-encompassing nature. In 2013, the Plenum that year had issued a long list of promises about more vigorous reform and marketization within the rubric of the one-party state. In 2014, the following Plenum had been about the need to create rule by law, though again with the imperative to avoid any set-up where courts might remotely think they could challenge the CPC. In 2015, the meeting had been to launch the Thirteenth Five-Year Plan. Throughout there had been movements and campaigns to promote the notion that the Party, and the Party alone, had a comprehensive plan, that it was the one entity that fitted all the complex parts of China together and could make sense of things.

This complex interlinking of different strands of ideas and languages about different policy areas has had one immense challenge, however. And that is the simple one of how to reach the core audience, Chinese people, and how to engage with them in ways which combine intellectual and emotional sources of appeal. This was the most comprehensive ambition of all. Precedents for this were, nevertheless, problematic in a Chinese context. Mao Zedong Thought had been a living faith, at least in the period of most intense fervour in the Cultural Revolution. It had brought Chinese people together in one belief community in ways that had never happened before, defying the syncretic traditions of the past. This proved to be a searing moment of self-understanding and self-recognition, creating the tumultuous results referred to in Chapter 4. The succeeding ideological phases of the Party were characterized by their diffidence as a result of the experiences of the Cultural Revolution and the cautiousness this resulted in. Ideology has had a limited, functional role, focussed on addressing specific challenges. But under Xi, the trend of modest purpose has been bucked. There is a remarkable return to comprehensiveness, and the ambition to stand by all-inclusive ideological positions. One massive question nags away at this project, however. For all its grand aims, does anyone actually believe in any of it? Followers of Mao Zedong Thought might have been deluded, but they did believe in what they were saying. Until, of course, they stopped believing, when the Cultural Revolution ended, with all the repercussions that flowed from that in terms of disappointment and disillusion.

For the Four Comprehensives under Xi, there has been the continuous challenge of who, why, and how people might believe in such a complex, layered system, with the antecedents it has been built on, its dense accumulated vocabularies, and its hybridity which places sinified Marxist notions next to the market capitalist realities people live, breathe, and work in. Ironically, to sustain themselves in this often schizophrenic world where officials say one thing and the world seems to operate in another way, the average Chinese needs to draw on all the skills gleaned from the syncretic intellectual history of their forebears, rather than embracing comprehensiveness and trying to unify everything.

All of this is vividly illustrated by the Nineteenth Party Congress speech, delivered by Xi on 18 October 2017, a three and a half hour epic, which combines all of the narrative, ethical, and ideological issues covered in this book. The achievement of that speech, and the Congress overall, was to promote Xi Jinping Thought to the Party constitution, placing it on a level with Mao Zedong Thought, and introduce a new notion: modernization of socialism with Chinese characteristics. This is to be achieved by 2035.

What can one make of such a grand, abstract formulation? One way to address this question is to look at the core vocabularies through which so much of this was conveyed.

Xi's Keywords

Like many leaders, Xi has used a specific series of words with a high level of frequency, which have therefore become associated with him. Concentrating on these 'keywords' gives some idea of what the core, underlying ideological preoccupations are in his China, and how they relate to political strategies and practices. Cambridge scholar Raymond Williams had popularized the concept of keywords in the 1970s. He had looked at 100 words which had proved influential and important in the discourse of left-wing political development in the UK, moving beyond their original etymologies to their change over time according to the different social, cultural, and political contexts they had been used in, showing how these contributed to their later meanings.[11] For Xi, there are twelve distinctive terms that have been promoted as part of a campaign since 2014 to support 'socialist values'. These are the key terms of his time, carrying its main ideological messages. They are indicative of the complexity and hybridity of the era, because almost all of them do not fit easily into the standard Marxist-Leninist or Maoist lexicon. They combine traditional notions drawn from history, notions imported from outside but adapted to Chinese circumstances, and more modern concepts. They are words disseminated in written ideological material and also through spoken statements by Party leaders. They are also physically manifested on roadside banners and signs, sometimes with delicate illustrations.

The first is *fuqiang* (富强) – 'strong', a term with deep resonance in modern Chinese rhetoric and practice. 'Strong' first appeared combined with 'nation' in the late Qing, at the end of the nineteenth century, when it was deployed by modernizers like Kang Youwei and Liang Qichao to indicate their desire for a more confident, autonomous China which was able to emulate the Meiji-era reforms of the mid-1860s in Japan and accelerate industrialization, the construction of a modern military and education system, and administrative change. 'Strong' got linked with 'rich' in the Republican period, and then, in the interim between the Republicans and the PRC, a third term was added, 'powerful'. After 1949, the term remained within domestic political discourse despite the radical political changes being introduced, with Mao, Deng, and almost every other leader using it to highlight the aspiration of building a country that would never again be a victim of foreign aggression. In the China Dream Xi talks of, the achievement of a 'strong, rich country' lies at the heart of this.

The second is *minzhu* (民主) – 'democratic'. As the Chinese official and scholar Yu Keping has made clear, despite the assumption that in a state where only one party has power, this word would be taboo, in fact, 'democracy is a good thing'.[12] The Party, however, has made sure that it is a term used in a very specific context: 'democracy with Chinese characteristics', literally 'power of the people', means following the mass line, represented by the CPC. Mao Zedong had written extensively of the term 'new democracy' in January 1940, in which he had stated that 'the Chinese democratic republic which we desire to establish now must be a democratic republic under the joint dictatorship of all anti-imperialist and anti-feudal people led by the proletariat, that is, a new-democratic republic'.[13] Use of 'democracy' in recent years in Chinese political discourse has pushed back against the perceived annexation of this term by Western liberal democracies. This operates as an indigenized iteration, one which, as made clear in the so-called 'Document Number Nine' issued by the Chinese propaganda organs in early 2014, is uncontaminated by ideas of Western bicameral parliamentary systems, multi-party democracy, and separation of powers. 'Democracy' here means democracy for the Party, by the Party, on behalf of the Party, which act as a servant to the people who serve it. It is a highly managed and circumscribed idea.

The third is *wenming* (文明) – 'cultured'. This is linked to notions like 'improving the quality of the population' that had appeared in the mid-1990s, when it had often figured on notice-boards and in slogans written in the countryside in public spaces. *Wenming* asserts a notion of social civility with Chinese characteristics, based on its '5,000 years of continuous civilization' with its associated conventions, modes of behaviour, and underpinning etiquette. It offers resistance to the idea of a country that is backward and undeveloped. The Chinese educational system, with its combination of classical, scientific, and ideological training, seeks to produce cultured citizens.

The fourth is *hexie* (和谐) – 'harmonious'. Discussed above in the context of Hu Jintao, who had made frequent use of this term in the 2000s, and linked to classical concepts in ancient philosophers from Confucius to Mencius, 'harmonious' asserts the underpinning stability of the Chinese cultural and philosophical world-view, with the idea that 'everything under heaven' (*tianxia*) had its rightful place. It offers a counterpoint to the great fear of chaos and instability, arising from China's dramatic historic experiences of natural calamities and popular uprisings. It also relates to another term closely related to it, that of 'stability', which feeds off the desire for social and political predictability and is achieved either through consent or through force. The priority is order at all costs. 'Harmonious' as a term draws its emotional power from the reference it makes to real threats of disruption to China. These fears are based on the memory traces left from history, and from a widespread acknowledgement of the vulnerability of China's social set-up and ecological situation. The Party, therefore, in taking ownership of this term through such frequent and privileged use in its language, makes clear that it stands for order and security.

The fifth is *ziyou* (自由) – 'freedom'. Like 'democracy', this is a term which sits awkwardly within Chinese political discourse in the PRC, linked as it is to notions from outside of free elections and Western liberalism. The term is particularly loaded as it had appeared in the slogans of demonstrators during the 1989 June unrest. In the contemporary context, it occurs as a word purged of its less desirable aspects in the eyes of the Party of promoting Western notions of freedom based on individual social and political liberty. Instead, it means partly freedom in terms of being released from material want, and partly the freedom gained from eliminating feudalism, exploitation, colonialization, and other ills from the old society. In all of these, the CPC narrative places it in a dominant role.

The sixth term is *pingdeng* (平等) – equality. This is a word with a more contemporary focus. It is recognition of one of the most pressing problems in China now: the huge disparities that have started to show themselves in society as an outcome of marketization and economic liberalization. *Pingdeng* harks back to the socialist tradition of the Party, and to the commitment it has made to deliver a society where all are equal. Such an aspiration needs to deal with the reality that since the relative equality of the Maoist period (where people largely had an equal share of nothing), from 1978 China's Gini co-efficient, an internationally recognized measure of inequality, has reached levels comparable to capitalist societies like the US, Brazil, and elsewhere. Reconciling a society where there are more dollar billionaires than in the US but also 100 million living under US$2 a day has necessitated even greater rhetorical emphasis on the commitment to trying to achieve fewer extremes. It is not so clear, however, whether the Party can do anything here that will prove more successful than the patchy Western attempts to solve the same problem while also preserving dynamic aggregate growth.

The seventh is *gongzheng* (公正) – fairness. Closely linked to 'legality', the following term, this acknowledges the Party's duty to govern for and on behalf of all. It is also an admission that since 1978 the rights consciousness of Chinese people about this and other issues has risen greatly. Desire for fair treatment serves as the main motivation for the many millions of petitions taken to central government annually seeking outcomes for problems encountered at local levels, and the recourse to courts in the civil realm for a similar reason. But the ways by which to achieve fairness, and how best to define it, are ones the Party has also circumscribed. It ultimately controls the sources for the delivery of justice (appeal systems, court judgments), and in this way acts as the final arbiter. Fairness is seen in a broader context where the individual is still located in a complex nexus where their interests are subservient to those of the collective and of the larger social mission.

The eighth is *fazhi* (法治) – rule by law. This operates as part of a new discourse of law with Chinese socialist characteristics. The core principle here is that under the CPC, China has moved away from 'rule of man' (*renzhi*), as was the case in the Maoist era, to one of greater institutionalization, more predictability in society, and less decision-making by fiat and the will of one individual. Rule by law is the main tool with which to attack the pernicious residual influence of the informal networks of the old society, pervaded by sentiments of 'human bonds based on feeling' and self-centred relationships (*guanxi*) focussed on the individual, seeking to build social capital by getting close to those seen to be in power regardless of any objective considerations of right or wrong. Once more, there is the same issue of boundaries as there was with fairness. Rule by law exists under the CPC, and in the service of the CPC and its moral narratives. It does not exist in a space competing with the CPC, but supports it. In this setting, rule by law is objective, because it is implemented according to pre-decided procedures, but these are set by the CPC. Under the banner of rule by law, there has also been increased importance attached to the issue of punishment, something harking back to the ancient Legalist school under Han Fei and others over two millennia ago.

The ninth is *aiguo* (爱国) – patriotism. This is a continuing acknowledgement inherited from the Jiang period and developed further under Hu that one of the most important new sources of legitimacy for the Party is to appeal to its patriotic, national mission and, by implication, the moral narrative underpinning this. The 'patriotic' education campaigns in the mid-1990s stressed the ways in which a strong country (see the first term above) was also linked to a stable, strong Party, and the ways in which this was the sure means to delivering a nation which would never again be afflicted by the nightmares of humiliation endured from the mid-nineteenth to the mid-twentieth century. The more negative outcome of 'patriotism' has been increasingly assertive nationalism and its effects on China's relations with the outside world. Being patriotic is not optional in Xi's China. All Chinese, not just CPC members, have an imperative to be so. To be unpatriotic is one of the worst insults to throw at someone, and ranks beside 'traitor', 'national shame', and even, as Liu Xiaobo noted, derogatory sexualized language. Interrogation of the kind of nation that such patriotism is directed at, what its specifics are, is unwelcomed. To reflect on this term is the start of the slippery slope to questioning and violating it.

The tenth is *jingye* (敬业) – dedication. Despite being one of the least frequently used terms in the new Xi discourse, it is one of the most important. This is because it relates to notions of the CPC seeking not just people's physical loyalty, but also their deeper commitment, referred to in the previous chapter – the mission to conquer the inner person. The German Nazi propagandist Goebbels spoke of a core function of political messages being to move people from neutrality to enthusiasm and then to addiction. Studied, tepid following was no good. What was needed was absolute fervent conviction. Similarly, the CPC seeks a state of affairs whereby not only can people not oppose the Party, but they are unable to live without it. In the aim to create this addiction, patriotism about the great nation and the irreplaceability of the CPC in building this offers the rationale for demanding dedication. There is a necessitating logic operating here. One cannot have a great nation without the Party (as the Trinity referred to in Chapter 1 showed), and that demands the need for an appropriate emotional and spiritual posture, best exemplified by dedication.

The penultimate term is *chenxin* (诚信) – trust. Like the previous term, this has figured little in Chinese political discourse, in this instance owing to embarrassment about the plentiful evidence for the chronic lack of trust that Chinese people have tended to show their political leaders. This is contained in trust surveys which have shown that while doctors, teachers, and even sex workers enjoy decent levels of trust within the PRC, officials at the national and even more so the local level suffer from an immense credibility deficit. Concerns about this issue were the motivating factor behind Xi's November 2012 speech about the need to repair the damage done by corrupt officials within the Party, and close the gap between the rulers and the ruled. A great deal of his political strategy has been about rebuilding this trust through deepening the boundaries between the Party as a political entity and the commercial zone, and creating a stronger, more widely understood commitment to the CPC's moral narrative.

The final term is *youshan* (友善) – friendly. This promotes the notion that China, the Chinese people, and the CPC and government, are not a threat, but are friendly to the wider world, promoting 'win-win outcomes'. To this end, the Party has waged a number of soft-power campaigns from the 2000s, pushing forward the idea that 'China is a friend to all the world'.

These twelve terms taken together show a number of attributes. They indicate great hybridity, a willingness to utilize words more closely associated with China's classical philosophical heritage, and to 'indigenize' other terms and relocate them from their more common external roots and put them to use within a politicized Chinese cultural context. In this new situation they are linked to an overarching narrative supportive of the CPC's moral mission and its story about itself, its role in history, and its vision for society. Particularly good examples of this are 'democracy' and 'fairness'. These keywords circumscribe a terrain which is neither overtly intellectual nor emotional. They try to walk between these separate modes, achieving a synthetic balance. Twelve such different terms are, however, hard to meld together despite these commonalities. They are a complicated menu, in an environment where the public's realistic attention span is for perhaps three or four ideas, not such a long list. Those who look at the promotion of these terms on advertising boards in public space, or inside newspapers, or within speeches might feel afflicted by information overload. What is the relationship between daily life and this menu of very grand, sometimes very abstract terms? What is the common ideological position they are linked to and displaying? At the very least, they betray complexity. They show a Party which in the Maoist era was adept at distilling ideas in very succinct, comprehensible ways now facing a situation in which it is almost overwhelmed by the different directions in which it is being pulled. Comprehensive it might be. But there is a real question mark over whether it is that comprehensible.

Ideology: Final Words

Unified ideology matters profoundly to the CPC. It matters as a tool of power through its ability to organize at least the public expression of privileged ideas about politics and national aims. It matters because of the way it unwraps and explicates parts of the moral narratives connected to these national aims, giving them an underpinning intellectual justification. The CPC is also staking a claim to intellectual hegemony. Ideology since Mao has been accumulated, adapted, extended, reformed, all under the umbrella of dialectics and the ability to cope with contradictions. Finally, this organically accumulated ideology is part of the CPC's identity.

To master this accumulated mass of material, cadres at all levels retreat to the leafy precincts of the Party training centres scattered across the country. Amongst the most impressive of these is the Pudong Cadre Training Centre in Shanghai, a strikingly modern building designed by a French architect surrounded by splendid parks that give it an air of monastic calm. Here some of the most powerful people within the party-state apparatus come to ruminate on where the organization they are part of has come from and where it might be heading. Here they come to be nourished by the lectures of academics, experts, and fellow practitioners. This is a fundamental part of their training in the twenty-first century. Under Xi Jinping, it has become an even more important element of the formation of new CPC personnel, people intellectually, morally, and emotionally trained to deal with the paradoxes of a China on a historic mission, using semi-capitalist means within a socialist framework to achieve national greatness. Party Schools and other such centres of CPC learning make them fluent in the specific sub-dialect of Chinese that needs to be used by officials, full of the keywords mandated by Xi's master discourse above, which migrate down into the Party's wider language. In this discourse are embedded the conceptual tools they need to have to balance Marxism with the market. With this ideology, which is practical in origin, flexible and durable, they are now armed against the temptations in the world around them.

It is clear why, in terms of the unity it supplies and the discipline it gives, the Party feels that so much investment in this ideological work is merited. Like Latin in the European Catholic Church in the Middle Ages, the CPC ideological discourse with its key terms and current keywords supplies a common language across a deeply diverse and divided community. No one can overestimate how hard won the unity and consensus encoded in this language have been. They were forged through long processes of argument, political struggle, and upheaval. Before and after 1949, there were moments of severe pressure. The events of 1978 offered something close to an existential crisis. Maoism was almost buried. But the underlying ideological direction was saved. Those seeking to contest CPC ideology and its new primacy under Xi do so at their peril. Ideological instability portends the awful spectres of implosion and upheaval from the past. Best to let this particular sleeping tiger continue its slumbers.

How sustainable this situation might be, however, is a different question. No one at the top of the Party welcomes too much quizzing about this. They all have to be true believers. If the main elite representatives of the CPC were to stop openly declaring their faith in Marxist ideology with Chinese characteristics, if they were to adopt a social democratic model, what would happen? What if the Party were to try to map out a position which, to its critics at least, looks more in accord with the society around it, downgrading or even eliminating the need for a unifying ideology? That would mean jettisoning a crucial, perhaps the most crucial, part of its identity. It is a political party, as Xi said on 15 November 2012, but also an ideological one. No ideology means no heart. This ideology might be functional, it might be simply on the level of rhetoric (though clearly, as was stated above, the Party hopes this is not the case) – but that is the point. It is the scaffolding, and if it were taken away, the structure underneath, the whole body of the CPC itself, would crumble. Unified official ideology might be an illusion of twenty-first-century China, but it is a necessary one. In the past, leaders were prone to say that holding a correct ideological position was a matter of life and death. In the China of Xi Jinping, for very different reasons, and in very different ways, it still is.

7

The Aesthetics of the Party

The Communist Party is commonly presented in ways that make it seem like a political machine. Inputs go in, get processed, and come out, whose sole function is to promote its prime ambition – to be an instrument exercising organized political power. In the era since reform, the main raw input to the CPC machine until recently has been economic growth, which is subsequently converted to legitimacy and power. Seen in this way, if the CPC's ideology, messaging, and propaganda appeal to any particular emotions, then these are either fear or awe. This accounts for why the art it is associated with is often grandiloquent and bombastic: mass events like the opening of the 2008 Olympics with its 2,008 drummers or the theatre of military displays during events like that held to mark the seventy years since the end of the Sino-Japanese War in 2015. They are impressive. But they do not come across as particularly human, or, for that matter, humane.

The CPC is interested in art, and in the means of emotional engagement with Chinese people that art offers. This serves an important function in promoting its moral narrative. Throughout its history, it has held a number of postures towards art, far from the antagonistic relationship it has today to many of China's most prominently creative figures who are best known outside the country. In that history, as Chapter 1 showed, it has created a drama of its own development and its core redemptive role, a drama which is still continuing. Television stations even in the China of 2018 have programmes starring lookalikes of Mao Zedong or other early-era leaders, celebrating their heroic endeavours on the path to liberation. Events like the Long

March from the mid-1930s and the war against the Japanese figure
in this, alongside the great moment of victory in 1949. Even after
1949, there are key landmark moments, from meetings that were
important to the Party like the Lushan Cadres Conference in 1959
(which marked the first pre-Cultural Revolution divisions between
Mao and his internal critics), to events like the rapprochement with
the US in 1972. In the post-Mao period, a whole new set of dramatic
moments have been added: the 1978 Third Plenum of the Eleventh
Party Congress, which kicked everything off, for instance, and then
the Southern Tour by Deng to restart reforms in 1992. Alongside this
history, with its memorialization and drama now presented as positive, is the negative counter-history of the Cultural Revolution, the
great famines, and the 1989 uprising. These are often most conspicu-
ous by their absences, and occupy a position within China almost
akin to what American scholar of modern Chinese history Ralph
Thaxton has called 'whispered histories', known at some level, but
never candidly spoken of.[1] Over the last few decades, from this diverse
set of ingredients, the CPC has constructed a drama of its story and
the meaning of that story, with a whole set of symbols, events, and
signifiers to convey this. This drama is ongoing, and every Chinese
person is a player in it. It is truly a national psycho-drama, the soap
opera to end all soap operas!

Alongside this sits another set of considerations. The CPC as a
movement has always had a philosophical attitude towards art, and
a broad understanding of its importance, albeit located in a highly
political context. Art was always a major means of the Party appealing to the emotions of Chinese people, serving to recruit them and
gain their allegiance in the years before it came to power, and then
as it consolidated power after 1949. It had, and continues to have,
an ideological vision for art, and an awareness of the use art had –
spoken, written, performed – to convey key ideological points. For
this reason, art from previous eras of China's histories, because it was
viewed as conveying dangerous counter-ideologies (feudalistic, Confucian, conservative), was often condemned and destroyed. In the Cultural Revolution, as the term itself makes clear, the aim was not just
to remake the souls of Chinese people, and create new model Communist beings, but to reform and re-create Chinese culture itself. In
this new culture, through this new art, the Party became the hero in
its own story, positioned at the vanguard. New forms of art were
proposed, new ways of writing, attempts to fuse different art forms.
As in the area of ideology, attempts were made to combine traditional
Chinese influences with those from outside, resulting in something
new and exceptional. The Eight Beijing Model Operas from this era

typified this, using Western forms that were, in other areas, despised and condemned at the time, but justifying this because of their ability to convey radical messages of proletariat uprising and liberation. In the realm of art, the connection is finally made between intellect (ideology), morality, emotions, and the master narrative of the CPC. In this space, the imaginations of the inhabitants of contemporary Deep China can be reached. This, more than any other reasons, makes art of great importance to the CPC.

For all this clear importance art has had and will continue to have for the CPC, it is one of the most difficult areas to discuss, largely because the Party's posture has been described by its critics internally and externally largely as hostile, uncultured, and philistine. It is seen as wholly focussed on power. One does not have to look hard to see evidence that this might be partially true. As in so many other areas described in this book, cities have become physical embodiments of the power elite in China's current posture, crammed with the most outlandish and bold avant-garde structures, like the CCTV building in Beijing, constructed by Dutch architect Rem Koolhaas, to the ever-taller skyscrapers that sit atop the marshy land of Shanghai. Provincial cities have joined in this orgy, putting up museums, memorials, and massive new public buildings, setting in concrete, brick, and cement a mental attitude towards Chinese modernity. All of this has proceeded as ancient hutongs (i.e. traditional narrow streets), and other architectural remnants that have somehow managed to survive from the past, have been renovated to the point they may just as well have been rebuilt. A huge proportion have been wholly swept away.

Chinese cities today are monuments celebrating a hybrid view of modernity with Chinese characteristics and on China's terms. They are not just epic aesthetic statements but also ideological ones, designed to create a specific emotional response, of awe, pride, a sense of being part of the great national drama that is unfolding as one walks around these stage sets. For those who look a little harder, however, questions start to surface. They can see clues in the bombast and confidence that greets their eyes about identity shifts which are unresolved (the odd mix of Western and Eastern design styles in some structures) and issues within the deep culture of the country that seem contradictory. (So gleaming and new, and yet so hard to walk around, and get access to, as anyone has found who wants to perambulate Pudong in Shanghai.) Are these buildings really bold assertions of a unique Chinese sense of being modern, or slavishly derivative, with no real innovations of their own, admissions of confusion rather than clarity? Over this hovers the great question as elsewhere: is this all sustainable? How will buildings like the China National Opera House in Beijing, built around the turn of the millennium, with its multiple performance spaces and huge glass dome, look like in forty or fifty years' time, with decades of sand storms, pollution, and other environmental forces eroding and reshaping it? And for a country blighted by natural calamities throughout its history, how will Beijing, or Shanghai, or any other major city fare were there, God forbid, to be an earthquake or some other natural calamity? Would the buildings be able to withstand shocks like these?

The Maoist Attitude to Art

The CPC had one very specific difference with its counterpart in the USSR. Mao Zedong, who led it and brought it to power, was a significant poet. Not by any means a great one, but certainly accomplished and technically adept. Ironically, for a revolutionary his poetry was largely conservative in form. His calligraphy, as Simon Leys observed, was 'strikingly original, betraying a flamboyant egotism'.[2] The 1940s era in the revolutionary central Chinese refuge of Yan'an was the most significant till then not just in clarifying the Party's attitude towards its own history, but also in setting out a view of art and culture while it was there. This is contained in 'The Talks at the Yan'an Forum on Literature and Art' from May 1942. The context of this event was the influx of sympathetic artistic figures who had come to the area, and the attempt to harness their commitment and sympathy for Communist aims in ways which were controllable and (most important of all) unified.

Because of what transpired after 1942 – the purges, attacks on, and eradication of so many artists – it is difficult to read the talks given by Mao sympathetically. They are located in this very inglorious history. A rectification campaign waged almost as soon as the talks were over felled a number of significant writers. Some, like the novelist Ding Ling, were chastised and silenced. Other even lost their lives. This was to be the augur of a long series of campaigns to rein in the intellectuals and coerce those working in the field of art. Artists, writers, film makers, and poets were to fare badly after 1949, with many of the finest either falling silent, like the short-story writer Shen Congwen, or becoming puppets for the regime's message. The author Guo Moruo is the most infamous of the latter group, occupying positions of formal bureaucratic power in the 1950s and becoming a slavish adherent to the CPC line till his death. More ambiguous figures like the novelist and essayist Ba Jin were to walk a tightrope, compromising themselves during various campaigns under Mao in order to protect their own skins and those of others, and then being plunged in the more liberal era after Mao's death into regret and self-recriminations over those they felt they had let down.

Despite this context, if we look at the 1942 talks by Mao as an artistic manifesto for a political movement, we can see the document in a fresh light.[3] There are a number of aspects that are worth paying attention to. The idea was very clearly conveyed of the Party having within its wings a 'cultural army', a notion that was to come to the fore with a vengeance over two decades later during the Cultural Revolution. There is the alignment of artistic figures in the usual Maoist rubric of 'the enemies, our allies in the United Front and our own people'.[4] Stretching across the piece is the unifying theme of art having a responsibility to map the political struggle in the 'real world' by promoting class struggle and articulating class interests.

This final element stems from the strong awareness that Mao clearly has about two aspects of art. The first is a sense of responsibility towards the audience. The second is the ways in which it can fit in with the Party's moral narrative, and convey messages that support that narrative. Mao talks of the 'problem of audience – i.e. the people for whom our works of literature and art are produced'. He also talks of the way that 'literature and art fit well into the whole revolutionary machine as a component part, that they operate as powerful weapons for uniting and educating the people and for attacking and destroying the enemy'. Such martial language was informed by the notion of purpose, of there being things above and beyond art that art served. Mao's argument about audience tapped into discussions going back through Lu Xun to the intellectual Hu Shi in the early part of the twentieth century after the Second World War, and the creators of 'Bai Hua' (reformed, everyday) language, of a traditional culture so sophisticated that it lay beyond the reach of almost everyone except specialists. Chinese classical texts demanded high literacy. Even modern novels were in a language that made them inaccessible to most readers. As a political force seeking support in the countryside, somehow a bridge needed to be made to this vast community who had only folk art to reach them.[5]

Responsibility for this was laid at the door of the artistic elite: 'Since the audience for our literature and art consists of workers, peasants, and soldiers and of their cadres, the problem arises of understanding them and knowing them.' After all, whom are literature and art for? For the producers alone, as an enclosed, semi-private act for the small groups of cognoscenti around them? Or for the wider society, arising from a sense of social responsibility and service to them? 'Literature and art are for the people', Mao declares, eradicating any potential confusion about where he stands on this issue. They support a 'new culture' which is 'anti-imperialist, anti-feudal'. This posture is anti-high art, anti-esoteric, and politicized to its roots. Art here serves as a functioning tool: 'Our literature and art are first for the workers, the class that leads the revolution.' Service is key, as is the ethos of learning from those who are traditionally seen as the ones who should be doing the learning – the audience: 'Prior to the task of educating the workers, peasants and soldiers, there is the task of learning from them.' That mythical thing, the 'life of the people', is the area that the artists have to mine – their daily struggles, their fights, which through previous Chinese histories had been consigned to silence, and to voicelessness. In this Foucauldian upending of the usual power dynamics, Mao urges a mission of rectification.[6]

Artists under the Maoist vision are like cadres, going 'amongst the people', losing their individuality, eradicating their self-centredness, immersing themselves, becoming vessels through which larger and more important messages might flow: 'Intellectuals who want to integrate themselves with the masses, who want to serve the masses, must go through a process in which they and the masses know each other well.'[7] The relationship of the individual and the masses is a problem that needs to be solved in the same way as that of officials and other Party members. They must pursue the same kind of selflessness and impose on themselves the same codes of combating any form of individualism as Liu Shaoqi had urged in his 1939 *How to Be a Good Communist*. In this way, artists are co-opted into a cultural wing of a party and become part of its all-embracing mission, servants of its grand vision. The choice given them in 1942 was a simple one: to serve or dissent. History was to subsequently show that the same regimes of discipline were to be used against them as against cadres: struggle sessions, self-criticisms, the harrowing processes of inner self-reformation which Lifton and others documented in the 1960s.

In the Maoist understanding, the function of art was a simplistically moral one. It was a tool in a righteous struggle, armoury in the battle to deliver justice for the wronged Chinese masses. Art betrayed one's side in this battle by showing class allegiance – support for the good proletariat, farmers, and oppressed, or for the bad capitalists, landowners, and feudalists. In a world-view saturated with signs of power, like a weapon art can be used for good or ill. Its power could be wholesome or pernicious. This was not a technical issue because technically good art can have bad values: 'The notion of universal love so much promoted in Enlightenment literature is spurious,' Mao continues: 'We cannot love enemies, we cannot love social evils, our aim is to destroy them.' The proper artist has a moral mission: 'All the dark forces harming the masses of the people must be exposed and all the revolutionary struggles of the masses of the people must be extolled: that is the fundamental task of revolutionary writers and artists.'[8] The Party's mission is a grand redemptive one, and that of its cadre of artistic figures is to serve this. The criterion for the value of art is not in the pure realm of aesthetics, but in political, ideological, and moral utility.

Mao's Vision of Art in Practice

After the forum at Yan'an in 1942, Mao was to attempt to implement this vision of art through a great act of fusion which involved lifting the grassroots, native art forms of peasants to the mainstream, copying ideas from Soviet Realism, and generating a unique CPC style of aesthetics. Central to the effort to unite the national story of reconstruction and resurrection after the tragic mode of the majority of China's early modern history with the redemption mission of the Party. From this moment, the CPC became not just a lead player in this great national story, but also its director and scriptwriter. It had the agency and power to increasingly figure as its own source of drama, creating a perpetual series of actions throughout the period after it came to power in 1949 which it could then ask artists to dramatize. The Party became a great propaganda asset. It resulted in a style of literature, of performance art, and of built environment aesthetics rich in the signifiers of promotion and glorification of the CPC's redemptive role. This captured the energy of fast development, of moving away quickly from the disowned and dark past towards a bright utopian future.

Scholar Chang-tai Hung, in his study of political culture in the Maoist period, makes clear just how comprehensive this aesthetic project was.[9] *Yangge*, the creation of a specific form of folk opera, made peasant life noble, observing the edict from Mao of 1942 to lift up the everyday, the graft and life of China's underclass, the peasants, which had never had an appropriate voice in classical literature, and make this infused with meaning as part of the redemptive CPC moral narrative.[10] Society in the era of mass mobilization campaigns from 1950 was febrile with parades and mass events. These allowed public participation in the drama of Communist life in the new China. In these, the people became not just observers but actors in this grand new play.[11] The physical landscape also became the servant of this story. The so-called 'ten monumental buildings' in Beijing, from the Great Hall of the People, to the Beijing Railway Station, to the

Military Museum, were constructed at breakneck speed, with the first put up in a little under a year.[12] The speed of their creation exemplified the sense of energy and purpose of the era in which they were built, guided by the urgency to deliver on the CPC promises in its moral historic narrative.

The Party did far more than this. It created an iconography founded on the charisma of its elite leader, Mao. It created a whole set of symbols, myths, and narratives, conveyed in a unique language, a language made accessible to most people by using newly simplified, not traditional, more complex characters. There was the cult of the everyday hero, the soldier Lei Feng, whose diary and life figured in official propaganda from the early 1960s before his early death promoting selfless behaviour and values, or Iron Man Wang, a Chinese Stakhanovist figure from the Cultural Revolution who was made a national work hero. Alongside these stood a community of martyred saints from the era of struggle before the CPC came to power. Figurative art portrayed Mao and leaders around him in stirring, heroic poises. These infiltrated the most intimate spaces of people's lives, with Mao's portrait hung on living-room and bedroom walls. With the great reconstruction of society, new apartments, new organizations like work units, and a gallery of associated images of sinified futurism being brought about by Marxist-Leninist visions of progress became the lived reality of people's lives. They existed in a landscape promising utopia and Chinese-style modernity. This was real, not something abstract and other-worldly.

Scholars of modern Chinese history and politics David Apter and Tony Saich in their study of the Maoist discourse refer to this whole process as a 'narrative reconstruction of reality'. Reality was something muscular Maoist intervention could change through its ideology, its narratives, and its aesthetic vision. This was a vision saturated by the potency of the CPC's power, with Mao's person and its symbolic power at the heart of this. 'Far from simply adapting Marxism,' Apter and Saich explain, 'Mao invented his own form of inversionary discourse out of the immediacy of the Chinese experience, and in doing so assumed the role of a cosmocratic leader, a kind of radical Socrates.' The project of this 'radical Socrates' for modern China was to reconstruct not only the grand narratives of history, but the ways in which people saw their experience in daily life, defining a new kind of aesthetics where the demotic, the moments and phases of each day, became contributions, for every single person, towards revolutionary struggle and final liberation. The battle between good and evil was not some titanic struggle occurring in the skies above. Class enemies were real, visible in the worlds around people, standing beside them in their work units, their societies, even living within their own homes. In the fight to eradicate influences like these, people had a role in the larger drama. The Party's mythologizing of its miraculous rise to power as a proof of its moral function managed to create a political story and, by extension, a style of politics that reached into people's emotions, conquering their inner worlds. Yan'an, 'which came out of a virtually biblical experience', and then 'the Long March[, which] was also a creation of carefully composed social texts, magic realism and dialectic logic', presented an 'overcoming and inversionary variety, following lines of the original master–slave relationship of Hegel [and] portrayed Chinese society as having fallen into a condition of disintegration, a state of anarchy'. The remedy for this was simple: 'Only a revolution with its own language would allow China to be restored to health.'[13]

Maoist Aesthetics in Action: The Cultural Revolution as Theatre

Anyone gazing at photos taken from the time of the Cultural Revolution will almost immediately pick up the ways in which, for all its inner complexity, on one level at least (that of the spectacle) it was an immense drama, an act of grim theatre in which large swathes of society were recruited to play particular roles. Underlying this was the core Manichaean vision described above, of there being people in Chinese society who were good and people who were bad. The Cultural Revolution was the moment China had arrived at in which it had to wage a war across all fronts in order to achieve the final victory of justice against those seeking to undermine, destroy, or jeopardize the Chinese party-state's national mission. The brutal clarity of this division within society, and the tensions and clashes it generated, had a similar logic to that created in Nazi Germany in the 1930s or Cambodia from 1975 under the Khmer Rouge. What was different, however, was the specific iconography and the vast completeness of the theatre of the Cultural Revolution. It was the ultimate 'real-life' drama. When French Situationist philosopher Guy Debord talked almost contemporaneously with the movement in China of a social condition in which 'all of life presents itself as an immense accumulation of spectacles', where images dominate, and the sense of sight is elevated above all else, the Cultural Revolution fits neatly into this.[14] It was a grand, grim festival of images, sights, and graphic representations.

Paul Clark in his history of this period makes a valid critique of the available accounts of events in China after 1966. Most of these, in Chinese and English, or other languages for that matter, concentrate on the political, or social, aspects of the movement. But this is odd, because the word 'culture' is so evident and prominent in the ways in which it was, and is, described inside and outside China to this day. It was initially not a political revolution, but one presented in the realm of culture. As Clark explains, 'an account of cultural practices in the Cultural Revolution offers another way to understand what life was like for most Chinese in these ten years'.[15] For some, the standard issue had been that from 1966 there was no culture. Books, poems, plays, music, everything was frozen. Only the editions of some of the works of Lu Xun, and those of Marx, Mao, Engels, and Lenin, were allowed. The Eight Beijing Model Operas were exhaustively performed across the country. But this era can just as well be seen as a period of innovation and experimentation, a period, as Clark states, in which there was an attempt to commit to social reform, close the gap between remote, classical art and the everyday as Mao had promised in the 1942 Yan'an talks, and modernize often moribund genres in Chinese theatre and performance art. This does not deny that its implementation was to result in obnoxious and tragic outcomes. It does, however, recognize the idealist intentions driving it, and partially explains why its impact was so huge. It educated and complicated the world-view of a whole generation of young people coming into adolescence or adulthood at the time who went on to be artistically productive and more daring in the post-revolution period.

One powerfully representative figure for the idea of the Cultural Revolution being a battle in the zone of culture, and being focussed on cultural issues and cultural life, would be the much maligned Jiang Qing. Wife of Mao since the 1930s, in the early era she had been sidelined from any form of political or public activity despite her youthful career as a film starlet in Shanghai. By 1966, however, she became much more visible, taking an active and increasingly prominent role in the radical reformation of art. Jiang herself had no specific well-worked-out intellectual programme as such. Her comments from the time are epigrammatic and curt, lacking any systematic completeness. For that one must look to the main ideologues of the era *qua* cultural revolt such as Yao Wenyuan, a writer from Shanghai who was the hired pen producing lengthy attacks on the main enemies appearing in Mao's vision. For Jiang herself, however, the political ambitions driving the whole movement were clear enough. The objective was to touch the soul, to undertake a final definitive struggle using the pen, not weapons. (This was a popular motif of cartoons of the time portraying muscular-looking Red Guard activists impaling miniature enemies on the nibs of their sharp-tipped ink pens.)

Jiang's fiery public speeches to various literary groups typify the self-dramatization of the CPC's own story. They show the ways in which Party leaders around Mao, and Mao himself, became key actors playing out an immense psycho-thriller. A very typical Jiang Qing production was that delivered on 12 November 1967 to cultural figures in Beijing. Demanding that the attendees needed to take part in the 'revolution of the theatre and of music', she talked of the two battalions in the current proletariat struggle: the creative and the critical. These were part of the 'objective rhythm of class struggle'. Their work was therefore within this rules-based development to 'struggle, criticize, and change'. Once she had announced this, her simple follow-up was to demand that 'enemies be dug up'. Self-criticisms by artistic figures needed to be undertaken, the contradictions in society between the enemies and the good needed to be waged to the bitter end. Ominously, she stated that 'the situation in the artistic zone was complex'. Enemies were sly. They were able to infiltrate and undermine. Culture was the weapon to use against them.[16]

Jiang's role as a cultural and artistic leader did not end in the realm of performative arts. She was even willing to set out her opinions on the novel widely regarded as the greatest ever written in Chinese, Cao Xueqin's *Dream of the Red Chamber* (in Chinese, *Hong Lou Meng)*, the vast mid-eighteenth-century epic of manners revolving around two separate branches of the Jia family. The novel itself has held a special place in the affections of literate Chinese since the era in which it was hand-copied and passed amongst an increasing army of new readers. By the time the PRC had been founded, it was already recognized as the core modern novel, written in a style which, while often difficult, was markedly different to the classical Chinese that had prevailed through the centuries before. The symbolic importance of this *magnum opus* works on a number of levels. It typified the best of the 'old culture', with its sophisticated wordplay and densely interlocking narratives featuring different characters. But it also had a plot rich in references to the kinds of traditional family relationships and kinship structures that the Communists had risen to power opposing, and had been so busily trying to clear away since their victory in 1949.

The set of interviews between the American writer Roxane Witke and Jiang Qing undertaken in late 1972 where she outlines her views of the novel subsequently came to acquire a certain level of infamy once they were published in 1977. The interviews overall were largely sympathetic, and tried to show a more human side to someone who had been portrayed in the international press as a fearsome demagogue and extremist. But Simon Leys, for one, argued that Witke had proved naïve in allowing herself to be used by warring propagandists, some of whom were connected to Zhou Enlai and knew that showing the wife of Chairman Mao engaged in the elitist practice of tending delicate orchids in her private garden in Guangzhou, as Witke did, while the rest of the country was in turmoil was only going to damage her.[17] Indeed, by the time the book had appeared, she was already under arrest. She had lasted only a matter of weeks after Mao's own death in September 1976.

Jiang's comments on the *Dream* are almost comically self-important and purblind. 'I am,' she declares, 'a semi-expert on *Dream of the Red Chamber.*'[18] She then proceeds to give a masterclass of the ways in which high-Maoist ideology, the ubiquitous politicization of society, and the various discourses and critical tools it had used, when brought face to face with an authentic work of classical Chinese literature, produced results beyond parody. 'Don't read the novel as it if were just a story,' Jiang solemnly tells Witke, 'but see it as a book of history which demonstrates class struggle.'[19] Later on, referring to Mao's interpretation of the work, Witke explains that 'the Chairman had also taught ... not to focus upon the obvious – the love story. [Readers] must ferret out the theme of class struggle, bearing in mind the fact that more than twenty of the characters die as a result of it.'[20] Jiang herself simply felt that 'the novel should be analysed by the method of dialectic materialism. All the issues it raises stem from the basic question of how to accept the cultural inheritance.'[21] Cao Xueqin's book was placed in the category of those that 'made so powerful an assault on the ruling class that officials were compelled to ban it'.[22] It reflected a struggle between characters who, Jiang wryly commented, were 'big rightists', but who were at least 'resolute in their opposition to feudalism'.[23]

There are scholars like Mobo Gao who argue that the Cultural Revolution did at least create new forms of expression and positive innovative cultural models which did try to address the fundamental problem that Mao had outlined in Yan'an in 1942 of the immense distance between so much of high Chinese culture and the vast mass of the people. But the kind of intellectual straitjacket Jiang used as someone highly representative of this era because of her particular status and set of responsibilities shows that the bankruptcy of the Party's phase of most intense radicalization was as evident in the artistic field as it was in the economic. In 1978, therefore, there was a moment of recognition not just of need for material, organizational changes in China, but also for cultural adjustment. As Chinese people were returned to a world where individuation and personal networks were tolerated, they were also restored to a more familiar cultural terrain, in which the Party jettisoned its most extreme posture on artistic issues as it abandoned the framework of the universality of class struggle and the Manichean moral universe this relied on. The question from 1978 was therefore how to redesign the relationship between art and the Party's revised mission. This did not mean relinquishment of the grand popularizing project of Yan'an in 1942. It meant, as in the ideological and narrative space, adaptation and revision.

The Party's Aesthetics after 1978

As has been stated before, 1978 meant more than just a transformation in the economic sphere. It heralded change that eventually swept across society, reaching into the inner lives of people. All of this meant that the identity of the Party, and its overall function, changed. It acquired a new role in society where it identified specific spaces it wished to control but also had to jettison others. This metaphor of Party space is a useful one. From stretching across the inner and outer spaces of Chinese lives, as had been the case in the late Maoist era, almost trying to cause the annexation of the former by the latter, the Party from 1978 contracted and withdrew behind more limited boundaries. Its narratives became more defined. It no longer overtly held out large holistic outcomes for society. It involved itself with processes around tangible material enrichment, leading to the creation of the kind of two-track society described previously, one guided by the rhetoric of Party cadre selflessness, the other a society enjoying a carnival atmosphere of individualism, sometimes almost verging on anarchy. This at least was the ethos that prevailed until the more ambitious era of Xi.

The impact on art in China was complex, with multifaceted outcomes. 'Wounded literature', a genre that started to appear around the end of the 1970s and into the 1980s, serves as a good example. It was one manifestation, sometimes a very powerful one, of a restoration of voice to authors less guided by state-ordained uniform restraint along the lines dictated by Mao in 1942 and more concerned with addressing the specifics of harm and trauma that the Cultural Revolution had entailed. This type of literature offered a counter-narrative, and came from an alternative space in which expression could exist that was not bound by the ideas, language, and aesthetic prescripts of the Party. There had been underground literature in the period up to 1978, but with no public existence. Even the relatively small space accorded this new post-1978 literature was a radical change.

This and other phenomena in performance and figurative arts showed a process of Party retrenchment. It no longer supplied the drama, as it had in the 1960s and 1970s, with its model operas and literature theatricalizing its own history and present. Space opened up for increasingly radical expressions that either ignored, or openly violated, the Yan'an decrees. The artists Ai Weiwei, Yue Minjun, and others created works sometimes of breath-taking cynicism. The 1980s into the 1990s, however, saw a parallel movement. On the one hand, the Party itself sponsored an aesthetics which was conservative, and largely continued to convey messages about the importance of its own past in creating an increasingly rich and strong China. This was most typical in grand films supported by the state, which involved re-enactments of events like the Long March, or key moments in the Sino-Japanese War. These received the full support of the state film distribution service, and immense amounts of promotion, with ready-made audiences. Their true appeal tested against proper market mechanisms was limited. The most infamous was *The Opium War*, a vast, star-studded account of the circumstances in which Hong Kong had first been ceded to Britain, which played across China to mark the hand-back of the island in 1997 but was largely regarded as critically risible. With typical perversity, the Chinese films most popular abroad were those that the state either tried to ban, or regarded as being made simply for foreign taste forever critical of China.

As reform China proceeded, there was a paradoxical phenomenon of new-style art and its position in all of this. A vibrant avant-garde developed which lived in an ambiguous territory where some days it antagonized the Party authorities, and on others it was a source of cultural pride and cachet for them. This was because of the rising commercial value of the work of this group as the 2000s wore on. The aforementioned Yue Minjun is a good example of this, a figure whose trademark is grinning faces dominating each of the canvases he produces. The value of these rose in auction rooms in Hong Kong, the US, and Europe over the 1990s into the 2000s, to such an extent that he stood accused of opportunistically churning out highly standardized fare for a greedy market that was willing to pay whatever he or his representatives might ask. Director Zhang Yimou was a much more contentious figure. Part of the fourth generation of film makers alongside the highly regarded Chen Kaige, his earliest works, like *Yellow Earth* (1984), and *Raise the Red Lantern* (1991), were immensely popular in Western art cinemas, and garnered awards at Cannes and elsewhere. But he fell foul of the censors in the 1990s, particularly over *Ju Dou* (1990) and *The Story of Qiu Ju* (1992), whose stories started to shift from the more remote past to the present day, and risked interpretations implying criticism of the current government. For this he was rewarded by bans. His response was to make increasingly palatable and domestically successful films on epic historic themes from 2001 onwards. This culminated in his creative directorship of the 2008 Olympics Opening Ceremony. Was this a rehabilitation or a capitulation? He had fierce critics and supporters in equal measure. At the very least, his personal journey showed how treacherous and difficult it was in contemporary China to be an artist even despite the commercial power that art had now gained.

British sinologist Julia Lovell in her account of the Chinese hunt for Nobel Prizes tells of how the party-state from the 1980s latched onto appreciation and validation of the country as a soft power, depending on using old and new artistic assets outside the country as a key tool to achieve this.[24] The dream of gaining Nobel Prizes was a path beset by disappointment and misunderstanding on China's behalf, with only two successes in the era up to 2010 across all the prize areas. Both were the deeply embarrassing and unwanted Nobel Prizes for Peace, for the exiled Dalai Lama in 1989 and dissident Liu Xiaobo in 2010. Finally, in 2011, the writer Mo Yan was awarded the literature prize, and, in 2015, the scientist Yu Tutu won the shared prize for medicine. The fact that China from the 1980s was seeking this affirmation of its intellectual and artistic status is most revealing, whatever the actual results. It showed that the Party had a strategic aim partially mobilizing its artistic, intellectual, and cultural assets. Inevitably, politics played a big role. All success was fed back into the meta-narrative the CPC had, contributing to the idea of creating a powerful, strong country, thanks to the Party's guidance. No area was out of bounds for this mission. It operated far beyond the realm of Nobel Prizes. Li Nana, the tennis player, someone who had dropped out of the state system to pursue her own training regime, was unwillingly dragooned back into the system when she returned from winning the Australian Open in 2014. A photo showed her freshly arriving from Melbourne to her home province of Hunan after this victory regarding with stony face a local official handing her a large congratulatory cheque. Clearly, it was the contribution her sporting success had made to the national, politicized meta-narrative that she was being rewarded for. Equally clearly, she was not wholly happy with this.

This tension between, on the one hand, a Party aesthetics of support for products that conveyed ideas of national greatness and pride and, on the other, the actual work of Chinese artists successful beyond the confines of the country reflected tensions in the PRC itself. It vividly illustrated the ways in which the CPC, with its all-important moral narrative and cadre ethics still promoting collectivism, sacrifice, unity, and self-abnegation, was ranged against a society which was plural-istic, centred on individuals and their achievements, and dynamic. Much art that had real resonance and following inside and outside China came from this second level. Art associated with the Party world-view got political support, but often came across as contami-nated by propagandistic messages which had limited emotional reach for people and sounded alien. It did not help the CPC cause that it attempted to achieve obedience from artistic figures through the same kind of coercive campaigns used against businesspeople and cadres. In the 1980s, these took the form of the spiritual pollution struggles. There were subsequent clampdowns in later periods, though the main pressure was through banning works, cutting down funding oppor-tunities, reducing access to audiences, and engaging in a game of cat and mouse where police closed down what were viewed as subversive events, or harassed writers who strayed too far from the permitted lines.

In reform China, there were modifications and adaptations in the ideological and economic realm. But the ethos of the Yan'an 1942 talks in the artistic zone still stood. There were no new pronounce-ments by figures like Deng, or Jiang, or Hu, on the question of what artists specifically needed to do to reflect changes in other areas. Instead, it was a case of them observing their social responsibilities as Mao had required, deploying the large but increasingly meaningless 'art for the people' slogan. In painting the Stars (*xingxing*) movement, and in literature the Scar (*shangheng wenxue*) movement, were two examples of groups engaged in a subversive critique of the Maoist posture who were clearly talking in a way that proved this grand notion of a unified audience was no longer tenable. But these groups were marginal, and easily contained. The CPC attitude was a dismis-sive one: individualist art was an unfortunate side-effect for a society undergoing reform and change. It would eventually be cleaned away. Then proper, healthy socialist art would take its place.

The 2008 Olympic Carnival

The culmination of the CPC holding its Maoist line on a collective, mass aesthetics was the 2008 Opening Ceremony for the Olympics in Beijing, despite the fact that Mao's image did not physically appear during the event itself. The right to host this event had been a hard-won achievement for China, with one attempt in 1994 failing by a mere two votes because of residual criticism over the handling of the

1989 uprising. The news in 2000 that China had succeeded in its second bid was greeted in Beijing by jubilation, fireworks, and all-night revelry. Its preparation reportedly involved US$45 billion of investment, more than the GDP of some countries. Parts of Beijing were redesigned, with the Bird's Nest stadium presented as the most iconic building, based ironically on a design by Ai Weiwei, a figure who was becoming increasingly critical of the government by this time.

Almost every aspect of Beijing 2008 was drenched in symbolism. It started at eight minutes past eight in the evening, on the eighth day of the eighth month, August, eight being a homonym for wealth and therefore a lucky number in Chinese. Pyrotechnics was used during the opening moments, reminding the audience that the Chinese had invented gunpowder centuries before the West. A group of 2,008 drummers started the whole event off, followed by a large, seemingly miraculously dangling scroll portraying the whole sweep of Chinese history. The event was geared towards creating a sense of awe and respect, for Chinese history, for its richness and complexity. Confucius seemed everywhere. Admiral Zheng He, the eunuch seafarer of five centuries before, also received generous attention. (He had, according to some, discovered America before the Europeans.) A history once dismissed under Mao as feudal, full of backwardness and oppression, was now a source of glory and pride. But that was because the Maoist collectivist 'art that serves the people' attitude, despite all the surface changes, still dominated the public aesthetic zone. In an eerie way, with its onus on arousing and manipulating mass sentiment, the 2008 Opening Ceremony was reminiscent of the Red Guard rallies of the late 1960s. The most significant difference was that Mao had been replaced as the centre of worshipful focus by China, the country. The 2008 Opening Ceremony was an act of worship for a nation, not a man.

As the CPC made a highly pragmatic new deal with the past of the country it was in charge of, so too did the creative director Zhang Yimou come to peace with his own more radical roots. The firebrand who had scandalized Chinese cinema-goers by dressing the great beauty actress Gong Li in peasants' clothes as a petitioner in the gritty story *The Story of Qiu Ju*, and who had been rewarded by several bans on his work, now became the admired, highly compensated mastermind, someone who bragged about the fact that, unlike in the West, with its pesky work union and other restraints, in China tens of thousands could be press-ganged into appearing as dancers, or extras, largely at the order of the state. Zhang's overarching vision for the event clearly allowed no space for admissions of human failure. The most infamous piece of intervention was the fact that in the standard dance festival by representatives of China's fifty-five ethnic minorities, it transpired afterwards that all those performing were of Han ethnicity. Even worse, the young girl singing a song before the observing President Hu Jintao was dubbed, because the owner of the voice was regarded as not good-looking enough to appear on such a grand stage.

While it observed Maoist collectivist principles, the Olympics Opening Ceremony did give evidence of the Party broadening its aesthetic appeal. There was the pragmatic acceptance that constant focus on its own narrow story and the receipts that might be gained from this in terms of public emotional support had now been superseded by attention to the more promising, richer story of China – the China that had existed prior to 1949. In the 1990s, as international relations expert William Callahan and others had pointed out, patriotic education campaigns had stressed the need for love of country.[25] This had necessitated a deeper attention to the identity of that country, and to its assets in the fields of thought, art, and performance. Mao's Yan'an strictures about the remoteness of so much classical Chinese art from the people no longer had the same impact, because people were now much better educated. A lot of this culture that was once esoteric was now no longer so. And with the discrediting of the Cultural Revolution, the smashing of the old society, and the viewing of art through a class prism articulated by figures like Jiang Qing became risible. Art was part of a glorious national identity, an asset in the creation and then celebration of the newly acquired greatness, power, and strength the country had. Art like this, pointing to the traditions of the past, was there to be used as a means of creating an emotional attachment for the Party which its own complex identity and narratives could not achieve. Within this explanatory framework, 2008 was a great annexation – the Party moving back into the remote past and stealing cultural assets it did not have itself to speak to Deep China. It was also a pact. The dreaded feudal past and the current world were brought into a great Mencian-style unity. Harmony, one of the keywords of the Hu era, had been achieved, at least on the surface.

In the febrile atmosphere of the socialist market economy of post-WTO China, however, art also figured as part of the money-making economy. An exhibition director in the UK at this time specializing in Chinese modern art, when referring to dealing with Chinese artists, complained about how it was hard to get them off the subject of fees and the huge auction house amounts their work was making. In 2014, according to one list, Cui Ruzhou's *Landscape in Snow* (2005) sold in Hong Kong for US$23 million. Zeng Fangzhi's *The Last Supper*

(2001) came a close second the year before. The pyrotechnic artist Cai Guoqiang sold one piece from 2007 for US$7 million.[26] These were comparable to the sorts of amounts that the greatest classical European artists were getting. There was a kind of kudos that such attention garnered for China. It manifested status. That this highly lucrative art often appealed to memes of subliminal, or overt, criticism of the Chinese political system or social conditions in China was mostly brushed aside. In many ways, there was an expectation outside of China that contemporary art would carry this kind of message conveying a negative attitude towards the country's current political situation because these were more marketable.

Ai Weiwei has become the most celebrated contemporary artist occupying a position combining creativity and subversion. His criticism of the Party from the era of the mid-2000s to today has resulted in his incarceration for three months in 2011 (ostensibly for tax reasons) and an ongoing campaign of harassment. He was also refused leave to travel from 2011 until 2015. Critical assessment of his work itself has varied. Large public pieces like 100 million individually painted sunflower seeds displayed at Tate Modern in London during 2010–11 have been appreciated as spectacle, and their provocations interpreted as freighted with criticisms reflecting back on life in contemporary China. But as one assessment put it, while Ai is a hugely courageous and effective dissident, his art in and of itself is less compelling.[27] Past pieces like his smashing of a 2,000-year-old piece of Han Dynasty pottery typify a more theatrical bent. He has also, like the modern British artist Damian Hurst, been very effective at self-promotion.

Art as marketable commodities is not a subversive subject for the Party. But art which dabbles with its core iconography and its narratives and myths steps closer to the 'zone', the space where things suddenly become illicit, forbidden, and dangerous. Areas like these are of compelling fascination to artists, who like to test and violate boundaries. But the risks of producing an image of Chairman Mao construed as disrespectful can be high. The costs can be even more severe for doing the same with living Chinese elite figures. A cartoon of Hu Jintao in 2006, even despite being extremely mild (it showed him weeping while reading a letter from a schoolgirl whose father had died of overwork), earned the artist, Kuang Biao, suspension from his work.[28] And while Xi Jinping has been more amenable to having his image rendered in friendly cartoonists' or artists' work, only those safely outside of China, or wishing to visit one of the country's detention centres, dare to produce unflattering, mocking portraits of the current elite leadership.

Xi Jinping and the New Yan'an

From 1978 to 2013, in the CPC's aesthetic narrative, its rhetoric stuck by the Maoist Yan'an line of art to serve the people, though in practice it adopted a mostly laissez-faire attitude. Elite CPC leaders opined publicly that art needed to promote decent spiritual values, a stable society, a hard-working ethos, and, as time went on, the promotion of a strong, powerful country. Censorship was widely practised, with phases of varying intensity. On the whole, though, the duality between CPC rhetoric and practice offered an example of cohabitation. As Danielle Stockman showed in her study of television and print media over this time, the new dynamic placed promotion of core ideological statements and messages alongside the simple need to make money.[29] New television stations sprung up dependent on advertising revenue, and therefore on attracting viewers. A mass of new magazines and newspapers also appeared, driven by the same imperative. Artistic figures, writers, and directors had to walk the same route, seeking commercial viability in an era in which state patronage of art was changing, and where the most lucrative and rewarding opportunities existed in areas outside of the party-state's direct purview and involvement. It could be argued, too, that the CPC, through commission of some of the most radical buildings being constructed in the world, had allowed the avant-garde to infiltrate its own practice. The Party over this period, however, continued to have its designated aesthetics with artworks associated with these, largely built on celebrating its history, and its role in creating a powerful, confident, strong nation. It had a cadre of artists, organizations, and figures to promote this. It put significant resources into it. The message was an intrinsically conservative one, with a lot of the art produced this way being derivative, backward-looking, sometimes almost nostalgic.

As in other areas discussed before in this book, the Xi era has shown its ambitiousness by adopting a new, revised attitude towards art, and one that brings it under the umbrella of a comprehensive Party view. This is, after all, the period of the ideology of the Four Comprehensives, where the CPC aims to stretch across all areas of society, implementing its grand moral narrative, tied inextricably to the mission of national rejuvenation. This is an era in which emotions are once more on the rise, where messaging is important. There is a need for the CPC to engage with Chinese people through stories that reach into their inner lives, that speak more to their ideals, so that they feel linked to the Party and its mission in deeper and more dependable ways than simply following their pragmatic, economic interests.

Xi himself has a story, as mentioned before, an autobiographical narrative, which has elements with dramatic power: his difficult youth, his gradual rise through the Party system, and his marriage to the celebrity singer Peng Liyuan, a perennial favourite of the CCTV gala watched by hundreds of millions every Chinese New Year. Xi's speeches since 2012 have carried frequent mentions of Chinese writers and thinkers, largely from the classical era. This simply did not occur under Hu Jintao. A large part of the effectiveness of this personal narrative is how it echoes, often faintly but sometimes very clearly, that of Mao (both, for instance, spent part of their lives living in caves). It is therefore unsurprising that in 2015, addressing a large group of eminent cultural figures, Xi announced an updated approach by the CPC to the art field.

This was Yan'an Two for the new generation.[30] But this time, the audience were not radical activists and firebrands fleeing from the cities to the countryside to be part of the underground political cultural resistance being waged by the Party, but people living in the period when the CPC was secure in its power whose lives were devoted to one particular area of cultural activity. In his 2015 address, Xi discussed five tasks. The first belonged to the nationalistic theme. It acknowledged the intrinsic importance of a flourishing Chinese culture to the revival of the people. This related to the mission of the Party as a redemptive vehicle, restoring justice to Chinese people. What a terrible history we had, Xi stated, but, throughout, culture kept us going, especially in better times, where the quality of the art spoke for itself. The second task was the celebration of cultural amalgamation, with a reference to other world civilizations and their influence. Here the onus was on the search for parity. This also referred to the dependency of the nation's revival upon adequate material resources. The third task was the delivery of clearly articulated values. The current urgent need is to create timeless works of excellence. 'The most fundamental part of pushing for cultural flourishing is to create excellent works that do not let down our great nation in this great era'. There was a responsibility derived from the first two tasks for artists in contemporary China from whatever field to remember they were ambassadors, they had a public role, they were representatives of a Chinese national mission rather than a specific individual one, and that therefore they needed to stay close to these public values. Fourth was a purely political aim. Art had to 'maintain creative focus with the people as core', the recalibration of CPC values from the era of Hu that has lasted into the Xi period. Taking people as the core meant meeting their spiritual demands, reclaiming the attention of the inner person that had been so neglected by the CPC since 1978.

As the Party in the period of material reconstruction made its mission to ensure Chinese were at least fed and clothed, in the new era they have to be well nourished with cultural works, with new art, which places them at the heart of the great, stirring story of the regeneration of the nation they are part of. 'Only by following the people's wishes, reflecting the people's concerns, can [art] be full of life.' This is not quite the direct demand of Mao in 1942 for art to reflect the life of the proletariat and directly refer to their daily experiences and travails. It recognizes, unlike the Maoist framework, that there are no clear-cut class distinctions and identities in a China now more diverse and plural than ever before. But despite this surface difference, the underlying philosophical starting-point for both Mao in 1942 and Xi in 2015 is the same: to commit to a notion that art needs to refer to concrete social reality. And in this grand new plot, Chinese people are not just actors in their own drama, directed by the CPC. They have become the stars.

Xi's approach to art in this speech is a utilitarian one. In that respect it does not differ greatly from the 1942 Mao talks, despite all the intervening changes. Art's content cannot be for its own sake, but needs to be related to specific goals and ideas. It has to have a moral purpose, conveying messages supportive of the idea of a meaningful progress for history and a final good outcome. Artists have to conduct themselves with a sense of responsibility to this message. As Xi put it in his 2015 speech:

> This is not to say that art should not reflect the flaws of society, but it's a matter of deciding properly how best to reflect them. ... If creative works merely describe the status quo, essentially displaying the bad, but without any praise of the good, inspiration of hope, guidance for morality, [art] cannot motivate people to progress.

Violating Oscar Wilde's edict that art is for art's sake, this approach belongs to the school where art has a use, a social function. The Party has a role here as the transmitter of modernity. It is not just a case of using Chinese culture as the basis for new art, but adapting it for an iteration of modernity on China's terms. There were also institutional issues that Xi touched on: the need to strengthen and improve the leadership of the CPC towards creative work, including the imperative (an old Maoist refrain) to develop new institutions and practices by which to promote and protect new art forms and the necessity of art to be critically received.

A striking refrain of Xi's 2015 words was that of competitiveness. Chinese-style art is a crucial part of the promotion of China as a country abroad. It figures in its armoury of soft-power attributes, and as a means of legitimizing its status as a great modern nation, one based on unique values and exceptional artistic achievements. Jiang Qing in the Cultural Revolution had referred to the battle being one of words, not weapons. In the new era, art and culture figure as an instrument of external power, of promotion. They need to garner prestige for China, to gain it understanding. As with Mao, so with Xi, in almost every domain, the common link is to legitimize its power by linking it ever more closely with the nation, and the nation's rejuvenation and strength. In Xi's China, even the realm of the imagination is colonized by the CPC's moral master narrative. It, too, delivers something for the project of a China finally risen from the ashes and restored to its just position at the centre of the world.

Xi's Politics: The Party as a Vessel for Emotions

When the technocrats took over the elite leadership of the Party, in the time of Deng Xiaoping as paramount leader, they adopted a discourse of technical governance, their speeches sprinkled with statistics and the articulation of managerial outcomes. They were the lords of the tangible. Their brand of socialism with Chinese characteristics allowed no space for abstract appeals to things happening in the distant future, or in realms other than the physical present. To get rich was glorious, and the Party spoke of how to do it. And only in this way did it aim to energize and recruit people's emotions. It delineated a space in society during its rehabilitation after the deep catastrophe of the Cultural Revolution where it could get on with its new obligation: maintaining stability, pumping out GDP growth, and building the governance and administrative infrastructure to make this kind of enrichment possible.

   Emotion and idealism do not have a good pedigree in modern Chinese political history. Their apogee, or Armageddon (depending on which angle one wishes to take), was, as in so many things, the decade of extremity from 1966, when emotion became the guiding force behind Chinese politics. Everyday life became a theatre. The Chinese people were unified as never before with a belief system, a unified ideology, with its accompanying moral codes. This was driven by the emotions of love (for Chairman Mao) and hate (for China's enemies, of whom there were many). The volatility of public emotions in this era is testified to by the public mass events, the most famous of which were the vast Red Guard rallies held in Beijing over 1966 into 1968 in which Mao, as the sun god come down to earth, walked amongst ecstatic crowds. The standard descriptions of these events are filled with fervour, giving the sense of an epic, emotion-filled landscape amongst which people walked in a state of perpetual ecstasy. 'At five minutes past seven on the evening on the 15th of September 1966, I saw our most most most most most dearly beloved leader Chairman Mao!' goes one student's account:

> I have seen Chairman Mao! Today I am so happy my heart is about to burst. We're shouting, "Long live Chairman Mao! Long live! Long live!" We're jumping! We're singing! After seeing the Red Sun in Our Hearts, I just ran around like crazy all over Beijing. I so much wanted to tell everyone the great news! I wanted everyone to join me in being happy, jumping, and shouting.[31]

Such intense ecstasy was short lived. By the mid-1970s, Chinese people were exhausted by the psycho-drama they had been unwittingly recruited into. The endless campaigns and the ups and downs of elite politics of the time, with one week's hero being the next week's arch villain, necessitated the need for a quieter era, one where the onus was simply getting on with things, reconstructing the country, and living more quietly. No wonder that, for all its dryness, the elite leaders' neutral language of mechanical outputs and business was welcomed. In the grey decades of the 1980s and 1990s, the Party did not do political emotion, beyond standard themes like celebrating successes, and declaring that the country's time in the sun was imminent.

And yet, as American political scientist Martha Nussbaum stated in her study of this subject, 'All societies are full of emotions.'[32] She continues:

> Such public emotions, frequently intense, have large-scale consequences for the nation's progress towards its goals. They can give the pursuit of those goals new vigor and depth, but they can also derail that pursuit, introducing or reinforcing divisions, hierarchies, and forms of neglect or obtuseness.[33]

In her view, the criticism of and perspective on the development and use of emotions help in maintaining a healthy, balanced atmosphere. But in China, this lack of critical apparatus means that emotions, when they well up into public expression, even in the era in which Deep China has received more space and recognition and where the CPC needs to talk to it, can take an unpredictable and ugly turn. Massive outpourings of anger and grief occurred when the Chinese embassy in Belgrade was bombed by NATO in late 1998. Similar explosions of public anger occurred during clashes with Japan in the mid-2000s, sometimes simply ignited by China's defeat in a football match.

The Party's campaign to engage with the public in a more emotional way after its technocratic phase has been highly strategic. An outcrop of this has been the tolerance, and even encouragement, of rising levels of nationalism and patriotism. Nationalist sentiment first reared its head in the 1990s, when bloggers like Wang Xiaodong and others wrote *The China That Can Say No*. A decade on, and they produced an even more inflammatory work, *China is Not Happy*, berating their leaders for their failure to defend Chinese interests in international affairs, and to look after food safety at home.[34] That art in the form of figures like Ai Weiwei and the writer Han Han, a hugely popular blogger and racing driver, was able to offer an alternative source of emotional mobilization was of concern to the Party. It is not surprising therefore that it has engaged in moving beyond its technocratic functions post-1978, to become an entity which is able to use the great resource that emotion carries in art and the close alignment with a notion of traditional Chinese culture that this offers.

French political scientist Dominique Moïsi in his study *The Geopolitics of Emotion* describes how, today, people, unsure of their place and seeking greater identities, 'have replaced ideology as the motor of history, with the consequence that emotions matter more than ever in a world where media are playing the role of a sounding board and a magnifying glass'.[35] Hope, fear, and humiliation – the three key emotions that Moïsi highlights in the subtitle to his book – all figure in the current Chinese climate, with the first in the ascent, but plenty of fear (about stability, sustainability, and other issues) and humiliation (from the past) also worked into the mix. On Moïsi's account, the strong optimism about China's future, the Party's narrative of the great moment of national rejuvenation, give the CPC a huge advantage. Whatever their feelings about Marxism-Leninism (probably typified by indifference), or the CPC, Chinese people, in that vast, largely unexplored, emerging place of Deep China, have been emotionally engaged by this nationalist message. They love their country. They love its histories, and its current wealth, and the signs present before them every day that for the first time in modern history it looks to be winning. For that reason, the confident, expansive register of Xi in his speeches, the kind of messages sent to the population by his physical appearance and through his many journeys around the world, are crucial. They convey a message which is not just a political, economic, or technocratic one but at heart emotional.

Conclusion
The Party's Great Historic Mission

From its earliest days, the Party was always willing to buck the trend. When under Mao's emerging leadership it retreated from the main cities, particularly Shanghai, and sought support in the countryside, it started to acquire a distinctiveness. Its ideology became differentiated from that of the Soviet Union, with a stress on agrarian, not urban, struggle. This was the first great schism, and part of the attempt to make something *sui generis*. In the words of historian Jerome Ch'en, when the Nationalists tried to wipe it out as a force in 1927, the CPC 'had to have an army, a territory and a government. In other words, it had to make a state within a state.'[1] As part of this creation of a stronger, clearer identity, it also acquired a very specific outlook. That involved an attitude to its followers which treated them almost as though they were chosen people, mandated with a mission which was about more than just acquiring power. It was about the use of Western modernity, and an ideology which originated in the West, to reform and save the Chinese nation. This nation had a history which was uniquely ancient as a culture. It was also one which had suffered immeasurably during the modern era, a victim of the aggression and interference of others. The CPC sought a mandate to deliver justice to this entity, to ensure that it rose again as a strong, rich country which would never again be done down. The Party from this foundational era committed to a master narrative which was about positive progress in history, and the moral mission to deliver a necessary, just outcome for Chinese.

Over the last nine decades of its existence, while the CPC has not shifted from commitment to this grand master narrative, it has travelled in a great arc. It its initial period in power after 1949 it became involved in almost every aspect of life to the point where in many ways *it was* the daily life of most Chinese people, structuring everything from meetings, to marriage, education, and mealtimes. From 1978, with the crisis brought about by the Cultural Revolution, the CPC tactically withdrew, occupying more carefully defined spaces. It became an entity to help China in its mission to first enrich itself materially, and then convert this to status and power. Economy was the core discourse, with a largely technocratic leadership who spoke the language of outputs, one which was laden with data, numbers, and figures. Under Xi Jinping, however, there has been a concerted attempt to restore the Party's centrality, to, as it were, bridge the great gap between the lives, inner and outer, of the Chinese people and the role that the Party plays. This book has described the nationalist campaigns which have aimed to achieve this, along with the real challenges that the Party addresses in bringing about this new accommodation. The most one can say at the moment is that this is a work in progress. It indicates a great deal, however, about Xi's ambition, and the politics that he is using to validate China's great campaign for national rejuvenation, with the Party and the unity it provides at the heart of this.

Most studies of China's political economy, society, and development from 1978 have tended to view that date within a predominantly economic framework. The changes from this time in China are seen as being about introducing into the highly politicized, idealistic, utopian, and largely disastrous polity under Mao a much more pragmatic results-orientated approach. This book has taken a different tack. Although 1978 did mark a significant turning-point, it was much more profound than simply changing the material circumstance of society. The Party itself mandated a series of repositionings, in which its ethical vision, its ideology, and its aesthetic views fundamentally transformed. The liquid individualistic networks of Deep China, a place linked to a past before Mao even existed, came back into existence, or were allowed space to at least operate openly again. The selflessness and crushing of the ego under the old Party vision from the 1930s only became relevant for cadres. For the rest of society, individualism became permissible. That more than anything else had revolutionary implications which impacted not only on the material structure of society and the way it was organized but also on the most intimate inner lives of the Chinese people themselves. That most understudied place, Deep China, has figured a lot in this book. It is somewhere that even Chinese have a hazy knowledge of. But it is a place that increasingly Chinese politicians are needing to speak to, with the more emotional language used since Xi's rise to power amongst elite figures.

For this place, the place of the manifold individual interests, aspirations, fears, and beliefs of different Chinese people, the Party occupies a particular position – more, in the modern context, of a custodian of a specific narrative – the most powerful link between the two eras of before and after 1978. It is true that China either side of that date comes to look increasingly different, almost as though it were two different countries. And yet the continuity at the deepest level is supplied by the Party narrative – a narrative which promises to Chinese people as a nation the deliverance of justice, of liberation forever from victimization and the dark past, with its humiliations and sufferings. Across almost all areas, this is the core mobilization. The Party with this moral vision of history, a history guided by scientific progress, dialectics, and orderly laws, is able to deliver this final deal – a rejuvenated, powerful, strong, proud country, one able to win the battle of modernity on its own terms. This moment is not remote. It is imminent, just around the corner, coming into sight. With the 2021 First Centenary Goal, China will become a middle-income country. More importantly, it will become one which is entering a new era of modernization – a modernity entirely suitable to China's national conditions, and one that will deliver it moral retribution.

Part of this, of course, will involve a subliminal justification of the Party's own errors. The argument is simple. As the 1981 Resolution made clear, in the Mao era mistakes were made – particularly in the Cultural Revolution. But in the post-Mao history, the main effort has been in the Party, through penance, through service and transformation, undergoing a renewal of its own. After all, it is the holder of the historic covenant, derived from the idea that history as it develops in modern times has a meaning, and that the shocking suffering from the 1950s into the 1970s will be redeemed by the final massive achievement: for the first time in modern history, a powerful, strong, autonomous China looking at the world that once victimized it not just as an equal but as a superior.

In these various accounts, therefore, 1978 was an epistemic, moral, and spiritual shift, rather than a purely physical one. It carried within it the seeds of a transformation far beyond the merely material and administrative. Dwelling on this aspect of the changes since then allows one to understand a bit better just why the Party has till now been so successful at surviving. It is an entity into which a great deal of cultural and spiritual capital has been invested, not for its utility as a political force obedient to the tenets of Marxism-Leninism, but because of its becoming, since the time of Mao, a repository of the national mission, something unique and exceptional for a unique and exceptional nation. Mission was the word referred to at the start of Xi Jinping's mammoth speech at the Nineteenth Party Congress in October 2017. Mission is what the Party under Xi is about. Marxism-Leninism is merely the means. The end is a great, powerful nation. In an odd way, this, more than anything else, shows the ways in which, even in contemporary China, Chineseness, Chinese identity, the sense of Chinese civilizational values, stands like a religion, despite the impressive revival of Buddhism, Daoism, and other forms of belief. It is the one thing that unites people across the many other socio-economic, ethnic, and religious boundaries that divide them.

Deep within this vision, however, are a series of profound structural problems. They point to the kinds of challenges of sustainability that figure so large in the environmental and economic realms. These derive from the viability of asserting that socialism with Chinese character-istics can really continue to be the unique governance and political structure of China, and manage to hold together and supply coherence in the other spheres: moral, intellectual/ideological, and aesthetic. In many ways, China since 1978 has consistently managed to square a circle. It has had the rhetoric of socialism and the reality of capital-ism. It has been trying to combine two wholly different kinds of thinking: non-competitive, unitary, often repressive and controlling political institutions marching alongside highly competitive, often deeply pluralistic, and sometimes anarchic social and commercial realities. I have captured this in this book by the Bakhtinian notion of carnival. In many ways, China is the archetypal carnival society. But it is a carnival held in a state-controlled space where the festivities are happening on government land, and using government-provided utilities and services.

This book has argued that there is a huge challenge in the Party somehow sustaining parallel moral discourses, with the cadre elite and their networks under Xi expected to remain faithful to the selfless creed of the Liu Shaoqi era, and the rest of society being run on more diverse, more ancient, and, until very recently, more contentious forms of local ethical thought. Confucius, Mencius, Xun Zi, and a host of other ancient voices have made comebacks. There are even academics arguing that these ideas have validity in the West, with their lack of abstract metaphysics and concentration on pure action.[2] Party dis-course in the area of ideology has become even more vexed, with the seemingly unbreakable commitment to Marxism-Leninism and Mao

Zedong Thought figuring like a strange, elite dialect largely indecipherable to an unheeding wider society. Ideology still has a functional value for the Party, and gives it cohesion and unity, as I have argued in the chapters on this subject above. But the issue is more about the deep divisions that exist in a society now restored to its highly networked, fragmented default, a society where the Party's language of ideas seems wholly different from that of the vast majority of the other citizens.

In his seminal work from the 1970s *The Cultural Contradictions of Capitalism*, Daniel Bell referred to the many ways in which, through its institutionalization of envy, and its privileging of the future over the present, the constant state of hunger, expectation, and unsatiated desire kept capitalism in a state of perpetual crisis. He talked of a 'revolution of rising entitlements' by people.[3] In this world, 'the seduction of the consumer has become total'. It is a place where hedonism has run riot. This is 'a world of make-believe in which one lives for expectations, for what will come rather than for what is'.[4] Hedonism, interestingly, has become the term of greatest critical force used against cadres in China who have lost sight of their service ethic, and become servants instead of their own limited networks, family or otherwise.

Bell paints a dystopian picture of how this scenario pans out. His vision has proved prescient. Social media and the rise of 'fake news', along with even greater service to the ego and its curated online presence, have proved corrosive and disorientating for individual self-confidence and mental health. China as a society has undergone more change than almost any other, more quickly and on a greater scale. So the tensions between the Party in charge, with its missions and powers, and the people ranged around it, and the dynamic between these two, have become complex and hard to manage. This is compounded by the fact that no one can mediate between the two. They have to sort out their problems on their own.

In an era in which we often see the greatest challenges in China as involving the environment, water, governance, and economic growth, these issues of ethical sustainability and the ability of the Party to continue to preserve at least some authority over its use of ideology, even if the belief in the content has long gone, have been neglected. And yet, with the moment of great national rejuvenation so close, it is perhaps proper that we remember in its early era how much time and effort the Party spent on getting these various areas right. These have formed a fundamental part of its culture, precisely in the way that Bell spoke of. Its use of myths, symbols, practices, and an accompanying language have been crucial components of its ability to hang on to power. It is therefore only right that they be given attention. After all, in the twenty-first century, should the Party succeed in its great mission, its vision of Chinese-style modernity, because of the importance and status of China itself, will have global relevance. At that moment, we will all need to start paying attention to what the Party is, what its culture is driven by, and how we can relate to its moral, aesthetic, and historic vision.

Notes

Introduction

1 'Princeling' is a term referring to current elite leaders related to similarly high leaders from a previous generation – usually at Vice Minister level or above.

2 'I am seeking to rescue the poor stockinger, the Luddite cropper, the "obsolete" hand-loom weaver, the "utopian" artisan, and even the deluded follower of Joanna Southcott from the enormous condescension of posterity.' E.P. Thompson, *The Making of the English Working Class*, reprinted with new preface (Harmondsworth: Penguin Books, 1981), 12

3 One should acknowledge here that, of course, domestically, in China, the Party has plenty of voice. But the point here is about how this is received and understood in the outside world.

4 Liu Yunshan, 'Five Dimensions in Understanding the Communist Party of China', Speech at the 'International Seminar of the CPC in the Eyes of European Scholars', 11 June 2014 (record of speech given in Copenhagen, unpublished).

5 See Kenneth Lieberthal, *Bureaucracy, Politics and Decision Making in Post-Mao China* (Berkeley: University of California Press, 1992), Introduction, 'The Fragmented Authoritarian Model and Its Limitations', 1–31; Steve Tsang, 'Consultative Leninism: China's New Political Framework', *Journal of Contemporary China*, vol. 18, no. 62 (2009), 865–80; David Shambaugh, *China's Communist Party: Atrophy and Adaptation* (Berkeley: University of California Press; Washington, DC: Woodrow Wilson Center Press).

Chapter 1 Redemption from the Dark Past

1 Louise Lim, *The People's Republic of Amnesia: Tiananmen Revisited* (Oxford: Oxford University Press), 2014.

2 William J.F. Jenner, *The Tyranny of History: The Roots of China's Crisis* (London: Penguin, 1992). I use the plural for 'histories' and 'pasts' here because, despite the moment a unified Chinese political entity appeared, in the era of the First Emperor, the Qin, in 221, there has been no easy single line of Chinese history. Periods of stability in the Han up to the third century AD, the Tang from the seventh to the tenth century, and the Ming and Qing from the fourteenth century onwards were interspersed with moments of cataclysmic fragmentation. There were also very significant differences even between the unified dynastic entities. The use of the plural is therefore an acknowledgement of this complexity.

3 Constitution of the People's Republic of China, National People's Congress website, http://www.npc.gov.cn/englishnpc/Constitution/2007-11/15/content_1372962.htm.

4 Full Text of Constitution of Communist Party of China, *People's Daily* website, Xinhua, 2013, http://english.cpc.people.com.cn/206972/206981/8188065.html.

5 The injustice of modernity is about more than just how bullying Western nations came to pick on a China with its magnificent, ancient history. It is also about how China in its pasts was an innovator and great scientific power, one which invented the core creations behind modern development – the magnetic compass, printing press, and gunpowder – earlier than anyone else and yet, despite this, was robbed of its own industrial revolution. This has been called the Needham question, after the great British sinologist Joseph Needham. His monumental *Science and Civilization in China* (Cambridge: Cambridge University Press, 1954–present), was unable to effectively answer this question. For China and the Japanese war, see the work of Rana Mitter, in particular *China's War with Japan: The Struggle for Survival 1937–1945* (London: Allen Lane, 2013).

6 Mao Tse-tung, *Selected Works*, Vol. III (Beijing: Foreign Languages Press, 1965), 177.

7 Ibid., 180.

8 Ibid., 184.

9 Ibid., 194.

10 Ibid., 213.

11 Ibid., 210.

12 Ibid., 217.

13 Michael Harris Bond (ed.), *The Psychology of the Chinese People* (Hong Kong and Oxford: Oxford University Press, 1986), 279.

14 Mao Tse-tung, *Selected Works*, Vol. III, 217.

15 'Every Communist must grasp the truth: "Political power grows out of the barrel of a gun".' Mao Tse-tung, 'Problems of War and Strategy' (6

November 1938), in *Selected Works*, Vol. II (Beijing: Foreign Languages Press, 1966), 224.

16 Mao Tse-tung, *Selected Works*, Vol. III, 194.

17 Ibid., 197.

18 Ibid., 196.

19 For instance, Frederick C. Teiwes and Warren Sun, *Paradoxes of Post-Mao Rural Reforms: Initial Steps Towards a New Chinese Countryside, 1976–1981* (London: Routledge, 2015).

20 'Deng's time in Jiangxi strengthened his conviction about how far behind China was and how much it needed to change. His experiences gave him insights into the extent of the Great Leap's failure that other party leaders, who were continually reading exaggerated reports of local achievements, had difficulty evaluating.' Ezra Vogel, *Deng Xiaoping and the Transformation of China* (Cambridge, Mass.: Belknap Press of Harvard University Press, 2011), 56.

21 'Resolution on Certain Questions in the History of Our Party since the Founding of the People's Republic of China', available at https://www.marxists.org/subject/china/documents/cpc/history/01.htm.

22 Deng was called 'paramount leader', though not in Chinese materials at the time he was alive, largely as recognition of the paradox that from 1978 he was the most powerful leader in China but had no formal job title indicating this. He was a Vice Premier to 1982, and thereafter Chair of the Central Military Commission up to 1989. He also sometimes sat on the Politburo Standing Committee, and chaired a leadership group made up of 'retired leaders' which was meant to be informal, but clearly made the main decisions about the handling of the unrest in 1989. Despite this, Zhao Ziyang, who was the General Secretary of the Communist Party from 1987 to 1989 and therefore, on paper at least, the supreme power holder, acknowledged to Japanese journalists in 1989 that no major decisions were made without getting Deng's imprimatur.

23 Deng Xiaoping, *Selected Works of Deng Xiaoping, 1975–1982* (Beijing: Foreign Languages Press, 1982), 276–7.

24 Ibid., 284.

25 Ibid., 287.

26 Roderick MacFarquhar, *The Origins of the Cultural Revolution: Vol. 1. Contradictions Amongst the People, 1956–1957* (New York: Columbia University Press; London: Royal Society of International Affairs, 1974); *Vol. 2. The Great Leap Forward, 1958–1960* (Oxford: Oxford University Press; New York: Columbia University Press, 1987); *Vol. 3. The Coming Cataclysm, 1961–1966* (Oxford: Oxford University Press; New York: Columbia University Press, 1997). Yan Jiaqi and Gao Gao, *Turbulent Decade: A History of the Cultural Revolution*, trans. and ed. D.W.Y. Kwo (Honolulu: University of Hawai'i Press, 1996). Frank Dikotter, *The Cultural Revolution: A People's History, 1962–1976* (London: Bloomsbury, 2016). Michael Schoenhals (ed.), *China's Cultural Revolution, 1966–1969: Not a Dinner Party* (Armonk, NY: M.E. Sharpe, 1996).

27 See in particular Gao's splendidly provocative *The Battle for China's Past* (London: Pluto Books, 2006).

Chapter 2 Winning the Historic Mission: The Party under Xi

1 See Joseph Fewsmith, *China Since Tiananmen: From Deng Xiaoping to Hu Jintao* (Cambridge: Cambridge University Press, 2001), for a comprehensive overview of this crisis of belief, particularly from 81 onwards.
2 See Xiaoying Wang, 'The Post-Communist Personality: The Spectre of China's Capitalist Market Reforms', *The China Journal*, no. 47 (January 2002), 1–17. This will be analysed in some detail in Chapter 4.
3 Arthur Kleinman, Yunxiang Yan, Jing Jun, Sing Lee, Everett Zhang, Pan Tianshu, We Fei, and Guo Jinhua, *Deep China: The Moral Life of the Person: What Anthropology and Psychiatry Tell Us About China Today* (Berkeley and Los Angeles: University of California Press, 2011).
4 *Zhongguo Gongchandang Lishi 1949–1976* (History of the Communist Party of China 1949–1976) (Beijing: Party Archives Press, 2011), Vol. 1, 5.
5 Ibid., 7–10.
6 Ibid., 15.
7 Ibid., 16.
8 Ibid., 59.
9 Ibid., 40.
10 See, for instance, Xuan Loc Duan, 'Xi Jinping Seems Destined to Become China's New Mao', *Asia Times*, 29 October 2017, http://www.atimes.com/xi-jinping-seems-destined-become-chinas-new-mao-zedong/.
11 *Xi Jinping Jiang Gushi* (Xi Jinping Telling Stories) (Beijing: Renmin Chubanshi, 2017), 9.
12 For the Xinhua biography, see Xi Jinping, *The Governance of China* (Beijing: Foreign Languages Press, 2014). For the use of his personal biography, see Kerry Brown, *CEO China: The Rise of Xi Jinping* (London and New York: I.B. Tauris, 2016). For the lack of biography about Hu Jintao in his political persona, see Kerry Brown, *Hu Jintao: China's Silent Ruler* (Singapore and London: World Scientific, 2012).
13 *Xi Jinping Jiang Gushi*, 2.
14 David Shambaugh deals with this, critically, in *China Goes Global* (Oxford: Oxford University Press, 2014).
15 This is most famously captured in the opening lines of the great classic novel *Romance of the Three Kingdoms*: 'The empire, long divided, must unite; long united, must divide. Thus it has ever been.' See Luo Guanzhong, *Three Kingdoms: A Historical Novel*, trans. Moss Roberts (Berkeley and Los Angeles: University of California Press; and Foreign Languages Press: Beijing, 1991), 5.

Chapter 3 Being a Good Chinese Communist: The Search for a Moral Narrative in Xi's China

1 See Tan Hecheng, *The Killing Wind: A Chinese County's Descent into Madness During the Cultural Revolution* (Oxford: Oxford University Press, 2017), for a particularly dramatic and harrowing example of this.

2 This proved to be particularly ironic in view of Wen's family's direct links to immense wealth and trading interests. See David Barboza, 'Billions in Hidden Riches for Family of Chinese Leader', *New York Times*, 25 October 2012, http://www.nytimes.com/2012/10/26/business/global/family-of-wen-jiabao-holds-a-hidden-fortune-in-china.html.

3 See Andrew Wedeman, *Double Paradox: Rapid Growth and Rising Corruption in China* (Ithaca, NY, and London: Cornell University Press, 2012).

4 Wang was to stand down from this position in 2017, to be replaced by Zhao Leiji. He was, however, to be appointed as Vice President in 2018, a position he did not need a seat on the Politburo to occupy.

5 Wang Xiaofang, *The Civil Servant's Notebook*, trans. Eric Abrahamsen (London: Penguin, 2012).

6 Richard McGregor, *The Party: The Secret World of China's Communist Rulers* (London and New York: Allen Lane, 2010).

7 See Frank N. Pieke, *The Good Communist: Elite Training and State Building in Today's China* (Cambridge: Cambridge University Press: Cambridge, 2009), 1:

Cadre training also highlights the fact that China's contemporary administration is Mao Zedong's worst nightmare become real. Gone forever are first-hand revolutionary experience and direct involvement in the life and work of China's toiling masses. Instead, cadres have become a ruling elite who worship book learning and formal educational qualifications. As the embodiment and chief instrument of the party's leading role in society, cadres are to be leaders, managers, moral exemplars and faithful servants of the Party at the same time.

8 Cary Huang, 'Mao Zedong Granddaughter on Rich List, Prompting Debate', *South China Morning Post*, 9 May 2013, http://www.scmp.com/news/china/article/1233208/mao-zedong-granddaughters-addition-rich-list-prompts-debate.

9 Bruce J. Dickson in *The Dictator's Dilemma: The Chinese Communist Party's Strategy for Survival* (Oxford: Oxford University Press, 2016), 142. In the table there, based on surveys of county, provincial, and central leaders, the lower levels of government were trusted the least.

10 For an up-to-date overview of the deep challenges faced by the Party from corruption in China, and a pessimistic assessment of whether it will be able to surmount these, see Minxin Pei, *China's Crony Capitalism: The Dynamics of Regime Decay* (Cambridge, Mass.: Harvard University Press, 2016).

Chapter 4 Back to Basics: The Roots of the Party's Moral Crisis

1 Liu Shaoqi, *How to Be a Good Communist* (New York: Prism Key Press, 2011), 7.
2 Ibid., 8. It should be made clear that Liu uses 'he', and his language was not sensitive to gender neutrality. There were female activists in the early CPC era. But to this day, it remains a male-dominated force: 80 per cent of current members are men; on the Politburo from 2017 there were only two women; there has never been a single woman on the full Standing Committee; and there have only been three women heading provinces as governors since 1949.
3 Ibid., 9
4 Ibid.
5 Ibid., 23.
6 Ibid., 27.
7 Ibid., 37.
8 Ibid., 38.
9 Ibid., 45.
10 Ibid., 47.
11 Ibid., 48.
12 Mao Tse-tung, *Selected Works*, Vol. I (Beijing: Foreign Languages Press, 1967), 112–13.
13 Ibid., 291.
14 Fei Xiaotong, *From the Soil: The Foundations of Chinese Society*, trans Gary G. Hamilton and Wang Zheng (Berkeley and London: University of California Press, 1992), 60–1.
15 Ibid., 65.
16 Ibid., 66.
17 Li Zhengsheng, *Red-Color News Soldier*, ed. Robert Pledge (London: Phaidon Press, 2003).
18 Mao, *Selected Works*, Vol. 1, 28.
19 Robert Jay Lifton, *Thought Reform and the Psychology of Totalism: A Study of Brainwashing in China* (London: Victor Gollancz, 1961).
20 Robert Jay Lifton, *Revolutionary Immortality: Mao Tse-tung and the Chinese Cultural Revolution* (Penguin: Harmondsworth, 1970), 53.
21 Ibid., 72–3.
22 Ji Xianlin, *The Cowshed: Memories of the Chinese Cultural Revolution*, trans. Jiang Chenxin (New York: New York Review Books, 2016), 118.
23 Yang Jiang, *A Cadre School Life: Six Chapters*, trans Geremie Barmé (New York: Readers International, 1983).
24 See, in particular, Arthur Koestler, *Darkness at Noon* (London: Macmillan, 1940).
25 Ba Jin, *Random Thoughts*, trans. Geremie Barmé (Hong Kong: Joint Publishing Co., 1984).

26 Yasheng Huang, *Capitalism with Chinese Characteristics* (Cambridge: Cambridge University Press, 2008), 20.
27 Wang, 'The Post-Communist Personality', 1.
28 Chuihua Judy Chung, Jeffrey Inaba, Rem Koolhaas, Bernard Chang, and Sze Tsung Leong (eds), *Great Leap Forward* (Cambridge, Mass.: Harvard Design School, 2001).
29 Wang, 'The Post-Communist Personality', 3.
30 Ibid., 4.
31 Daniel Bell, *The Cultural Contradictions of Capitalism* (New York: Basic Books, 1976), 22.
32 Wang, 'The Post-Communist Personality', 7.
33 Ibid., 9.
34 Ibid., 11.
35 See, in particular, Simon Leys, *The Burning Forest: Essays on Chinese Culture and Politics* (London: Paladin, 1988).
36 Wang, 'The Post-Communist Personality', 12.
37 Liu Xiaobo, *No Enemies, No Hatred: Selected Essays and Poems*, ed. Perry Link, Tienchi Martin-Liao, and Liu Xia (Cambridge, Mass.: Belknap Press of Harvard University Press, 2012), 309–10.
38 Ibid., 47.
39 Ibid., 65.
40 Ibid., 165.
41 Ibid., 170.
42 Ibid., 155.
43 Ibid., 164.
44 Ibid., 166–7.
45 Uradyn E. Bulag, *The Mongols at China's Edge: History and the Politics of National Unity* (Lanham, Md, Boulder, Colo., and Oxford: Rowman & Littlefield, 2002), 63ff.
46 Liu, *No Enemies, No Hatred*, 170.
47 Ibid., 173.
48 Chan Coonchung, *The Fat Years*, trans. Michael Duke (New York: Doubleday, 2011).
49 The Bo case is dealt with succinctly by Jamil Anderlini, *The Bo Xilai Scandal: Power, Death and Politics in China* (London: Penguin, 2012), and John Garnaut, *The Rise and the Fall of the House of Bo: How a Murder Exposed the Cracks in China's Leadership* (London: Penguin, 2012).
50 Wang Qishan, http://dangjian.people.com.cn/n1/2017/0717/c117092-29408660.html.
51 Leys, *The Burning Forest*, 194.
52 Zheng Wang, *Never Forget National Humiliation: Historical Memory in Chinese Politics and Foreign Relations* (New York: Columbia University Press, 2012), xii. Wang's own suggestion is to look for the clue to this 'inner life' mystery in the notion of historical memory.
53 Kleinman et al., *Deep China*, 30.

54   Ibid., 185–6.
55   Ibid., 268.
56   Mark Elvin, *Changing Stories in the Chinese World* (Stanford: Stanford University Press, 1997), 177. The first belief system had been the traditional Confucian order, prevailing ostensibly up to 1949.
57   See Kleinman et al., *Deep China*, 285–6.
58   Figures in Ian Johnson, *The Souls of China: The Return of Religion after Mao* (New York: Random House, 2017), 31.
59   Lu Xun, *Jottings under Lamplight*, ed. Eileen J. Cheng and Kirk A. Denton (Cambridge, Mass.: Harvard University Press, 2017), 186.
60   Roderick MacFarquhar and Michael Schoenhals, *Mao's Last Revolution* (Cambridge, Mass., and London: Belknap Press, 2006), 370.
61   Guobin Yang, *The Power of the Internet in China: Citizen Activism Online* (New York: Columbia University Press, 2009), 25.
62   For background and analysis of this speech, see Brown, *Hu Jintao: China's Silent Ruler*, 161–2.
63   F.W. Mote, *Imperial China: 900–1800* (Cambridge, Mass.: Harvard University Press, 1999), 83.
64   C.T. Hsia, *The Classical Chinese Novel: A Critical Introduction* (New York: Columbia University Press, 1968), 20.
65   Quoted in Shaoyang Zhang and Derek McGhee, *China's Ethical Revolution and Regaining Legitimacy: Reforming the Communist Party through Its Public Servants* (London: Palgrave Macmillan, 2017), 231.
66   Ibid., 245.

Chapter 5 The Drama of Ideas: The Party and Ideology

1   Huang, *Capitalism with Chinese Characteristics*, 210.
2   Ibid., 212.
3   Ibid., 212–13.
4   Wang Hui, *The End of the Revolution: China and the Limits of Modernity* (London and New York: Verso, 2009), 6–7.
5   Pieke, *The Good Communist*, 59: 'In 1995, there were already considerably more than 2,000 party schools in the whole of China.'
6   Terry Eagleton, *Ideology: An Introduction*, new edition (London and New York: Verso, 2007), 1.
7   Hans van de Ven, *From Friend to Comrade: The Founding of the Communist Party of China, 1920–1927* (Berkeley, Los Angeles, and Oxford: University of California Press, 1991).
8   Mao, *Selected Works*, Vol. I, 311.
9   Ibid., 216.
10   Ibid., 345.
11   Mihai Craciun, 'Ideology Shenzhen', in Chung et al. (eds) *Great Leap Forward*, 117.

12 Ibid., 89.
13 John Wilson Lewis, *Leadership in Communist China* (Ithaca, NY: Cornell University Press, 1962), 35.
14 Ibid., 35.
15 Ibid., 38.
16 Ibid., 66–7.
17 Ibid., 67.
18 Wang, *The End of the Revolution*, 6.
19 A. Doak Barnett, *Cadres, Bureaucracy, and Political Power in Communist China* (New York and London: Columbia University Press, 1967), 429.
20 Franz Schurmann, *Ideology and Organization in Communist China* (Berkeley and Los Angeles: University of California Press; and London: Cambridge University Press, 1966), 30.
21 Ibid., 61–2.
22 Li Junru, *What Do You Know About the Communist Party of China?* (Beijing: Foreign Languages Press, 2011), 6.
23 Ibid.
24 Like so many of Deng's important phrases, however, no one quite knows for certain when he first used these terms – or if he did. But they have a reality through being taken as indicative of his thought.
25 It is fair to say that the best recent scholarship on the myth of the seamless victory of Deng has shown that it was just that – a myth. The battle to accept more pragmatic policies was an intense one – largely because it did impact so profoundly on the identity of the Party. Teiwes and Sun do a magnificent job of showing, in one particular area, how epic this battle was. See their *Paradoxes of Post-Mao Rural Reform*.
26 Huang, *Capitalism with Chinese Characteristics*, Chapter 1.
27 Willy Wo-Lap Lam, *Chinese Politics in the Hu Jintao Era: New Leaders, New Challenges* (London: M.E. Sharpe, 2006), 156.
28 Deng Xiaoping, 'Excerpts from Talks Given in Wuchang, Shenzhen, Zhuhai and Shanghai', *China Daily*, 18 January–21 February 1992, http://www.chinadaily.com.cn/china/19thcpcnationalcongress/2010-10/26/content_29714457.htm.
29 OECD, 'Economic Survey of China 2005', http://www.oecd.org/china/economicsurveyofchina2005.htm.
30 Bruce Dickson and Jie Chen, *Allies of the State: China's Private Entrepreneurs and Democratic Change* (Cambridge, Mass.: Harvard University Press, 2010).
31 Teresa Wright, *Accepting Authoritarianism: State–Society Relations in China's Reform Era* (Stanford: Stanford University Press, 2010).
32 Chen Guidi and Wu Chuntao, *Will the Boat Sink the River? The Life of China's Peasants* (New York: Public Affairs, 2007).
33 On village democracy, see Kerry Brown, *Ballot Box China: Grassroots Democracy in the Final Major One-Party State* (London: Zed Books, 2011).

Chapter 6 The Ideological Fightback under Xi

1 Jonathan Unger, Anita Chan, and Stanley Rosen, *On Chinese Democracy and the Chinese Legal System: The Li Yizhe Debates* (London: Routledge, 2015).

2 See Andrew Nathan, *Chinese Democracy* (London and New York: I.B. Tauris, 1984).

3 For a fuller treatment of Deng and his work and importance, see Kerry Brown and Simone van Neuwenhuizen, *China and the New Maoists* (London: Zed Books, 2016), 60–85.

4 See Su Shaozhi, 'Dang Buneng Shiyu Shi "san ge daibiao" ('The Party Can't Begin to Say What "Three Represents" Is'), BBC website, 29 June 2000, http://news.bbc.co.uk/hi/chinese/china_news/newsid_811000/8113931.stm.

5 Shambaugh, *China's Communist Party: Atrophy and Adaptation*, and Neil Munro, 'Democracy Postponed: Chinese Learning from the Soviet Collapse', *China Aktuell*, no. 4 (2008), 31–61.

6 Jamil Anderlini, 'How Long Can the Communist Party Survive in China?', *FT Magazine*, 20 September 2013, https://www.ft.com/content/533a6374-1fdc-11e3-8861-00144feab7de?mhq5j=e5.

7 Yang Hengjun, 'China Is Not the Soviet Union', *The Diplomat*, 14 June 2014, https://thediplomat.com/2014/06/china-is-not-the-soviet-union/.

8 Full text, 'New Party Chief Xi Jinping's Speech', 15 November 2012, http://www.bbc.com/news/world-asia-china-20338586.

9 Despite the use of the word 'virtues', these were more about organizational, Party-centred necessities. They were the principle of upholding the socialist path, the principle of upholding the people's democratic dictatorship, the principle of upholding the leadership of the CPC, and the principle of upholding Mao Zedong Thought and Marxism-Leninism.

10 Perry Link, *An Anatomy of Chinese: Rhythm, Metaphor, Politics* (Cambridge, Mass.: Harvard University Press, 2013).

11 Raymond Williams, *Keywords* (New York: Croom Helm, 1976).

12 Yu Keping, *Democracy Is a Good Thing: Essays on Politics, Society, and Culture in Contemporary China* (Washington, DC: Brookings Institution Press, 2009).

13 Mao Tse-tung, 'On New Democracy', in *Selected Works*, https://www.marxists.org/reference/archive/mao/selected-works/volume-2/mswv2_26.htm.

Chapter 7 The Aesthetics of the Party

1 See Ralph A. Thaxton Jr, *Catastrophe and Contention in Rural China* (Cambridge: Cambridge University Press, 2008), 301–2.

2 Simon Leys, *The Halls of Uselessness: Collected Essays* (Collingwood, Victoria: Black Inc., 2011), p. 335.

3   Mao, 'The Talks at the Yan'an Forum on Literature and Art', in *Selected Works*, Vol. III, 69ff.

4   Ibid., 70.

5   Ibid., 70–1.

6   Quotes ibid., 75–6.

7   Ibid., 96.

8   Ibid., 91.

9   Chang-tai Hung, *Mao's New World: Political Culture in the Early People's Republic* (Ithaca, NY, and London: Cornell University Press, 2011), 75–92.

10 The work of David Holm on the peasant operas from Yan'an is particularly interesting: David Holm, *Art and Ideology in Revolutionary China* (Oxford: Clarendon Press, 1991).

11 For a caustic but accurate analysis of the notion of 'the people' and how managed and circumscribed its meaning was in post-1949 Party discourse, see the writer Yu Hua's *China in Ten Words*, trans. Allan H. Barr (New York: Random House, 2011), 3: 'I can't think of another expression in modern Chinese language that is such an anomaly,' Yu says, 'ubiquitous yet somehow invisible.'

12 Hung, *Mao's New World*.

13 David E. Apter and Tony Saich, *Revolutionary Discourse in Mao's Republic* (Cambridge, Mass.: Harvard University Press, 1994), 13.

14 Guy Debord, *Society of the Spectacle* (Detroit: Black and Red, 1970), 1. From a French edition originally published in 1967.

15 Paul Clark, *The Chinese Cultural Revolution: A History* (Cambridge: Cambridge University Press, 2008), 3.

16 'Jiang Qing Tongzhi zai Beijing Wenyi Zuotanhuishang de Jiang Hua' (Comrade Jiang Qing's Speech at a Seminar for Artistic Figures in Beijing), in *Wuchangjieji Wenhua da Geming Shengli Wan Sui* (Beijing: People's University Press, 1969), 265–70. Translation my own.

17 Simon Leys, 'Review of *Comrade Chiang Ch'ing*, by Roxane Witke', *New Republic*, 25 June 1977, 23–7.

18 Roxane Witke, *Comrade Chiang Ch'ing* (London: Weidenfield & Nicolson, 1977), 280.

19 Ibid., 278.

20 Ibid., 287.

21 Ibid., 289.

22 Ibid., 290.

23 Ibid., 289.

24 Julie Lovell, *The Politics of Cultural Capital: China's Quest for a Nobel Prize in Literature* (Honolulu: University of Hawaii Press, 2006).

25 William Callahan, *China: The Pessoptimist Nation* (Oxford: Oxford University Press, 2009).

26 'Who are the Top Ten Most Expensive Living Chinese Artists at Auction?' *Artnet News*, https://news.artnet.com/market/who-are-the-top10-most-expensive-living-chinese-artists-at-auction-240285.

27 Jed Perl, 'Noble and Ignoble: Ai Weiwei, Wonderful Dissident, Terrible Artist', *New Republic*, 1 February 2013, https://newrepublic.com/article/112218/ai-wei-wei-wonderful-dissident-terrible-artist.

28 'China Cartoonist Suspended for Drawing Hu Crying', *Epoch Times*, 14 September 2006, https://www.theepochtimes.com/china-cartoonist-suspended-for-drawing-hu-crying_1730104.html.

29 Danielle Stockman, *Media Commercialization and Authoritarian Rule in China* (Cambridge: Cambridge University Press, 2014).

30 'Xi Jinping: Zai Wenyi Gonzuo Zuotan de Jianghua' (Xi Jinping Speech at a Working Meeting of Cultural Figures), 14 October 2015, http://news.xinhuanet.com/politics/2015-10/14/c_1116825558.htm.

31 Bei Guancheng, 'I Saw Chairman Mao!!!', in Schoenhals (ed.), *China's Cultural Revolution 1966–1969*, 148.

32 Martha Nussbaum, *Political Emotions: Why Love Matters for Justice* (Cambridge, Mass., and London: Belknap Press of Harvard University Press, 2013), 1.

33 Ibid., 2.

34 This book is analysed in Brown, *Ballot Box China*, 118–21.

35 Dominique Moïsi, *The Geopolitics of Emotion: How Cultures of Fear, Humiliation and Hope are Reshaping the World* (London: Bodley Head, 2009), 4.

Conclusion: China's Great Historic Mission

1 Jerome Ch'en, 'The Chinese Communist Movement to 1927', in John K. Fairbank (ed.), *The Cambridge History of China: Volume 12. Republican China 1912–1949, Part 1* (Cambridge: Cambridge University Press, 1983), 526.

2 One of the most lucid of these attempts is by Michael Puett and Christine Gross-Loh, *The Path: What Chinese Philosophers Can Teach Us* (New York and London: Simon and Schuster, 2016).

3 Bell, *The Cultural Contradictions of Capitalism*, 23.

4 Ibid., 70.

Suggested Readings

Just as there has been a narrative about its own history and development by the CPC, so there has been a parallel narrative by those outside of China, observing, describing, and trying to make sense of the Party, its role in Chinese politics, and its decision-making structures and unique culture.

Amongst the earliest works was Edgar Snow's classic *Red Star over China* (London: Victor Gollancz, 1937), the seminal account, and a highly sympathetic one, of the first encounter between an American journalist and the new Communist leadership produced during their fugitive years in the remoter parts of Shaanxi, central China. Snow was subsequently to visit China long after Mao had come to power, and wrote updates, of which perhaps the most striking (largely because it was by one of the few foreign journalists allowed into the country at the time) is *The Other Side of the River* (London: Penguin, 1963). The latter work has been criticized for what is claimed to be almost deliberate myopia about the clear mismatch between the idealist rhetoric of the leaders Snow talked to and the harsh reality of Chinese lives at the time.

In the 1950s and 1960s, a group of scholars analysed the Party and tried to work out the relationship between the ideology guiding it and its actual practice. In view of the severe limitations on getting hold of primary source material, undertaking field research, and even talking to actors in all of this, it is remarkable that these works were as accurate as they were, and have proved as enduring as they have. Amongst the most important are John Wilson Lewis's *Leadership in Communist China* (Ithaca, NY: Cornell University Press, 1962), Franz

Schurmann's *Ideology and Organization in Communist China* (Berkeley and Los Angeles: University of California Press; and London: Cambridge University Press, 1966), and A. Doak Barnett's *Cadres, Bureaucracy, and Political Power in Communist China* (New York and London: Columbia University Press, 1967). The volume by Schurmann in particular is a masterpiece of comprehensiveness and synthesis, concisely emphasizing the ways in which the CPC's belief system mattered to the manner it behaved, and that understanding one demanded a good comprehension of the other.

In terms of histories of the CPC, Hans van de Ven's *From Friend to Comrade: The Founding of the Chinese Communist Party, 1920–1927* (Berkeley, Los Angeles, and Oxford: University of California Press, 1991) offers a complete account of the early era of the CPC when it was a renegade force in the rural areas, and in particular in central provinces such as Hunan. This gives useful context to the path that the CPC followed in the 1930s and the era of greater dominance by Mao. Jacques Guillermaz's *History of the Chinese Communist Party 1921–1949* and *History of the Chinese Communist Party 1949–1967*, trans. Anne Destenay (New York: Random House, 1972), is out of date, but its narrative drama has enduring value and its descriptions of the decades in which the CPC was a guerrilla force have particular authenticity given that the author was a French military officer. The late Arif Dirlik's *The Origins of Chinese Communism* (New York and Oxford: Oxford University Press, 1989) is, like other parts of his oeuvre, a work of formidable scholarship and inventiveness. Nor should or could we forget Lucien Bianco's *Origins of the Chinese Revolution, 1915–1949*, trans. Muriel Bell (Stanford: Stanford University Press, 1971), which accurately depicts the centrality for Mao of class theory and class struggle.

Coming to terms with the figure of Mao would take a bibliographical note in its own right. The early account by Snow was helpful, but over-admiring. In recent years, accounts have veered between the scathingly critical – such as Jung Chang and Jon Halliday's *Mao: The Unknown Story* (London: Jonathan Cape, 2005) – and the much more balanced – such as Alexander Pantsov and Steven Levine's *Mao: The Real Story* (London: Simon & Schuster, 2012). Pantsov and Levine's version of Mao is 'real' in the sense that it is based on not only Chinese but also Russian sources, giving new insights. The picture of the Chairman their work conveys is of a person traumatized and dehumanized by his early experiences as a revolutionary and a guerrilla leader. This at least gives some idea of the inner workings of Mao, rather than presenting the brutal, superhuman face of an autocrat that is often presented to the world. Jerome Ch'en's *Mao and the*

Chinese Revolution (London: Oxford University Press, 1965) was an early and admirably neutral description of Mao's relationship with the Party he had brought to power. The classic account of Mao Zedong Thought is contained in Stuart Schram's lengthy introduction to *The Political Thought of Mao Tse-Tung* (Harmondsworth: Penguin, 1969). Frederick C. Teiwes and Warren Sun have worked for over four decades on establishing an accurate account of the era from late Mao into the early reform period, and their work is rich in detail. It often contests the neat frameworks that are sometimes supplied about how, and why, things mattered. *The End of the Maoist Era: Chinese Politics During the Twilight of the Cultural Revolution, 1972–1976* (Armonk, NY: M.E. Sharpe, 2007) is a typical example of their ground-breaking work.

In terms of Deng Xiaoping, the two most important works are *Deng Xiaoping and the Transformation of China* (Cambridge, Mass.: Belknap Press of Harvard University Press, 2011) by Ezra Vogel, a veteran expert on Asia, and *Deng Xiaoping: A Revolutionary Life* (Oxford: Oxford University Press, 2015) by Alexander Pantsov and Steven Levine. As Pantsov and Levine point out in their work, however, for all Vogel's sweep in his epic biography, he devotes a tiny proportion of his work to the seven decades of Deng's life up to 1978. They rectify that balance, and point out more succinctly the key strategic decisions Deng made, why he made them, and why they had such impact. For leaders after Deng, the most useful works are Willy Wo-Lap Lam's *The Era of Jiang Zemin* (Singapore: Prentice-Hall, 1999), Kerry Brown's *Hu Jintao: China's Silent Ruler* (Singapore and London: World Scientific, 2012), Willy Wo-Lap Lam's *Chinese Politics in the Hu Jintao Era: New Leaders, New Challenges* (Armonk, NY, and London: M.E. Sharpe, 2006), and Kerry Brown's *CEO China: The Rise of Xi Jinping* (London and New York: I.B. Tauris, 2016).

Overviews of how the CPC actually functions and frameworks it might best be located in can be found in David Shambaugh's *China's Communist Party: Atrophy and Adaptation* (Berkeley: University of California Press; Washington, DC: Woodrow Wilson Center Press, 2008), Kerry Brown's *Friends and Enemies: The Past, Present and Future of the Communist Party of China* (London and New York: Anthem Press, 2009), and Richard McGregor's *The Party: The Secret World of China's Communist Rulers* (London and New York: Allen Lane, 2010). Shambaugh's volume is particularly strong on giving an account of what lessons the CPC learned from the collapse of the Soviet Union, and how often it has returned to this issue, seeking some illumination about the ways it can help them avoid a similar fate. McGregor's is most striking for describing the CPC almost like a major corporation, with a clear link to profit and economic performance. In some ways, the Xi leadership has attempted to counter this view.

More nuts-and-bolts descriptions of the CPC as an organization can be found in Yongnian Zheng's *The Chinese Communist Party as Organizational Emperor: Culture, Reproduction and Transformation* (London; New York: Routledge, 2010). Zheng, a Singaporean-based scholar of the Party, is strong on combining Western analytic political science concepts and frameworks of the CPC in a credible and well-thought-out fashion. His notion of the CPC being the emperor of modern China, rather than any particular figure, is one rich in suggestiveness and implications. Li Junru's *What Do You Know About the Communist Party of China?* (Beijing: Foreign Languages Press, 2011) is a straightforward insider's view of the CPC, why it matters, what its function is, and what its relationship now is to Mao. Li is worth attending to because he was formerly deputy president of the Central Party School in Beijing, the core think-tank on CPC matters. He was also involved in drafting leaders' speeches for congresses. Tony Saich's *Governance and Politics of China*, Fourth Edition (Basingstoke: Palgrave Macmillan, 2015), describes the relationship between the Party and the government, one of the most mysterious and difficult links to get right in contemporary China, in objective and analytic terms.

The vexed issue of internal factions and the composition of different tribal allegiances in the CPC originated in research at the time of the Cultural Revolution in the early 1970s about how best to understand the clashing groups vying for influence around the ageing Mao Zedong. The classic account is Andrew J. Nathan's 'A Factionalism Model for CCP Politics', *The China Quarterly*, no. 53 (Jan./Mar. 1973), 34–66, which was in turn critiqued by Tang Tsou, with a response by Nathan, in 'Prolegomenon to the Study of Informal Groups in CCP Politics', *The China Quarterly*, no. 65 (March 1976), 98–117. Cheng Li, from the US Brookings Institution, in his *China's New Leaders: The New Generation* (Lanham, Md: Rowman and Littlefield, 2001), gives a more recent, more elaborated factionalist model, this time looking at the transition in leadership between the Jiang and Hu eras. Cheng Li has returned to this issue in subsequent papers and books up to the period of the Xi leadership. Zhiyue Bo's *Chinese Elite Politics: Political Transition and Power Balancing* (Singapore: World Scientific, 2007; revised 2012) has exhaustive detail on the composition of Central Committees in the CPC and where the power between these lies. Alice L. Miller does an elegant job of critiquing the factionalist position in 'The Trouble with Factions', *China*

Leadership Monitor, no. 46 (Winter 2015) (https://www.hoover.org/research/trouble-factions). Kerry Brown, 'Factions in Modern Chinese Politics: A Help or a Hindrance?', *The Journal of the Oriental Society of Australia*, no. 47 (2015), 61–72, wades in with a summary of previous positions, and an argument for how the complexity of the Xi era means that it is difficult to find any factionalist model of allegiance in the elites that does not end up at the level of each individual being a discrete faction on their own.

The Cultural Revolution has figured a great deal in this book. Luckily, in English, there is a rich corpus of material about its social and political importance. The standard English-language narrative account of the whole decade of activity is in Roderick MacFarquhar and Michael Schoenhals's *Mao's Last Revolution* (Cambridge, Mass.: Belknap Press of Harvard University Press, 2006). Impeccable in its sourcing and historical veracity, it is largely confined to the intricate machinations amongst the elite leadership. Mobo Gao's *The Battle for China's Past: Mao and the Cultural Revolution* (London and New York: Pluto Press, 2008) is a passionate, provocative revisionist work, defending aspects of the Cultural Revolution and its guiding intentions. Gao's arguments are based on his own experience as an activist living through this period. Andrew G. Walder's *Fractured Rebellion: The Beijing Red Guard Movement* (Cambridge, Mass.: Harvard University Press, 2009) looks at the battles between groups based at elite universities in Beijing and shows just how divided and complex the whole era was, even at the most local level. Journalist Tan Hecheng's searingly powerful and often harrowing *The Killing Wind: A Chinese County's Descent into Madness During the Cultural Revolution* (Oxford: Oxford University Press, 2017) represents the very best example of Chinese scholars, journalists, and writers undertaking research, often in highly sensitive areas in the past of their own country, and producing magnificent material, full of detail and insight.

On Deep China, and the moral life of contemporary Chinese people, the inevitable starting place is Liu Xiaobo's *No Enemies, No Hatred: Selected Essays and Poems*, ed. Perry Link, Tienchi Martin-Liao, and Liu Xia (Cambridge, Mass.: Belknap Press of Harvard University Press, 2012), a work which has figured in much of what has been discussed in this book. Liu derived particular authority from his remaining in China despite the very high price this carried, and speaking from a position as an insider criticizing the system rather than as someone removed and outside. This is not to denigrate Wei Jingsheng, whose *The Courage to Stand Alone: Letters from Prison and Other Writings*, trans. Kristina M. Torgeson (London and New York: Viking, 1997) contains the essential texts for which he was incarcerated for so long. But whereas Wei's focus is largely political, Liu probes into the moral and cultural underbelly of Chinese society. His criticisms and insights are incisive and troubling. This can be supplemented by the two other works I have drawn on extensively: Arthur Kleinman, Yunxiang Yan, Jing Jun, Sing Lee, Everett Zhang, Pan Tianshu, We Fei, and Guo Jinhua's *Deep China: The Moral Life of the Person: What Anthropology and Psychiatry Tell Us About China Today* (Berkeley and Los Angeles: University of California Press, 2011), which gives a superb analytic framework with which to understand this vexed issue, combing fieldwork from within China, insights from Chinese scholars, and psychological techniques from outside. Beyond its many commendable academic qualities, this book is exemplary in the ways in which it offers a model of intellectual collaboration between Chinese and non-Chinese in a fresh area. Xiaoying Wang's essay 'The Post-Communist Personality: The Spectre of China's Capitalist Market Reforms', *The China Journal*, no. 47 (January 2002), 1–17, has offered stimulation to me for over a decade, and introduced a wholly new way at looking at contemporary China. Ian Johnson's *The Souls of China: The Return of Religion after Mao* (New York: Random House, 2017) is a beautifully written account of the rise of local and imported religions in China in the last three decades and the way these have also competed for space in Deep China.

On political reform, the most useful works to date are Bruce J. Dickson's *The Dictator's Dilemma: The Chinese Communist Party's Strategy for Survival* (Oxford: Oxford University Press, 2016), because of the rich opinion survey data it is based on, and Yu Keping's *Democracy Is a Good Thing: Essays on Politics, Society, and Culture in Contemporary China* (Washington, DC: Brookings Institution Press, 2009), as the well-argued and well-structured position of an official on questions around democracy in the system. Daniel A. Bell's *The China Model: Political Meritocracy and the Limits of Democracy* (Princeton: Princeton University Press, 2015) offers a spirited but controversial argument for the strengths of the meritocratic system in China as it now stands. As he admits, the China Model, alas, is only applicable to China itself, although it perhaps has some similarities to the model used in Singapore.

Index